Debunking ADHD

Debunking ADHD

10 Reasons to Stop Drugging Kids for Acting Like Kids

Michael W. Corrigan

ROWMAN & LITTLEFIELD
Lanham • Boulder • New York • London

Published by Rowman & Littlefield
4501 Forbes Boulevard, Suite 200, Lanham, Maryland 20706
www.rowman.com

Unit A, Whitacre Mews, 26-34 Stannary Street, London SE11 4AB

British Library Cataloguing in Publication Information Available

Library of Congress Cataloging-in-Publication Data

The hardback edition of this book was previously cataloged by the Library of Congress as follows:

Corrigan, Michael W.
  Debunking ADHD : 10 reasons to stop drugging kids for acting like kids / Michael W. Corrigan.
     pages cm
  Includes bibliographical references.
  1. Attention-deficit hyperactivity disorder—Diagnosis. 2. Attention-deficit-disordered children—Medical care. 3. Diagnostic errors. 4. Psychiatric errors. I. Title. II. Title: Debunking attention-deficit hyperactivity disorder.
  RJ506.H9C675 2014
  618.92'8589—dc23   2013048147

ISBN 978-1-4758-0654-0 (cloth : alk. paper)
ISBN 978-1-4758-2737-8 (pbk. : alk. paper)
ISBN 978-1-4758-0656-4 (electronic)

∞™ The paper used in this publication meets the minimum requirements of American National Standard for Information Sciences—Permanence of Paper for Printed Library Materials, ANSI/NISO Z39.48-1992.

Printed in the United States of America

I owe a special thanks to my wife, kids, family, friends, and editors who gave me the courage and support to write this book. But most of all, this book is dedicated to all of the kids in the world who have not quite mastered the behaviors many adults expect, and for their parents, who need a little help in getting through this thing we call parenthood.

CONTENTS

ILLUSTRATIONS

FIGURES

TABLES

PREFACE

Why Write *Another* Book on ADHD?

Most books on attention deficit/hyperactivity disorder (ADHD) offer good advice to help kids who display annoying levels of the commonly observed childhood behaviors associated with the ADHD diagnosis. A few of the books, however, also tiptoe around the possibility that what is used today to diagnose ADHD might be contributing to overdiagnoses or misdiagnoses of ADHD. This book does all of that but goes a bit further.

My goal is to share with you everything (and I mean everything) a concerned adult should know about ADHD and the unfortunate connection it has to children. But before we begin, I want you to understand that this book is much different than most books on ADHD. By starting with a little clarification on the two main explanations for writing this book, I think you will understand what I mean.

EXPLANATION #1: ADHD DOES NOT EXIST

This book is written to help adults protect children from being labeled for displaying the behaviors associated with the symptoms of ADHD that basically all children display to some extent nearly every day. After researching this conveniently invented mental disorder for close to seven years as I debated whether or not I should write this book, and watching the trend of diagnosing children for ADHD grow further out of control (a 41 percent increase over the last decade according to Centers for Disease Control and Prevention data), like many others I became convinced that ADHD is basically a sham that has given far too many a license to pill children for acting like children. Sadly, it has seemed at times as if I were investigating and writing about one of the largest, strangest, and most evil experiments ever attempted—an experiment where kids serve as the guinea pigs, taking experimental pills that even the pills' manufacturers claim to have no idea what they actually do.

This book shares a large body of evidence and a healthy dose of common sense to help you connect the dots as to why ADHD should by no means ever be considered a mental disorder for children. After connecting the dots you also will see that ADHD should not be considered a chronic disease or condition. Displaying the behaviors associated with the symptoms used to currently diagnose ADHD (which are related to kids being highly energetic, creative, communicative, and full of imagination and wonder) should not be something we stigmatize and medicate. Instead such behaviors should be viewed as a gift parents and educators should embrace, nurture, and celebrate.

When it comes to diagnosing kids, ADHD in its current form is nothing more than just another highly questionable label on the long list of overdiagnosed and misdiagnosed mental disorders being measured inaccurately and identified incorrectly. In the land of reality where science, evidence, facts, and common sense actually matter, ADHD the mental disorder does not exist.

At best for kids, the diagnosis for ADHD in its current form serves as basically a *diagnosis of normal*, using eighteen very generic, commonly observed childhood behaviors (or, as the insurance industry, pharmaceutical industry, and some medical doctors and mental health practitioners refer to the behaviors justifying the label, *symptoms*). Coincidentally or conveniently, ordained by the all-knowing creators of ADHD as *proof* of ADHD's existence, these eighteen childish behaviors (in their infantile or developmental stages) seem to drive parents and educators crazy at some point in time nearly every day. This is where the brilliance of those behind the ADHD movement starts to come into play. If one were going to create a fictional diagnosis to justify drugging children for acting like children, one might as well make the symptoms reflect annoying childhood behaviors that many adults observe often but would like to see disappear quickly.

Many of these common childhood behaviors (or supposed symptoms) associated with ADHD, however, are also many of the same traits we use to identify giftedness. When these same ADHD symptoms are used to identify giftedness, they are used to identify kids who are highly intelligent and have traits that, if nurtured, could help them become amazing students. These behaviors, when harnessed and focused, can help children become incredibly creative, insightful, and successful individuals in adulthood. Unfortunately for some kids who have not yet learned how to harness the power of the behaviors that ADHD and giftedness have in common, such behaviors when displayed might seem annoying and immature.

The fact that some incredible kids labeled with ADHD have not yet quite figured out how to use their special powers in a less annoying fashion is just one example confirming that the symptoms of ADHD might also just be a sign of a temporary or delayed developmental issue. Regardless, if such behaviors are related to delayed child development, a sign of giftedness, or in many cases normal not-so-enjoyable childlike behavior, the annoying nature of these supposed ADHD behaviors will decline with time to some extent. Sometimes the annoying immature behaviors will completely disappear altogether. But quite often, even when such behaviors do remain and are harnessed, they become the behaviors that define a person. They become the behaviors that make a person special, unique, and quite possibly distinctive, artistic, extraordinary, and successful.

ADHD is just a negative label that some not-so-altruistic or possibly misguided people want you to believe is real. Not unlike the many wonderful stories about unicorns, fairies, and leprechauns, the diagnosis of ADHD is a brilliant work of fiction. Beyond being used as a label to identify a highly questionable mental disorder specifically created and branded to justify drugging children for acting like children, ADHD does not exist.

EXPLANATION #2: THERE IS NO
SUCH THING AS A MAGIC PILL

My biggest reason for writing this book is my desire to show you that the practice of medicating children for acting like children in the name of ADHD is, in two words, wrong and dangerous. Despite the grandiose claims of the mega-pharmaceutical companies selling ADHD drugs to concerned parents, prescribing pills to young children trying to learn how to become young adults is just a quick fix void of any long-term benefits.

Research on the practice of drugging children for ADHD only offers weak evidence of temporary and minimal benefits to modifying children's behavior. Research to be shared in this book also documents that ADHD drugs come with a long list of serious health risks, warnings, and possible short- and long-term side effects, some of which are permanent. Overstimulating incredibly energetic children into a state of drug-induced compliance, is neither a healthy nor safe approach to achieving optimal growth when it comes to their ethical, academic, psychological, neurological, or social development.

My two main explanations for writing this book—denying that ADHD is a real mental disorder and claiming children should never be drugged for such a diagnosis—might seem outlandish and unsubstantiated to some. But the evidence and logical arguments presented in this book will document that such views are neither outlandish nor unsubstantiated and that I am not alone in my beliefs.

My intention is to share with you a comprehensive view of valuable information every adult should know in order to better understand, manage, nurture, and guide the behaviors associated with ADHD. This book offers insight, research, and advice about how to help kids harness the power of the behaviors negatively associated with ADHD. In the following chapters we will also learn how the science and evidence falls far short of actually supporting ADHD, which is the real disorder, and we will debunk the justification behind prescribing dangerous ADHD drugs to children. If you want to research any of the topics and issues I discuss on your own, I've provided a large number of the sources I consulted, listed by chapter, in the references section.

Even if you accept and use today's popular view that the ADHD diagnosis is real and identifiable, the evidence provided in this book will show you that the disorder is currently most assuredly at the very least overdiagnosed and misdiagnosed. As a result millions of children diagnosed with ADHD have likely been wrongly diagnosed with a mental disorder or the wrong mental disorder. This means millions of children are taking dangerous medication they have no real need to be taking.

ADHD is currently by default wrongly diagnosed—that is, overdiagnosed and misdiagnosed—because the diagnostic criteria are not being used as recommended. Also, the diagnostic criteria (the way we supposedly measure and identify ADHD) are not supported by science. And if the powers behind ADHD readily admit there is no reliable or valid way to measure or test for it (shortly, we'll see how the powers that be readily admit this is the case), then how can they either claim it exists or hope to come close to offering an accurate diagnosis capable of identifying it? Rest assured, the pro–ADHD experts make many contradictory claims related to not having evidence of the disorder, ways to identify the disorder, or knowing the effects of the drugs they are pushing on kids.

Don't Believe the Hype

Believe it or not, for decades experts in child development, psychology, psychiatry, and neurology have produced evidence and repeatedly warned us of this farce being touted as fact. For example, Dr. Gerald Golden, a professor of neurology, stated in 1991 that "the response to [ADHD stimulant medication] cannot be used to validate the diagnosis. Normal boys as well as those with ADHD show similar changes when given a single dose of psychostimulant." For decades, numerous respected international health organizations (e.g., the International Narcotics Control Board and World Health Organization) and even the U.S. Congress have expressed concern as to whether prescribing drugs for such a questionable diagnosis is warranted or safe. Unfortunately, the propaganda campaign fueled by those behind the ADHD movement has quite successfully distracted millions of parents and educators from discovering the real facts.

The research, however, documents that this whole movement to paint inattention and hyperactivity-impulsivity in children as a disease or some sort of abnormality of the brain is just a hoax growing further out of control. If there were real evidence countering the claim that it's a hoax, then after almost sixty years during which pharmaceutical companies have marketed stimulants for children and the American Psychiatric Association has tried to justify this label for kids, pro-ADHD experts wouldn't continually state in publications such as the *Diagnostic and Statistical Manual of Mental Disorders* (DSM-5) and many ADHD drug medication guides that "no real causes have been identified for ADHD," "no biological marker is diagnostic for ADHD," "brain scans *still* can't confirm ADHD's existence," or "tests of attention, executive function, or memory . . . are not sufficiently sensitive or specific to serve as diagnostic indices [measurements identifying ADHD]."

If pro-ADHD experts had real evidence that ADHD is a disease or chronic condition, real medical tests (e.g., blood test, DNA tests, or brain scans) would actually test for it. Instead most specialists still only use a pencil or pen to put a check mark on a simple piece of paper next to a few of the eighteen common behaviors associated with ADHD that all children exhibit *often* to some degree. This surreal hoax is fed by an arm of the pharmaceutical industry making billions of dollars every year by scaring concerned parents into believing their claims. Sadly, it is further perpetuated by a few doctors, the medical-insurance industry, mental-health practitioners, and educators, who have either been misguided or hope you don't take the time to learn the real facts explaining what the real deal is when it comes to children exhibiting ADHD *symptoms*.

So if you are ready and willing and you want to learn more about what I have discovered in my research into the mystical diagnosis known as ADHD, then I urge you to keep reading. What you are about to discover is that for kids ADHD is not a serious mental disorder or a disease you need to be highly concerned about.

The behaviors associated with ADHD are just signs that your child is young, still learning, still developing, energetic, imaginative, and most likely bored out of his or her mind at school. The behaviors associated with ADHD are just signs that you might have your hands full in helping a child develop into a responsible and well-behaved young adult—which is a given for nearly all of you who have raised children. And regardless of whether ADHD drugs seem to be a quick, convenient fix to drug a child into behaving the way some adults want them to behave, the reward is not worth the risk.

HOW IT ALL BEGAN

The day I realized just how strange and surreal life can be in the medicated world of students diagnosed with ADHD, I was standing in a crowded hallway in a small, rural elementary school, waiting in line for lunch. As a psychologist and researcher, I have worked with hundreds of schools during the past decade. And on this particular visit I had spent the morning studying children's and teachers' efforts related to one of my federal grant projects researching character development.

The principal had asked me to stay for lunch. There were a couple of classrooms of children rushing to get in the two lines entering the cafeteria that day. I stepped out of the way and decided to find my place at the back of what seemed like the longer line that had extended out into the hallway. The line I chose stretched along the far hallway wall all the way down to the door of the principal's office. There I was, once again standing and staring at a principal's door. I must admit it brought back some not-so-wonderful childhood memories.

The boy in front of me nodded at the sign on the principal's office door I was looking at and asked, "Did you get in trouble?" "Funny," I replied. The boy in front of him laughed and asked, "Did you get held back a grade . . . or twenty?" I smiled and said with my best kid impersonation, "Nooooo." My new friends giggled and wiggled even more as they continued to pelt me with endless fourth-grade humor.

At that point, the line of kids I was in seemed much more energetic, entertaining, and interesting than the shorter line across the hallway. As the last class came down the hallway to get in line, I let some more kids move in front of me. It was at this point that I noticed that the other line was moving much more quickly than the line I was in. At first this did not strike me as weird—I had simply picked the longer and apparently slower line on this day, I thought.

Yet upon closer examination, the other line was going straight into the cafeteria while my line was stopping at a hallway window getting what appeared to be drinks in little paper cups before going into the cafeteria. I stayed in the line thinking I was going to get a bonus cup of bug juice or something special.

As I finally made it to the window to get my juice, the school nurse behind the counter looked at me strangely and asked with a smirk, "Do you have a doctor's prescription for ADHD?"

"No, but I am a doctor, and I have been on TV," I joked.

"This is the line for ADHD medication, Dr. Corrigan, and though I hear you are slightly disruptive I am not sure I can give you any meds today."

To save face, and not look more clueless than I felt, I smiled and moved on, into the cafeteria.

What I Noticed

As I made my way slowly past each of the lunch ladies ladling out the loads of yummy gravy onto mashed potatoes, complemented by even more starch-filled carbohydrates and fat-laden proteins (the perfect recipe for inattentiveness and a strong desire to take an afternoon siesta), my tray was stacked with all the offerings. I was anxious to dig into the grub that rested in each little plastic molded sector of my nostalgia-inducing school lunch tray.

I decided to go sit at the table where some of the kids who had been in my line had taken a seat. As I ate my lunch, I noticed that the demeanor of my line's kids was different from others' in the cafeteria. As time passed, I noticed that only a few of the kids at my table would even make eye contact with others. Even the know-it-all, extroverted, smarty-pants kids I had stood next to in line were now slowly growing less boisterous.

As I continued eating my lunch, I also noticed that very few at my table were actually eating. As the lunch period progressed, I noticed some of the kids at my table were intensely focused on playing with their food and molding their mashed potatoes into strange starchy structures. Others, with an empty glare, gazed zombie-like into the distance in what I can only describe as a somewhat-catatonic state.

Some might wonder how taking ADHD stimulants could produce zombie-like gazes, because you might think that giving stimulants to children would amp them up more. Well, the process is sort of like eating too much sugar: Feed kids a little sugar, and they're bouncing off walls. But feed kids too much sugar and they crash like babies. It's a trick I learned long ago when babysitting my nephews when I was much younger. Technically, it is an effect of overstimulation. Yet the kids at my cafeteria table were now supposedly "good to go"—one of my Planet ADHD educational terms—now medicated sufficiently for an afternoon of "productive learning."

It was the longest lunch period I have ever experienced. Comparing the kids at my table to others in the cafeteria, and slowly watching these playful, creative, energetic, and funny children go from kids being kids to near expressionless robot-like entities, made me sick to my stomach.

Inspired to Action

At this point, my emotions were on a roller coaster that had started at confused, then crested at concerned, and finally went all the way downhill to just plain angry. I was mad. I looked closely at the kids sitting at my table and compared them again to the other kids in the cafeteria. My kids seemed to be skinnier, shorter, and, by the end of the lunch period, much less happy. It was as if I had mysteriously stepped through a portal into some similar yet strangely different parallel universe. It was as if I were on a different planet altogether.

Unfortunately, I have discovered that my experience at this school—though theirs admittedly had more out-of-control incidence of ADHD than appears in most schools—is not an uncommon occurrence in our education system. According to Centers for Disease Control and Prevention data, approximately 6.4 million kids in the United States alone are labeled ADHD, and 4.5 million are being drugged daily in the name of ADHD. To put this astronomical number into perspective, we are drugging more kids in the United States for ADHD than exist in Ireland's entire population. As I have also learned, on that day I had only seen the kids who had been given the cheaper, older drugs, which only last for three to four hours. There is a good possibility that twice as many kids had taken one of the newer extended-release (XR) pills for ADHD before they left home, which are designed to last all day.

AUDIENCE

Maybe you are an educator who is curious about what an outspoken psychologist (willing to speak out against the insurance-empowered pharmaceutical machine) would have to say. Maybe you are a concerned adult tired of watching this practice take place, and you want to know more. It's even possible you are a teenager, college student, or young adult previously diagnosed and possibly drugged for ADHD, seeking the truth about your diagnosis.

Maybe you are reading this book because you are among the millions who already agree that ADHD is highly questionable if not totally concocted. Or maybe, just maybe, you are a parent looking for just one person to be honest and say that this practice is deplorable while providing you with experiences, common-sense arguments, and research to back it up. Whatever your reasons for picking this book up, I sincerely thank you. As they say, knowledge is power and debate is healthy.

This book is mainly written for parents who are only now being pulled into this freaky world called ADHD. This book offers a sound body of evidence providing plenty of reasons for you to say no to the ADHD label and drugs. But hopefully many other parents and educators (possibly even mental-health and medical experts) who have already said yes to the ADHD label and drugs will consider what I have to say here.

I know that the message I share is going to make some of you uncomfortable: If what I have to share makes sense and successfully makes the case that ADHD doesn't really exist, it means millions have made the wrong decision. And no one wants to find out that they have made the wrong decision when it comes to diagnosing and drugging children.

Welcome to America's Nightmare

Call me crazy, diagnose me delusional, but I find it slightly surreal that we live in a society where millions of children are medicated daily in order to modify behavior that most experts in education, child development, psychology, and pediatric medicine would call normal or acceptable. It seems nearly Orwellian for parents to be told by an educator, mental-health practitioner, or medical doctor that their four- to ten-year-old child has ADHD and needs to take cocaine-like stimulants daily that have a long list of scary side effects.

Parents agree to this practice of medicating (or overstimulation) often not knowing that what is sold as a temporary step to help a child behave better and "focus more" becomes a long-term practice. The parents, after years of giving ADHD drugs to their kids, are then surprised when the doctor tells them that the child is now showing symptoms of disorders such as depression and/or obsessive compulsive disorder (OCD) and must be medicated further. Please note that the symptoms often associated with disorders like depression and OCD coincidentally are similar to the side effects that can come from using ADHD medications. I will expand more on this in chapter 4 when we explore what I call discombobulating disclaimers.

But after agreeing to more medications to treat the more serious diagnosis or diagnoses, parents later are informed that their once-precious little gassy baby is now exhibiting symptoms of bipolar disorder. Please note that the symptoms of bipolar are, coincidentally, similar to the side effects that often come from short- and long-term use of ADHD and depression medications. And when the ADHD drugs—combined with the depression, OCD, and bipolar drugs—lead to more abnormal behavior and possibly suicidal thoughts and the reality that their child might never move out of the basement or be able to live a normal life on his or her own, I can only imagine how alarming and discomforting it is for parents to hear the news I am sharing.

But despite the fact that I do not wish to increase the stress of parents stuck in the parallel universe on Planet ADHD, the truth is something that must be told. Whether or not after reading the evidence this book shares you agree that ADHD does not exist and that ADHD drugs are very dangerous, even using the accepted criteria today for diagnosing kids will still indicate that the majority of children labeled ADHD have likely been misdiagnosed.

A Large Margin for Error

Unfortunately, for the field of mental health, it wouldn't be the first time such mass levels of misdiagnosis have taken place. For example, a recent study in the *Journal of Psychotherapy and Psychosomatics* found that two-thirds of individuals diagnosed with depression in their study's sample of 5,369 participants did not meet the criteria for major depressive episodes. The study suggests that one reason why 66 percent were misdiagnosed might be that many cannot afford to see mental-health practitioners and instead go to general practitioners who do not necessarily follow the *Diagnostic and Statistical Manual of Mental Disorders* guidelines required to diagnose depression correctly. This same reason plagues the current ADHD diagnosis, because it is a recognized reality that millions of kids are being diagnosed with ADHD in ten to twenty minutes by a pediatrician or family physician (a.k.a. general practitioners).

The DSM, however, states that current diagnostic criteria (what it takes to be diagnosed) require documentation from several individuals observing the child in several different settings displaying the symptoms at an inconsistent developmental level for at least six months. Furthermore, the assessment tool for ADHD using eighteen simple child-like behaviors has no statistically significant findings gathered through sound research documenting its statistical reliability or validity. The current eighteen *symptoms* used to diagnose ADHD are so common to all children that it provides no reliable method to discriminate who actually has or doesn't have ADHD—what experts call *discriminant or divergent validity* in the field of psychometrics. The current eighteen symptoms used are so pathetically common to nearly all children that they could be replaced with the following single symptom: "Often breathes and has a heartbeat." Just these few facts begin to highlight that the math doesn't add up when it comes to diagnosing ADHD.

The severely flawed current diagnosis using eighteen commonly observed childhood behaviors is far too often not being followed as recommended, and the behaviors (ADHD symptoms) describe nearly every child. As a result, it is quite possible that nearly every child recommended for an ADHD diagnosis today is being diagnosed ADHD upon being seen by an "expert." The research and science used to justify ADHD does not come close to giving any doctors the privilege to drug children for acting like children and further exposes the nightmare that many seem to be unable to awaken from.

GOALS FOR THIS BOOK

Providing you with the total body of evidence you need to make a rational decision is my goal. I want to help you make a more informed decision when it comes to rejecting the diagnosis of ADHD and prescribing ADHD drugs to children.

Now trust me, I do understand why some adults are willing to consider being a part of this practice. I get it. I am a parent and professor, and I have also taught in a juvenile detention center (and worked outside of the detention center with many juveniles labeled as delinquents). Shamefully, at times I wished I could have medicated some of the children and students in my life. As one of my good friends likes to joke, "There is a good reason why some alligators eat their young." But I believe that all children should have the opportunity to experience childhood drug free.

I suspect some readers might be offended by my view. If so, I apologize now for my biased view about giving ADHD drugs to kids that have been labeled ADHD. If you want a book to make you feel better about drugging your child (or students) for exhibiting characteristics of somewhat annoying behaviors that nearly all children show signs of, there are plenty out there. If you personally have been diagnosed ADHD and find what I am sharing to be uncomfortable, I understand and apologize for being part of the angst you might be feeling.

But I suspect that if you read this book and push through the feelings of mental discomfort caused by new information that might conflict with your current view, knowledge, or beliefs (what we call *cognitive dissonance* in the field of psychology), the research and stories I will share are going to make you question this unfortunate trend as well.

HOW THIS BOOK IS ORGANIZED

The book is structured in two parts. Part I, A Parallel Universe, focuses on six factors that are contributing the most to this unfortunate practice of labeling and medicating kids for acting like kids. Part II, Multiple Realities, focuses on additional evidenced-based factors we can use to stop this trend and more holistically address such somewhat-annoying behaviors associated with today's ADHD label. In other words, part 1 focuses on the problems, and part 2 focuses on the solutions. Each chapter of this book is written to provide you with a concise summary of the facts you need to know, more insights on these facts, and suggestions on how to use the information to help children. Each chapter is written to provide you with ten specific evidence-based reasons why we should stop drugging children for acting like children.

ABOUT THE AUTHOR

I am an educational psychologist specializing in research on child development and the psychology of learning. I mainly teach human development, educational psychology, and research methods and statistical analysis. My grants and contractual research during the past decade have encompassed more than sixty thousand children in more than sixty school districts from coast to coast. My academic work and professional focus is dedicated to helping children live a better life physically, socially, and intellectually at home, in their community, and at school. My presentations, publications, and books are mainly focused on helping parents and our education system better focus on developing great kids.

I tender my credentials and interests because I want you to understand that I am not a clinical psychiatrist or psychologist, therapist, licensed counselor, or medical doctor. I do not have a license to diagnose or medicate. Unlike many of the published researchers who focus on ADHD, I am not funded by or connected to a pharmaceutical company. I am more of a research-focused psychologist. My expertise rests in designing sound methods and measurements to capture reliable, valid, trustworthy, accurate evidence.

I am a psychologist who uses real science to study the education process and the behavior and development process of children. From reviewing decades of research completed by others as well as personally researching children for more than a decade (as well as reflecting on my experiences working with kids in public-school settings, youth detention centers, and community outreach), I can assure you that all children develop gradually, sequentially (one stage at a time), and rarely ever on similar time lines. In other words, not every child in a third-grade classroom is going to be at the same stage of development behaviorally, physically, socially, or intellectually.

While some clinical colleagues, counselors, therapists, and pediatricians might want to tell you what is wrong with your child if he or she appears to be different than his or her classmates, I want to show you that a unique developmental issue or behavioral challenge does not always equal a disease, mental disorder, or learning disability. Instead of offering a diagnosis that provides a convenient label to finally offer an answer to describe your child's or some of your students' possibly awkward mannerisms or extreme behaviors, I want to share with you the same message I instruct my students to use in their careers working with children: What one might call a disability, disorder, or disease is actually quite often a sign of giftedness or a simple developmental issue that time, natural maturation, inspiring instruction, tons of love, and, most of all, good parenting can transform into something special.

A QUICK DISCLAIMER

Now, before the whole pharmaceutical industry and mental-health field declare war on me, I would like to be crystal clear before I continue. I am not against the whole pharmaceutical industry or doctors who prescribe pharmaceuticals. I am thoroughly convinced that many of the mental disorders in the DSM are real, and I admire the demanding work mental-health practitioners perform. I believe that many in the pharmaceutical industry and mental-health field are truly looking out for the public welfare, providing an essential service and doing incredible research and development.

I have a number of very close friends who suffer from a range of horrible diseases and disorders such as ALS (Lou Gehrig's disease), multiple sclerosis, and severe chronic depression, and I know that without medications their lives would surely be much less enjoyable. I personally know scientists who work in the pharmaceutical industry, and I know they are good people trying every day to the best of their abilities to do amazing things.

As an adult and parent, I am truly grateful for the medications they have created that reduce the pain associated with life-threatening health challenges and help so many to cope. I am not against prescribing medications for adults to cope with symptoms related to mental disorders (such as severe chronic depression) they have not been able to bypass—find a cure, if you will. As adults, we can make our own decisions if we feel medication is truly needed. As adults, we are no longer in the critical developmental years essential to our social, psychological, neurological, and physical growth.

ON BEHALF OF CHILDREN

This book is written to support all of the kids in the world who would like to avoid being singled out as one of the those who have to take their "medicine" before going to lunch or receive some special accommodations for taking a test. This might seem less important (or awkward) in elementary school, but as kids get older, such information can become quite harmful to a student's self-image and standing in class. Furthermore, this book is not just an attack on a small wing of the pharmaceutical industry that promotes drugging children, as some might say it is. I am an equal-opportunity critic, and I put equal responsibility on the few educators, health professionals, and individuals in the health-insurance industry who literally push parents to put kids onto the pharmaceutical freight train.

The good news is that not all pharmaceutical companies are selling such drugs for kids. The good news is that some health-insurance providers actually still pay for real therapy (talk therapy) and not just medication. The good news is that the majority of educators are very caring individuals who would never suggest to a parent that they need to have their child diagnosed with ADHD and put on drugs if they want that child to succeed in school. The good news is that a large population of doctors and mental-health professionals refuse to push these drugs or to play games with our next generation.

Even though some individuals associated with the pharmaceutical and health-insurance industries, education field, and health profession might be offended by the message, opinions, and information contained in this book, I know many others in their fields will applaud the effort. At the end of the day, the only people who can truly protect our children from such abuse are the educators, health care providers, parents, and guardians of our children: you.

As parents and educators we have to make the best choices possible when it comes to the difficult questions about how we will raise, educate, nurture, and discipline our children. The big question is whether you will regret having been the parent, guardian, or educator who accepted the claims of pharmaceutical companies or the advice of a health professional to put your child or children on drugs for a disorder that might not even exist but most assuredly is currently widely misdiagnosed and overdiagnosed. I urge you to delay answering this question until after you have read what this book has to offer. And I thank you for your willingness to listen.

INTRODUCTION

Greetings from Planet ADHD!

Imagine a not-so-distant parallel universe where there is a pill to treat anything that might trouble you. Depression? Aggression? There is a prescription. Can't fit into that fancy black dress or tuxedo? It's a safe bet you can find a miracle weight-loss formula. Child can't focus in school? No problem. No matter what your illness, Planet ADHD has a *magical* medication to relieve whatever your body or mind begs. It is a place where "medicines" exist to treat nearly every health challenge you or your family might ever have—and even a few more you would have never envisioned.

Sounds like a great place, doesn't it? But be careful what you wish for, because living on this strange Class-M planet (where M apparently stands for *medication*) can be very disturbing.

JOINING THE MEDICATION MOVEMENT

Planet ADHD is a disturbing place, because while the billion-dollar pharmaceutical industry has the resources to create so many medications to "treat" the pain and symptoms associated with psychological and behavioral challenges related to mental disorders, they seem to be unable to develop medications that can actually stop the symptoms from occurring or better yet "cure" disorders. Their efforts seem to run into the same challenges when it comes to curing real medical (not mental) diseases. Either way, as a result, we see medication more often used to mask symptoms than fix the problems.

Additionally, as many can attest from firsthand experience, when we take a medication to mask certain symptoms, we often encounter side effects. When we have side effects, we then *need* more medications to treat the side effects. For example, recently a foster parent shared with me how one of her new kids came to her on eleven prescribed medications, including treatment for ADHD, blood pressure, and sleeping. As she was told by her agency, most of these medications are needed to treat certain side effects of her foster child's ADHD and obesity drugs. This predicament and the foster parent's efforts to try and slowly wean her new foster child off these medications provide a picture of the many challenges in today's medicated world that is an all-too-common occurrence for adults and children.

When you become a customer of the pharmaceutical industry, you quite often remain a customer of the pharmaceutical industry. Due to the extreme side effects and severe withdrawal experienced when trying to quit the medications (such that one might question if withdrawal consequences are strategically designed into the medication—for example, nicotine added to tobacco products), it is hard enough to get off of one prescribed medication let alone another ten.

The extreme withdrawal experiences resulting from quitting ADHD or depression medications are perfect examples of just how painful quitting can be and a sign that quite possibly the prescribed drugs are extremely addictive—a fact that most if not all of the medication guides for the prescribed ADHD stimulants readily admit to. This parallel universe is also disturbing because some of these medications (which could in many circumstances actually help those fighting life-threatening diseases such as cancer, or at least improve one's quality of life) are frequently not affordable or accessible to the average citizen of Planet ADHD.

One of the most confusing and troubling aspects, however, is that millions of children have been recruited into this medication movement under the label of ADHD. What is truly scary is that adults (parents, teachers, and other professionals) are handing over these children to a life of drug use with little concern for

1. the legitimacy of how the disorder is currently diagnosed and, more importantly, concerns as to whether it is actually a real mental disorder,
2. the lack of conclusive research exploring the detrimental long-term effects of ADHD drugs on our youth, and
3. what it ultimately means for a child to be labeled ADHD.

TOO LEGIT TO QUIT

Of the hundreds of adults I have personally spoken to concerning ADHD, many are very concerned about medicating children, need help navigating this mysterious land, and want to know more. Although they may have been given a certain pharmaceutical company's marketing literature by the school or doctor's office that touts the legitimacy of the so-called science behind ADHD and the many benefits of the medication, or they were told by their doctor or mental health practitioner that "this is the best thing to do" for the child, there is still a little voice inside the heads of many adults saying "Find out more . . . This just doesn't seem right." And rightly so, for there is much to be concerned about when we agree to the diagnosis of ADHD and to medicate young children for acting like young children.

Regardless of whether you agree at this point that ADHD should not be considered a legitimate or real disorder, under current protocol and practices it would appear a large percentage of the children labeled ADHD have been *diagnosed* and provided a prescription by a pediatrician or mental-health expert during a single doctor's rather short consultation. So either we have some amazing doctors out there who can see the past and future quicker than a Long Island psychic in order to diagnose ADHD, or we are seeing firsthand the dismissal and mistaken use of the current criteria supposedly required for diagnosis of ADHD.

Such rushing to judgment is just partially responsible for the current misdiagnosis and overdiagnosis of ADHD. But as chapter 2 will show, the failing to follow protocol probably doesn't mean that much in the long run, given that every child basically meets the criteria for the currently recommended ADHD diagnosis.

One of the main focuses of this book in the beginning is to give you a close look at how little pro-ADHD experts use to diagnose ADHD and the strange path of disconnected medical discoveries (claims) they use to justify that ADHD is actually something real. Once you read the simple eighteen behaviors they feel represent ADHD today (by the way, kids don't even need to display any of them to be labeled ADHD, as we'll see shortly) and compare them to what ADHD was thought to be at a half dozen other times during the last one hundred or so years, you will see how the legitimacy of the ADHD label is indeed highly questionable.

The bottom line is that given the large likelihood of invalid diagnosis (overdiagnosis or misdiagnosis) taking place, the odds are quite strong that millions of children have been wrongly labeled with ADHD. In fact, studies shared in chapter 7 show how the youngest children in classrooms—those kids who don't always behave in the most mature ways—are two times more likely to be diagnosed with ADHD and put on ADHD drugs.

These studies suggest that developmental and behavioral issues related to the age (maturity level) of the child, in comparison to the older peers in the classroom, explain why about 2.5 million children are being misdiagnosed (wrongly labeled) with ADHD. The bigger question such research calls attention to, however, is what other simple explanations (beyond being the youngest of children in the classroom) clarify why the other four million kids are diagnosed with ADHD and possibly prescribed dangerous drugs.

THE LACK OF CONCLUSIVE EVIDENCE
AND ABUNDANCE OF RED FLAGS FLYING

As the following research will show, there is very little conclusive evidence on the developmental, social, psychological, neurological, academic, and physical effects (good or bad) resulting from the long-term use of ADHD drugs (see chapters 3, 4, and 6). Although the practice of medicating youth for ADHD-like behavior unfortunately has been going on for more than six decades since the creation of Ritalin, the pharmaceutical company's billion-dollar research arms have not provided enough longitudinal evidence to support the long-term use of these medications. They even readily admit within their medication guides that they have no proof (supposedly no idea) what the drugs even do to a child's brain (see chapter 4). The only real evidence pro-ADHD experts have is a lack of real evidence.

Doesn't it seem like companies with billions of dollars to spend on research that care about their customers would want to know whether their products are negatively affecting their customers—kids? Don't you think they would want to confirm that the drugs are not causing permanent brain damage? Since long-term use is being recommended, don't you think they would want to produce a massive amount of evidence showing that they are 100 percent sure that what they have to offer is safe and effective for long-term use?

The fact that they have good reasons to replicate studies to more soundly track the effects of ADHD medication on children over a number of years and ample resources to collect longitudinal evidence and yet are unable or unwilling to produce conclusive experimental research should serve as a major red flag.

The vast majority of the not-so-family-friendly arm of the pharmaceutical industry's evidence just supports that ADHD drugs are only capable of reducing behavior problems and improving the ability to focus in school for a short period of time. Meanwhile there is other evidence completed by the National Institute of Mental Health (NIMH) suggesting that such "improvements in behavior" are only reflective of the brain being medicated to malfunction. As we'll see in chapter 3, what the pro-ADHD pharmaceutical powers call behavior improvement is basically chemically induced brain failure.

Given that there are many effective alternatives to reducing behavior problems and improving a student's ability to focus that do not require drugs (see part 2 of this book), it seems reckless to justify the use of drugs when you compare the minimal short-term benefits possibly gained to the laundry list of possible negative (in some instances life-threatening) short- and long-term side effects that the ADHD drug manufacturers readily admit to in their medication guides.

FURTHER NEGATIVE IMPLICATIONS
TO CHILD DEVELOPMENT

From research collected inside and outside of the pharmaceutical umbrella, there is a strong possibility that many long-term detrimental effects and challenges to natural childhood development can come from taking such drugs for an extended period of time at such an early age. Information and research is readily available on the ADHD pharmaceutical companies' and the U.S. FDA's websites about the many unfortunate common side effects ranging from high blood pressure, decreased insulin sensitivity, diabetes, facial tics, weight loss and permanent growth suppression, and depression to suicidal thoughts. Sadly, such side effects can be even more severe with rare outcomes such as death occurring from heart failure or allergic reactions.

It also appears that the pharmaceutical powers that be would like for you to ignore research in child development and psychology that addresses how adults can help children manage the developmental and behavioral symptoms associated with the ADHD label without medication. Why? Because research completed inside and outside of the pharmaceutical umbrella (see chapters 3 and 7) shows that the behaviors associated with symptoms of ADHD—behaviors that so many want you to be very afraid of and immediately label and medicate—can be treated just as effectively (if not more) through an assortment of behavior modification and counseling efforts void of medication. Research also shows that typically, without the use of medication, such behaviors naturally gradually decrease in severity and in some instances disappear as a child matures.

IMAGE IS EVERYTHING

Beyond the questionable diagnosis and the effects of the ADHD drugs prescribed, what many haven't considered is what it means to a child's future and self-image when they grow up labeled with ADHD and receive special treatment and accommodations. Despite regulations tied to laws governing the practice of discriminating against persons due to disabilities and developmental delays, we must not forget that very few employers *want* to hire a person for higher-level positions if during the interview process the person explains they will be on drugs for ADHD and as a result will need special accommodations to perform their work duties. At some point in time, before becoming an adult, all children need (or at least need to be given the opportunity to try) to learn how to do what they do best (their career of choice) free of medication and special accommodations.

For example, I teach future counselors, therapists, and teachers, and on occasion I do receive notification from the university that a certain student has ADHD and will need special accommodations. Most often the requests involve providing extra time or special rooms void of distractions to take tests. It may be that such accommodations when a child is younger and has attention problems could be beneficial.

But at some point we must realize they will not get such accommodations in the business world, the real world. I do not foresee my education students diagnosed with ADHD explaining to their principal (their new boss) that since they need double the time to perform a teaching task, their students will need to attend fourteen periods of class a day rather than seven. I do not foresee a therapist or counselor explaining to one's client that they themselves have ADHD and, though most therapists only would need an hour to counsel them, they will need to charge for two hours to provide the same service. At some point we must start teaching students to catch up with their peers and not rely on special accommodations.

Helping children with special needs and providing accommodations to help with such special needs is what makes our education system one of the most admirable in the world. Unfortunately, with millions of questionable diagnoses like ADHD flooding the system, the services provided to the kids with more serious special needs are being watered down. But we also must realize that at some point, for many older special-needs children, it is quite possible such accommodations are only doing more harm than good.

Plus, as you are about to learn, a 2009 study published in the *Journal of the American Academy of Child and Adolescent Psychiatry* documents how ADHD drugs' effectiveness (e.g., ability to control behavior via medicating the brain into malfunctioning) decreases after fourteen months of use, and the drug-treatment advantage is gone completely after three years of use. Regardless of whether your child is already labeled with (and medicated for) ADHD, getting them off the drugs and teaching them how to think, behave, and perform drug free is of great immediate importance developmentally, neurologically, physically, emotionally, academically, socially, and professionally.

THE EBB AND FLOW OF ADHD LITERATURE

At this point I have to ask you whether this book is sounding or feeling like any other book on ADHD you have read. If you have not read any of the brave words written by individuals such as Dr. Fred Baughman, Dr. Richard E. Vatz, Dr. Diane McGuinness, or Dr. Peter Breggin, who for decades have tried to warn parents, educators, and mental-health professionals about the shortcomings of the ADHD diagnosis and dangers of ADHD drugs, I would venture to say your answer to my question would be no. As Dr. McGuinness wrote in 1989, "The past twenty-five years [have] led to a phenomenon almost unique in history. Methodologically rigorous research . . . indicates that ADD [attention deficit disorder] and hyperactivity as 'syndromes' simply does not exist. We have invented a disease [and] given it medical sanction and now must disown it. The major question is how we go about destroying the monster we have created. It is not easy to do this and still save face." In 1993, Dr. Vatz was even more candid, saying "attention-deficit disorder [ADD] is no more a disease than is 'excitability.' It is a psychiatric, pseudomedical term."

For decades respected experts have warned us of the lack of credibility and research behind this supposed disorder. But as you will learn in chapter 6, as the critics spoke out against ADHD, the pharmaceutical companies stepped up their game and flooded the market with a plethora of poorly designed and unethical research. Unfortunately, many of their propaganda efforts have worked to confuse the masses. As a result, the vast majority of recent books on ADHD and endless Internet resources (coincidently sponsored quite often by a pharmaceutical company selling ADHD drugs) endorse the diagnosis of ADHD and support ADHD medication.

But instead of giving you the whole story, the truth, these websites redirect your attention by providing misleading anecdotal evidence. Recently, however, many popular newspapers and magazines (*New York Times*, *Forbes*, *Wall Street Journal*, *Psychology Today*), as well as leading government agencies (the Centers for Disease Control and Prevention and the Substance Abuse and Mental Health Services Administration) have started to publish articles and studies suggesting that, indeed, ADHD is currently being misdiagnosed and overdiagnosed and needs to be studied more closely.

As you continue to read this book, though most literature published on ADHD in the last two decades has ridden the wave of ADHD's popularity, you will realize there are many questions when it comes to what has been written about ADHD's connection to kids. As discussed in chapter 6, the majority of what you will find written on ADHD is sponsored or funded by the pharmaceutical companies. Many of the so-called non-biased, nonprofit websites advocating for ADHD are often semicovertly sponsored by pharmaceutical companies selling ADHD drugs to parents. Much of what has been published and marketed supporting ADHD is riddled with shadows of bias and financial conflicts of interest. And when others not associated with the pharmaceutical industry publish conflicting and contradictory findings, they are often attacked.

By simply typing "Dr. Peter Breggin" (author of *The Ritalin Fact Book*, among others) into a search engine you can see what happens when an intelligent, qualified expert who cares about kids speaks out against the pharmaceutical machine. The typical route of attack starts with pro-ADHD experts basically calling you a quack and then using pharmaceutical mumbo jumbo and scientific or statistical language to confuse even the savviest of consumers and to act as if they have all of the answers. Again, don't believe the hype!

As a quantitative researcher, methodologist, and professor who teaches the mumbo jumbo known to the academic world as research statistics, I am well aware of how easy it is to confuse the masses with ivory tower "stat-a-neese" (the language of statistics). When it comes to analysis and statistical reporting, unfortunately, our academic and medical journals are plagued with studies pontificating, using *big* words, while at the same time using flawed methodologies and incorrect analysis, then overzealously touting inflated claims based on weak statistical findings.

What many outside of the science world don't understand is that findings claiming *statistical significance* can often be of little importance if the studies are (1) poorly designed, (2) the measures used to capture so-called evidence are meaningless, and (3) the outcomes, though statistically significant, are weak. Chapter 6 will expand on such limitations.

But regardless of the tsunami of misleading and misdirected literature on ADHD that has flooded our minds during the past decade or so, due to federal laws the pharmaceutical powers that be readily admit in nearly everything they publish that they don't have all the answers. This book is intended to help you make better sense of the science and claims associated with ADHD. This book is written to help you understand that, when it comes to ADHD, much of what is claimed to be fact is not necessarily so. The goal is to get you ask the question, What if?

WHAT IF?

What if the outspoken psychologist writing this book who wants to keep kids from being drugged for acting like kids is right? What if the pharmaceutical manufacturers, medical professionals, and educators who support medicating our youth for ADHD are wrong?

Think seriously about this simple, soul-searching question, because it is quite possible that pro-ADHD experts *are* wrong. The annual number of ADHD drug emergencies has quadrupled in six years, and according to a report released in August 2013 from the Substance Abuse and Mental Health Services Administration (SAMSHA), in 2011 ADHD drugs sent twenty-three thousand young adults to the emergency room. This same report, the DAWN Report, warned of heart and blood vessel damage being linked to stimulant use.

Furthermore, the DSM is the manual that mental-health practitioners use to diagnose mental disorders. Chapter 2 expands on the fact that numerous mental disorders in the DSM once touted as real mental disorders one should be very concerned about have been removed for various shortcomings and misguided assumptions. In other words, they have been wrong about mental disorders before.

On any given day on television you will see multiple advertisements recruiting individuals and families of individuals that have taken a certain medication or used a specific medical device that led to more serious medical conditions or death. There is an abundance of commercials promoting websites and services that connect such victims with law firms and organizations focused on helping individuals navigate the legal system. When you go to such websites you find a list of medications and medical devices once touted as wonderful now exposed for their many dangerous shortcomings.

Consider the cold, hard facts: more than one hundred thousand people die every year due to errors made by doctors. A 2006 report from the Institute of Medicine of the National Academies indicates that four hundred thousand preventable drug-related injuries occur each year in hospitals. The same report shows that another eight hundred thousand preventable drug-related injuries occur annually in long-term care settings, and roughly 530,000 occur just among Medicare recipients in outpatient clinics. More recent headlines bring attention to the unfortunate reality that our veterans returning from recent wars are being lost in the Veterans' Affairs system, overmedicated and not treated properly for horrible conditions such as post-traumatic stress disorder (PTSD).

There is an endless list of what-ifs we should be thinking about when it comes to ADHD:

- What if the doctor who wrote or wants to write a prescription for your child (or the educator who sent you to this doctor) has not considered the long-term negative effects of medication on a brain and nervous system that are still developing?
- What if the doctors making a handsome income by creating regular customers reliant on expensive office visits and pharmaceutical prescriptions are actually prescribing drugs that are harmful to the natural development process of the patient (e.g., children prescribed ADHD drugs who often have no choice in the matter)?
- What if all of the troubling symptoms that are used to justify ADHD and scare so many into becoming a part of the pharmaceutical phenomenon are symptoms that will typically disappear or at least decline gradually as a child naturally develops?
- What if many of the symptoms we are using to diagnose ADHD in young children are many of the same attributes we find in gifted children?

- What if the drugs for ADHD are actually injuring the child and insuring that children who take such drugs will never be able to live life (function) without medication?
- What if putting children on ADHD medication increases the chances they will become drug addicts as adults?

Unfortunately, all of these what-ifs are reality for far too many. These are serious questions that need to be asked.

So if the doctors might be wrong, what if the educators are wrong? As chapters 5 and 7 explain, despite the propaganda claiming that our newly revamped standards-based education system will help us become the best in the world once again, our standards-based education system has been performing at a less-than-stellar level in the United States for several decades. As research supports and millions of educators and parents will agree, the approach our educators are being forced to take is wrong.

In fact, since we adopted the standards-based achievement-test focus, our educational performance as a nation (as it relates to academic-achievement test scores) has declined steadily. According to international rankings, determined by the 2009 Programme for International Student Assessment (PISA) test scores, the United States was ranked as average, placing fourteenth out of thirty-four countries on reading skills, and as below average, placing twenty-fifth out of thirty-four in mathematics. The most recent 2012 PISA scores show little change or improvement for the US education system. Since adopting the initial standardized-testing model, we have gone from one of the best in the world to average and below average.

Although we have many wonderful educators, the systems and policies under which they are held accountable are forcing them to teach to a test (or at a minimum to focus on preparing for a test) and spend less time focusing on developing our children as individuals. When a teacher's job security rests on making sure the classroom or school increases test scores annually, that teacher may go to desperate measures. If you don't believe such a claim, take a moment to read about the nearly three dozen educators who were indicted in Atlanta for cheating on the standards-based tests. To many, something equally as bad as cheating includes drugging students who are "disruptive" in class, all in the name of ADHD. To many, this represents taking the easy way out at our children's expense and is morally and ethically wrong.

ADHD DIAGNOSIS DISCLAIMER

At an early point in my research into ADHD I believed that ADHD was an actual mental disorder and that it was just the medication that was being wrongly prescribed. At that time I was planning to explain that maybe for some children (and possibly adults) this diagnosis and the medication given to address such symptoms might be justifiable. I was going to take this approach in hopes of allowing some of the adults, with children who truly exhibit extreme "maladaptive" ADHD symptoms, to hold on to the belief they are doing the right thing.

As I continued my research, however, I made up my mind that I must be like Dr. Seuss's Lorax and be a voice for those kids, because those kids have no voice in this debate. Though I know it might anger many—and I am opening myself up to attacks from mental-health practitioners, medical doctors, educators, health-insurance providers, and an arm of the pharmaceutical industry—I will state right now that I believe that ADHD should not be defined as a disorder.

If a child is truly exhibiting extreme behavioral symptoms inconsistent with their development level, then by all means, have them see an expert. By all means, you and your child should get counseling. But I strongly suggest you explore more reputable diagnoses than ADHD. When a child showing signs of the eighteen very generic descriptors of *normal* child-hood behavior is on that basis diagnosed with ADHD it is my professional opinion that the child does not have a real disorder.

To better illustrate what I mean, take a look at the following—a few of the symptoms used to diagnose ADHD. A child with ADHD, according to this partial checklist,

1. is often "on the go," acting as if "driven by a motor"
2. often talks excessively
3. often fidgets with or taps hands or feet or squirms in seat.

If you were like many others when you were a kid (or how many adults still sometimes behave today) and find that all three of these symptoms describe you today or how you acted when you were a kid, then you are half way home to being fully diagnosed as ADHD Hyperactive-Impulsive. But don't be too alarmed. The totality of these symptoms only equates to a diagnosis of being a normal human being.

INTRODUCING THE DSM

The Diagnostic and Statistical Manual of Mental Disorders (let's just call it the DSM from this point forward to avoid spraining our tongues) is kind of like the great big book of everything wrong with us and then some. This is *the* book mental-health practitioners use to diagnose and code disorders in order to be paid by insurance companies. As chapter 2 shares, it has grown from 106 disorders in 1952 to more than 365 in the latest edition.

Inasmuch as the other 365-plus disorders discussed and documented exist in the book's fifth edition (DSM-5), so does ADHD. This statement is not intended to suggest that all of the disorders documented in the DSM are not real. Many are very real and accurately describe and diagnose mental illnesses that people unfortunately experience. But what is real?

The disorders in the DSM are real because mental-health experts (psychologists or psychiatrists such as Sigmund Freud) coined terms such as *narcissist* and then created descriptors to identify the coined term in order to identify (i.e., diagnose) a certain type of *abnormal* behavior in a person. The diagnoses are real for many folks—mainly adults—because they finally provide a name that encompasses so many of the unique symptoms and idiosyncrasies that one thought might be related to something seriously wrong with a person. For adults, who have reached a plateau when it comes to brain and nervous-system development, finding such labels or answers can be comforting and helpful.

Identifying disorders can lead us to discovering ways to cope or improve our health. For ADHD, however, and when it comes to kids (especially boys, since most kids diagnosed with ADHD are boys), exhibiting any of the eighteen symptoms that are quite normal behaviors we see in children does not even come close to capturing an abnormal behavior or mental disorder. These broad symptoms do nothing but tell us that everyone has ADHD; just read the symptoms in chapter 2, and put a check next to the ones that you exhibited when you were a child, or even still exhibit today.

I do this exercise quite often during talks I give on ADHD. I ask the audience to raise their hands if the symptom I read describes them today or when they were a child. After raising their hands for the first symptom, most people don't put their hands down as I read the rest of the symptoms. Given the defining symptoms for ADHD, we all have ADHD. It is quite possibly an accurate diagnosis of being human and most definitely a good diagnosis for identifying common childhood behaviors. This is why I suspect that nearly every child who has been sent to a pro-ADHD doctor to be diagnosed ADHD leaves labeled ADHD.

SUMMARY

Therefore, in acknowledging a diagnosis of ADHD in children, we should not be so easily persuaded to accept it. All of the symptoms associated with an ADHD diagnosis could easily be used to describe many aspects of a child beyond ADHD. They could describe signs of highly creative and analytical abilities, developmental delays and issues, immaturity, giftedness, and so much more. The symptoms may describe kids who have not yet given in to society's expectation of how they must behave or education's hope that they will focus on school work they are not necessarily interested in. The symptoms in most children show that instead of living in a well-behaved, well-focused, and hypothetical, orderly adult world, they choose to stay in tune with their own world.

Given that childhood is precious and fleeting, and given the many pressures of adulthood, such as having to make decisions about drugging or not drugging our children for behaving like children, who can blame them?

I

=

A PARALLEL UNIVERSE

Using a parallel-universe theme, the chapters in the first part of this book focus on the main factors contributing to the trend of, and possible outcomes resulting from, labeling and medicating youth for ADHD.

- In the first chapter we begin by addressing a very important question: What if? Children being medicated for ADHD will never know what would have happened had they been allowed to develop naturally, free of ADHD drugs. This point is illustrated through an embellished story—taking place in our parallel universe—narrating the drugging of a gifted young man named Leonardo da Vinci. This chapter sets the stage to further question if we are drugging our best and brightest (or even normal) students because their somewhat unique behaviors are perceived to be abnormal. This chapter explores why so many are being diagnosed ADHD.
- In chapter 2, by diving into the dubious diagnosis of ADHD, we will learn that the definition and use of the ADHD diagnosis has changed quite dramatically from its origins and is now being used in a way much different from its original intent. Furthermore, chapter 2 shares how the diagnosis is determined by identifying eighteen very general behavioral descriptors exhibited by nearly all people (and most definitely children) and showing how the lack of differential diagnoses being offered (alternative explanations for such behavior) is contributing to further misdiagnosis and overdiagnosis under the current diagnostic criteria being used improperly.
- In chapter 3 we learn more about the most popular ADHD drugs being prescribed and some of the mythology behind them. We learn what these drugs really do to a child's brain. Spoiler alert: what some want you to believe is a sign that the drug is helping kids behave

better and pay better attention is just the end result of a young brain experiencing a drug-induced malfunction that has been linked to permanent brain damage in lab animals.

- In chapter 4 we explore details of the many warnings and disclaimers about the ADHD drugs being used and how the side effects and the implications of long-term use are details that must be considered seriously before agreeing to allow children to become a part of the billion-dollar pharmaceutical industry. According to the medication guides provided by the pharmaceutical companies, side effects range from increased agitation, high blood pressure, permanent growth suppression, nervous ticks, anxiety, and death . . . This is a chapter you must read.
- Chapter 5 addresses how our educational system is still based on a century-old factory model and has far too many schools focused more on manufacturing students with high achievement scores than on developing the whole child, our future generation. This chapter confronts the existing practice or theory that believes that academic success at the classroom level will be easier to achieve if we label and medicate the kids who refuse to sit motionless and quietly or accept today's idea of what constitutes education.
- Chapter 6 explores the many limitations and flaws associated with pro-ADHD research. This chapter is intended to help you identify the bright red warning flags connected to the claim that ADHD is a disease or epidemic, and in the process I hope you'll become a more knowledgeable consumer and savvier critic of ADHD research.

1

DRUGGING DA VINCI

REASON #1: Due to many factors contributing to the current misdiagnosis and overdiagnosis of ADHD, it is highly probable we are labeling and drugging children who in reality are gifted, experiencing temporary developmental delays, or in many instances just exhibiting normal age-appropriate childhood behavior.

The internet provides us with a long list of famous historical figures who were hypothesized to have met the criteria for being diagnosed ADHD: Leonardo da Vinci, Thomas Edison, the Wright brothers, Pablo Picasso, Van Gogh, Albert Einstein, Abraham Lincoln, John F. Kennedy . . . The list goes on of creative *men* who have made an impact on our world through their talents, inventions, and actions.

Please note that the lists of famous historical figures with ADHD typically do not contain the names of famous women. This is an interesting tidbit that is most likely tied to the fact that the overwhelming majority of kids diagnosed with ADHD are boys. Additionally, historically women weren't allowed to develop their talents, inventions, etc., and so we're not even hearing about them, whether they were "well-behaved" or not. In decades and centuries past, however, we did not medicate our brightest and best children (regardless of their gender) based on whether they exhibited possibly annoying or eccentric childhood behaviors.

Even with all of their unique idiosyncrasies, these famous historical gifted figures who today may have been diagnosed with ADHD using existing diagnostic criteria were allowed to develop naturally, without the use of pharmaceuticals. One might venture to say that it was their unique and even sometimes bizarre behaviors that helped these individuals become some of our best thinkers, inventors, artists, leaders, and citizens. But for a moment let's imagine what would have happened had

FOCUS ON THE FACTS

- There is a long list of incredibly gifted and famous historical figures who exhibited the symptoms of ADHD as children yet were never medicated for these behaviors.
- Many of the same traits or symptoms used to identify giftedness are similar to the traits used to label students with ADHD, behavioral disorders, learning disabilities, and developmental delays.
- Family structures, custody battles, sibling rivalries, social challenges, and managing what we are gifted with through our genetics (e.g., IQ and temperament) are some of the inherent challenges of life that contribute to children exhibiting symptoms of ADHD.
- Such situational experiences in childhood produce challenges to children's behavior, development, and maturation that are contributing to the increased diagnosis of ADHD.
- The increase in ADHD in the United States is also connected to the testing-focused education policy in great need of repair that rewards schools for identifying more kids with mental disorders and learning disabilities.
- According to Centers for Disease Control and Prevention data, ADHD diagnoses have increased 41 percent in the last decade in the United States, where currently nearly 6.4 million children between the ages of four and seventeen have been diagnosed with ADHD, with about two-thirds of them on ADHD medication.
- The United States has an 11 percent average prevalence rate of ADHD that mysteriously increases annually, while the rest of the world is holding steady at 3 to 7 percent.
- In some regions in the United States, such as the highest poverty-ridden Southern states, about 23 percent of boys have been diagnosed with ADHD.
- Children covered by Medicaid have the highest rates of ADHD diagnoses: 14 percent according to Centers for Disease Control and Prevention data, about one-third more than in the rest of the population.
- If so many are being diagnosed with ADHD due to supposed abnormal behavior, at some point we must consider whether or not the behavior is actually quite normal.

we used pharmaceuticals (e.g., "medicines" or, in earlier times, alchemy) to dull the senses and genius of Edison and Einstein, to sedate Abraham Lincoln and John F. Kennedy, to silence or medicate the artistic creativity of Picasso and van Gogh.

Let's start this exercise and, for a moment, just imagine if the adults responsible for the young Leonardo da Vinci's care—his parents and a paternal uncle who helped raise him—had decided to drug the young developing brain of one of the most amazing individuals ever to walk this Earth.

RAISING DA VINCI

As a young child, Leonardo's family structure was probably slightly different than most kids who lived in his town. Born on April 15, 1452, in Vinci, Italy (hence his name, which translates literally into English as Leonardo of Vinci), he was the illegitimate love child of a land-owning, up-and-coming public official and notary named Piero, and a peasant girl, Caterina, who worked for Leonardo's father. Leonardo's years as an infant and toddler were spent living with his birth mother. Once his father and apparently the second of his four legal wives were unable at first to have kids, however, Leonardo's custody was contested, and he was taken from his birth mother at age three and given to his father.

Suddenly Leonardo had gone from the child of a young, peasant single mother living in poverty to what might appear to be a more *normal* upbringing, in a house with two middle-class parents. But digging deeper into his family upbringing, we see it was far from normal. Leonardo was the first—and only illegitimate—child of twelve, nine brothers and two sisters, who were raised by numerous stepmothers, as his father, who continued to grow more successful, was constantly traveling. In short, his childhood seems to have been less than ideal. As a result, young Leonardo probably had a great number of issues to cope with.

A Freudian Flip

Some 450 years after da Vinci's death, Sigmund Freud analyzed his childhood in what is referred to as a *posthumous diagnosis* and determined that Leonardo was most likely very resentful of and antagonistic toward his father. After all, his father had separated him from his birth mother at such a young age. And he would always have had the stigma of being an illegitimate child, which during that period in Italy, meant he would have been unable to join the middle-class clubs and unions to which his father had belonged, become a public official like his father, or attend a university, among other things.

These feelings of resentment and antagonism probably only increased when his father and his many wives went on to have numerous legitimate children, which most likely monopolized the attention of his constantly changing stepmothers' time and attention, leaving Leonardo feeling even more like an outcast. And when he was sent to live with a paternal uncle, Francesco, Leonardo's negative feelings certainly would have escalated.

Such childhood challenges often lead to behavior problems. And it seems quite likely that Leonardo's illegitimate stigma, his transient upbringing, and his diverse family structures were real challenges for the boy. At the very least they were less-than-ideal conditions in which to maximize development during his critically important early childhood years.

The Not-So-Funny Farm

Spending the majority of his middle childhood living on his uncle's farm, however, Leonardo probably spent a lot of his time playing outdoors and sketching. History confirms he was highly creative, fascinated by nature and excited by the many details that surrounded him. We can speculate that as a child he was probably a daydreamer with an active imagination, often seen studying nature with sketch pad in hand, scribbling furiously. As time passed, it probably became quite apparent to the young Leonardo that he was not like other children.

Beyond showing great promise as an artist, he also was a deep thinker. Once he began to think about an idea, it was hard for him to let go and listen to or focus on something different. Peers and adults would speak to him, yet it would appear that Leonardo wasn't listening. He would be deep in thought about something else. He was unable to change focus. It was as if he were living in his own private world.

For example, his writings document that he often was captivated by the concept of flight.

In reference to his fascination with devising a machine for flying, he explained in one of his adult diaries that from his earliest memory as a baby, he remembered how a hawk landed on him and stuck its tail feathers into his mouth, repeatedly hitting his lips. Freud thought this memory was a fantasy and tied to memories of Leonardo's mother breast-feeding him. But let's not digress down that rabbit hole, given Freud's introspectionist tendency to tie too many things to sexual obsessions with one's mother.

A Boy of Many Talents and Tribulations

Leonardo was also ambidextrous; in fact, it is believed that later in life he could write separate thoughts at the same time with both hands.

With so much talent and intelligence trying to come to the surface during his childhood, he was most likely a bundle of incredibly clever ideas entwined within a ball of energy, so focused on the task at hand that others did not know what to think.

He probably behaved in slightly abnormal ways and appeared to others a little strange. And if by chance you want to believe some of Freud's other insights into Leonardo da Vinci, or the legitimacy of a sodomy charge brought against Leonardo in his early twenties, he most likely also wrestled with the social challenges related to homosexuality in Italy during the 1400s.

Knowing these few historical details about his childhood, we can assume he was a child dealing with divorce, abandonment, sibling rivalries, anger, and quite possibly sexuality issues. He was no doubt smarter than his peers and probably often bored in what constituted schooling in his era. Like many children with a fondness for nature and science, he most likely would have rather been outside playing and exploring what he wanted to learn rather than inside listening to what he was expected to learn.

He was quite capable of teaching himself, however, as we know from his later years (he learned Latin on his own, without the help of Rosetta Stone®). As a result, though a smart student, Leonardo could have been a handful for teachers who may not have been ready for highly intelligent, high-energy, and creative students who tended to act quite differently from the "normal" students.

From historical details it would seem Leonardo was deeply loved by his father and uncle. One can only assume that his birth mother loved him just as much. So imagine, if you will, his father, uncle, and possibly his stepmothers and birth mother, with much love for Leonardo, trying to figure out what to do with this talented young man. Imagine them trying to decide what would be the best way to help such an amazing boy, the eldest son, who would not be allowed to go to university or follow in his father's footsteps. Now let's imagine what they would have done if the schoolmaster had told them that Leonardo's behavior was unacceptable and needed to be dealt with accordingly and that before he could return to school he should see the town's doctor.

The Dipping Point

We must remember that Leonardo's family did not know he would live to become one of the most influential artists, architects, scientists, and visionaries of all time. He was a kid who simply didn't fit in. He was probably a kid who knew it all and told you so. He obviously had a lot to say, write, and create later in life. And those who have a lot to say and write in adulthood were sometimes told that they were incapable of shutting up when they were young. In other words, Leonardo was quite possibly driving everyone bonkers, and they did not know what to do.

But first and foremost, they had to keep him in school. It was the best thing they could do for an illegitimate kid who lived in a society that rarely offered opportunity to those born out of wedlock. Given no other alternative to keeping him in the school, let's imagine they decided to go into town and see the doctor.

During their visit, the doctor seemed like a very caring and well-informed expert and told them of a new medicine created by an alchemist in Florence. The medicine was created for kids and was called Sedersi Zitto e Si Concentrano, which loosely translates to "sit down, shut up, and focus." Please note, alchemists didn't have expensive Madison Avenue advertising firms at this point in history to create snappy brand names for them.

The doctor gave them a sample of this medicine to take home and told them that if it appeared to help make young Leonardo a little more manageable they could get a month's refill at any time. The father, uncle, and Leonardo got in their wagon to head home. The ride home was very quiet. After much deliberation, before leaving the uncle's farm that evening, his father made Leonardo drink the potion and instructed his brother to do the same the next day in the morning and after dinner.

Medicinal Powers

The next week Leonardo was less conversational as he continued to take the new medicine. He was suddenly a quiet young man. His facial expressions had slowed, and his eye contact had changed. His eyes no longer looked intense and alert. He walked around showing little interest in doing the things he normally did. Instead of running out of the house excited for the day, his uncle had to explain to him everything he needed to do just to get ready for the day.

At school, the teacher was impressed that he sat still all day long in his seat, and the schoolmaster sent home good marks for behavior. Yet once he got home it became obvious that he was not as hungry. He did not want to play, read, write, or sketch. During the next week of school, after consulting with Leonardo's father, his uncle went to town and refilled the prescription.

The next month, and after a second refill of Sedersi Zitto e Si Concentrano, Leonardo's report card suggested that he was behaving much better in school. The teacher and schoolmaster stated that he seemed more like a *normal* student and was performing more like the other students now that he was focused on the lessons being taught and completing the assignments given. They suggested strongly that he remain on Sedersi Zitto e Si Concentrano until they and the doctor felt he might be ready to stop taking the medicine.

By the next year, Leonardo's physical growth had slowed considerably, and he seemed skinnier and had trouble sleeping. His uncle rarely saw him outside playing and daydreaming. The boy didn't draw anymore and no longer kept a diary in his sketchbook. He had abandoned writing with both hands and started using only his left hand, as he'd been instructed to at school. He was now a better behaved student and seemed like a more normal child. And as the saying goes, they lived happily ever after. The end.

What If?

Wow, now that is a happy story. Of course I am using sarcasm to provide a little comic relief to this not-so-funny embellished story. But can you imagine if *the* Leonardo da Vinci had been given a drug or potion (or medicine, if it makes you feel better) to make him normal? What would such a practice have precluded him from achieving?

The odds are quite great that it would have turned an amazing young man, one of the most intelligent people to ever walk this planet, into a *normal* student. It would have dulled his creativity and vision. And who knows what else? We might not be able to get on a plane today if it had happened. Given da Vinci's groundbreaking research into the human body, we might not be near where we are in the science of anatomy and medicine had his exploration been stunted by drugs. And as for what it might have done to his artistic ability, who knows?

Luckily, he was dearly loved by his family, and they knew that Leonardo was an amazing artist. They knew that his artistic ability could greatly help him rise above his illegitimate status. Instead of discouraging the behavior that might have made him seem abnormal as a child but would ultimately help him as an adult become one of the greatest minds in history, they nurtured it and eventually sent him to one of the best artists in Italy to become an apprentice, where his talents would be further nurtured. The rest of the story, as they say, is history.

PUTTING THINGS INTO PERSPECTIVE

This fictional twist to Leonardo da Vinci's childhood was written to summarize many of the initial ADHD experiences that parents have shared pertaining to their first experiences on Planet ADHD, which might explain why parts of the story reflected a few of your experiences. The story was intended to get you to imagine how misguided it would have been, just how weird it sounds, for the parents of *the* Leonardo da Vinci to have agreed to medication just because Leonardo behaved differently than others. Of course he behaved differently. He was *the* Leonardo da Vinci!

But how is such behavior any less acceptable, any less normal, for any other gifted, highly intelligent, or highly creative child? How is it acceptable to just drug a child behaving in a similar way if they are going through a family divorce, living with the challenges of poverty, or grappling with some other issue? The story also was intended to bring attention to the fact that our situational experiences in childhood produce challenges to our behavior, development, and maturation. Family structures, custody battles, sibling rivalries, being labeled, social challenges, and managing what we are gifted with through our genetics (e.g., IQ and temperament) are some of the inherent challenges of life children must learn how to cope with.

When it comes to addressing such behavior issues that arise from challenges, drugs should be the very last resort. This should not suggest that such behaviors be accepted and not dealt with properly, but we must remember kids are just kids and sometimes developing learned behaviors that are socially acceptable takes time. Drugs should be the last resort after years of exhausting every other alternative, because we do not know the what-ifs for every child.

The problem with childhood is that we are not adults. As adults, although we know such challenges in childhood can be or become serious issues for kids, the way kids sometimes react to such things often seems childish or even in extreme situations problematic. But as kids such challenges in life often seem like the end of the world. As kids we have not had the luxury of learning how to handle the daily challenges that seem to pop up at every corner. Therefore, often every little thing one faces as a child seems like a major obstacle that at first seems insurmountable.

Even as adults, we still have such days or weeks. Yet as adults we know that life requires patience. To a child the saying "This too shall pass" does not equate to sound advice. As such immovable obstacles begin to accumulate for children, however, it is only through experimentation that they can try to adjust in order to cope or survive. Unfortunately, sometimes such coping skills begin to produce bad behaviors and slowly redefine the child's personality and behavior.

The fact that children often do not react appropriately to unfortunate life events is quite normal. As a family we must put forth every effort possible to help them get beyond such challenges in life. As a family, we must work together to proactively make sure such behaviors does not turn into the behaviors some want to label as abnormal. As adults we must embrace the uniqueness of each child.

THE NORMALITY OF ABNORMAL

Some experts in abnormal psychology would like for us to believe that a fairly large percentage of the population suffers from or exhibits what is termed abnormal behavior. For example, given that feeling depressed is something most of us would not like to experience during a normal day, when one feels depressed this is considered by some to be abnormal behavior. But let's face it: going through life or even a day or week never feeling depressed is a rare occurrence for most.

Life is not always fair. And for most, during every day (at least every week), one has moments of depression—or at least moments of not feeling so positive. And given that pharmaceutical companies are now marketing a depression medicine to take to improve the effectiveness of the depression medicine one currently takes to treat depression, one might wonder if medication is the answer to relieving depression. Depression is normal. It is a part of life, and not even medication in many instances can help one completely escape this basically normal occurrence.

There are people who suffer from severe depression, however. They experience depression so often and so deeply that it greatly affects their day-to-day existence. This should be considered abnormal. The fact that only twelve out of one hundred thousand people in the United States commit suicide statistically suggests suicide is an abnormal behavior. But in the United States suicide is the second leading cause of death for young people between the ages of ten and twenty-four, and an average of twelve youths commit suicide each day. Such statistics blur the line between what is normal and abnormal. When such unfortunate mental challenges exist so often in so many, what might seem abnormal to some at times becomes part of a normal yet depressing day.

Science shows that when it comes to being human, nearly everything is normally distributed. For example, the bell curve illustrates how most of us are the norm and fewer are what might be referred to as *outliers*. The bell curve shows that in nature we all cover a spectrum. Figure 1.1 shows us how our IQ is normally distributed and that a few of us are geniuses (scores above 145), others are mentally challenged (scores below 70), and most of us are average—or the norm.

The same goes for our attention levels, energy levels, and so on. Some of us are more focused than others. Some are less energetic than others. Some daydream all day long about all kinds of different outcomes in life, and some never dream at all. Most are able to control their impulses, while others are severely challenged. Some are creative, and yet others think they don't have a creative bone in their body and need to be told everything. That is the beauty of human beings: we are individuals.

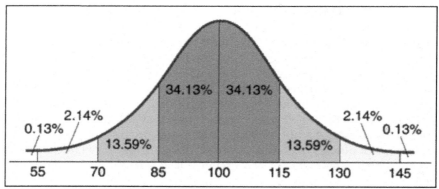

FIGURE 1.1 Normal Distribution of Intelligence

We all have unique, wonderful qualities, and we all have many less-than-wonderful qualities. We are not meant to be clones of one another. No matter how many clothing chains sell the same styles of clothes, we will always look different in them. For some, the clothes will fit, while others will find them uncomfortable. This is the beauty of life: we are all uniquely different.

Furthermore, we are all good at something. Maybe it's baking or cooking. Or maybe athletics comes naturally to us. Maybe we sing well or play an instrument beautifully. Some of us rock, and others just roll. We're all *good* at something, and a wonderful thing about growing up is that we get to dream about and discover what that special talent is—that thing we do almost effortlessly that brings us contentment.

Think about this for a moment. What are you good at? What do you enjoy doing the most? Has it really changed that much since you were a child? This is what childhood and becoming a young adult is all about: dreaming, exploring, and finding out who we are, what we're good at, and what we love to do.

But how can we expect a child to find that special talent, that thing they do every normal day that they are wonderful at, if they are medicated every day, year after year? How will they daydream, release their imagination, and get excited about things when they are drugged to do just the opposite? Do you really think children can reach their full potentials and discover their callings (what they love most) when they spend their childhoods medicated? When we put a child on medication for ADHD over the long term (and don't let them kid you—it is long-term use unless you say, "Enough is enough. Stop!"), the outcome in most cases is downright dismal. Being medicated daily should not be part of the American dream or achieving one's fullest potential. No matter whether you are on the inside of this ADHD phenomenon looking out or on the outside looking in, it's not pretty. Our children, your children, deserve better.

WHAT IS NORMAL?

There is a groundswell of concerned adults growing rather tired of watching children being medicated merely because the children do not yet understand social norms, do not yet behave the way adults (educators and parents) want them to, or do not fit the mold of the *normal* child. What is *normal*? More specifically, what does it mean to behave normally or to be normal, and who is in charge of defining what is normal? Most mental disorders are related to abnormal behavior, but when you have more than six million kids according to Centers for Disease Control and Prevention data being labeled with ADHD annually you might ask if these apparently popular behaviors associated with ADHD are actually abnormal behavior.

But who really wants to be normal? Many people spend their whole lives trying to become something special. Artists seek to define themselves as individuals. Musicians try to find their own styles. Professionals aim to break the mold and redefine the norm. And most parents try to be the best they possibly can be.

Many struggle with this idea of normalcy, because as an individual they have prided themselves on not letting society put them into some specific mold. Many have worked hard to not let their life circumstances hold them back from achieving their dreams. As a parent, the last thing many want to do is push their children to achieving only normalcy. Normal should rarely be the goal we set out to achieve in life, and, more importantly, at every turn we should try to steer clear of this parallel universe where the goal is to declare normal behavior abnormal.

The Pleasures of Parenthood

Parenting is extremely demanding and with a little luck and a lot of work can be the most rewarding experience we may encounter in life. We give life to wonderful human beings who at birth in the mystical glow of the delivery room have only endless potential. Most parents will never forget the magic that filled the delivery room in those first precious moments. After hours of painful labor, emotional swings, tears, and heartfelt happiness, we look into the beautiful shining eyes of the souls that will forever shape our lives.

These magical, mystical beings are born without prejudice. As philosopher John Locke proposed in the eighteenth century, children enter this world as blank slates—what he coined *tabula rasa*. As parents and guardians—and other adults in children's lives—we have the responsibility to shield our children from much of life's sadness, protect them from harm, teach them right from wrong, and provide all the goodness we experienced in life or possibly all that we wished we had been given as children.

The debate about the legitimacy of prescribing ADHD medications to children comes down to whether or not there are more healthy and holistic alternatives to get through the challenges of childhood. The bottom line rests on whether we adults are willing to put forth the extra love, compassion, patience, and due diligence needed to help our kids rise above the circumstances and allow the natural development process to nurture what some might call symptoms of a disorder into what others might believe to be signs of a gift. With the many dangerous outcomes associated with ADHD drugs, they only provide an unknown means to gamble our children's futures in exchange for a quick medicated fix that comes with far too many what-ifs.

DISORDER OR GIFT?

Regardless of the legitimacy of ADHD (to be discussed more in chapter 2), the list of famous historical figures as well as today's leaders, athletes, and movie stars who exhibited childhood qualities associated with ADHD symptoms is quite enlightening. The list provides evidence that clearly shows that being labeled with ADHD (or, more aptly, exhibiting the behaviors associated with ADHD) is not necessarily a bad thing and that exhibiting signs of ADHD ought not automatically provide a reason to medicate.

Instead, in some cases regarding these famous figures, the development of their unique and gifted qualities was probably encouraged and embraced by their families and educators. Their parents and educators probably had to work harder to help them to better manage social challenges and inappropriate behaviors. Instead of labeling such behaviors as abnormal or a disorder, their parents and educators most likely had to find the strength to implement better structures and routines to shape their children's character, being more patient in waiting to see who these not-so-perfect children might develop into. And most of those parents, if they were blessed to live long enough, were able to watch their children—who at one point were probably royal pains in the buttocks—grow, mature, and become amazing individuals. Every parent and educator deserves such an opportunity, and so does every child.

The behaviors associated with the symptoms of ADHD represent common and normal childhood behaviors. And sometimes, as the list of famous historical figures confirms, when the right combination of unique symptoms or behaviors exist, it is a sign of giftedness. If your child is exhibiting what pro-ADHD experts call symptoms of ADHD, it is not the end of the world or a call for desperate measures.

Though the behaviors associated with the ADHD symptoms might mean you are going to have your hands full as a parent in trying to survive your child's earlier years and possibly teen years, or as an educator trying to survive the school year with such a child, these same symptoms are signs that the child is quite capable of accomplishing wonderful things in life. To share more about how the behaviors associated with ADHD are connected to giftedness and many other childhood issues, I would like to share with you an exercise I do every semester with my students.

Unwinding the Web of ADHD

In the textbooks I use to teach human development (a course mainly focused on child development at my university) and educational psychology (which is a course basically on how people learn and how teachers should teach in order to help people learn), there is a chapter that discusses ADHD, which allows me to share this exercise. I often start the class, however, without explaining what the focus of the exercise will be. I divide the class into small groups and give a note card to each group. On each card there is a different term followed by seven blank spaces below the term. I instruct them to not tell any of the other groups what their card says. They are asked to discuss the term and list seven descriptions.

On one of the cards is the term *ADHD*, on the other cards are *genius or gifted kids*, *BD* (referring to students diagnosed with serious behavioral disorders), *developmentally delayed students*, *students who have a "challenged" teacher*, and *students who have a "challenged" home environment*. By *challenged*, I am trying to say in politically correct terms that the teacher needs extra help to manage and educate the students and that the parents or guardians need extra help to raise the children. I ask the small groups to use their texts, experience, knowledge, and even the not-so-reliable Internet to provide five to seven descriptions that might help us identify these types of kids if we were asked to go into an elementary or middle school.

I then ask them to go to the whiteboard and write just the descriptions they have determined. I tell them explicitly to not write the term on the whiteboard they were asked to discuss. Once all of the groups have written their descriptions on the board and have taken their seats, I ask the class to look at the different lists and see if they agree on any descriptions. During the group discussion, the class identifies similarities they see between all of the small groups' lists. What happens next has been repeated nearly every time I do this exercise.

"Well, we all agree they do not pay attention in class," says one participant.

"They also seem to be bored with school," says another.

Others continue commenting:

"They seem to daydream or have active imaginations. Maybe that is why they are easily distracted?"

"They don't necessarily either listen to or follow the directions given. Maybe this contributes to their being disorganized."

"They often blurt out answers or interrupt others. Looks like some called that being disobedient."

"Some seem socially awkward or immature."

"They don't know how to behave appropriately."

I find this part of the exercise enjoyable. I love having open discussions in class and hearing what students think. Quite often while they are sharing their thoughts on similar descriptions shared among the small groups, I draw lines on the whiteboard connecting the similar descriptions. And by the time they have finished sharing their insights the board looks like a spider web of connections.

A Consensus of Confusion

I then ask group #1 to tell me the term their seven insights were describing. I write it up on the board above their list. I then ask the second group and then the third group, and so on. And then I step back and ask if anyone is surprised that these descriptions were actually written for five different situations or disorders. The answer is usually a resounding yes.

It is a consensus that leaves many students scratching their heads in disbelief. They cannot believe it, because, in some instances, they have taken special-education or counseling courses, worked in schools, or read textbooks where they have been told that each of these different challenges to education or child development (e.g., ADHD, developmental delays, behavioral disorders) are real and distinct. They are told that these diagnoses are all uniquely different. But, in reality, the categories share much in common with the behaviors associated with ADHD.

Smart kids are often bored in class and as a result sometimes get more enjoyment out of disrupting class or choosing not to pay attention. When we move beyond identifying *gifted* as only the wonder kids who are already high achieving, cooperative, and incredible in the classroom, performing grade levels above their peers, we find that many gifted children are waiting to blossom even if they aren't yet showing obvious signs of blooming. Young gifted children (still developing) also are often unorganized, distractible, and inattentive, challenged socially, and challenged behaviorally. They sometimes have trouble fitting in and might be highly focused on unusual interests.

Young children that are developmentally delayed display similar behaviors and also daydream as they fidget at their desks for hours on end. Kids coming from challenged home environments often have not learned social norms or refuse to accept them, which results in similar ADHD behaviors being exhibited. Behavioral disorder (BD) students have even more challenges when it comes to behaving *normally*. The lists go on and on.

If you don't believe me, I urge you to get on your favorite Internet search engine and type in *gifted-children descriptions, developmental-delay descriptions*, and so on. Or try going to the library and reading some books on such labels. What you will find, if you go a little bit beyond the links to websites that have paid to come up first on keyword searches and read an assortment of books specifically written on the topics, is basically what my classroom exercise has produced every time. Many of the same traits we use to identify giftedness or genius are similar to many of the traits we use to label students with ADHD, BD, and developmentally delayed. Also, many of the same behaviors that stem from challenged classrooms and home environments produce similar behaviors associated with ADHD, BD, and developmental delays.

Houston, We Have a Problem

The problem is that we are basically using far too many simple behaviors that far too many kids display to identify too many disorders. This contributes to the existing overdiagnosis problem; our net of common childhood behaviors considered to represent abnormal behavior is catching far too many kids. We also are using many of the same behaviors (symptoms, if you will) to identify far too many supposedly unique and quite different possibilities. This contributes to the existing misdiagnosis problem.

Furthermore, categories such as ADHD or BD have become some of the catchall labels in far too many schools. To fuel this problem, we are rushing to judgment in our schools and doctors' offices, labeling kids at the earliest age possible when they exhibit certain behaviors. Some kids get lucky with such practices and are labeled gifted, but the majority fall victim to the more negative diagnoses.

In many instances the decisions related to these more negative assigned labels happen long before a medical professional with a license to medicate is consulted. These decisions are therefore set in motion at the home or school level, often connected to the subjective opinions and actions of the parents and educators involved. In other words, the diagnosis that is sought is often initiated and possibly predetermined based on a parent or educator's opinion as to whether the child is good, cute, or smart, or is misbehaving, annoying, and not so smart. As Dr. Fred Baughman Jr. pointed out, since the behaviors associated with ADHD basically describe about every child, ADHD is in the eye of the beholder.

Decisions, Decisions

Whether it's easy to hear the following message or not, parents are partially responsible for such decisions. Some parents, for numerous reasons, assume the worst when their child exhibits behaviors associated with ADHD (or when an educator brings problematic behaviors to their attention). Upon hearing such news, many parents opt to have their child given a more negative label and then request an Individualized Education Program (IEP) or a 504 Plan (a designation that ensures accommodations within a regular classroom for a child with a physical or mental impairment that limits one or more "major life activities"—a.k.a. learning).

Please note that typically an IEP or 504 requires that a student be diagnosed with a mental disorder or learning disability. Such designations are today's legal way of getting schools to provide extra time and one-on-one support for kids, something most schools had the time and commitment to do regularly in decades past. Many parents take this route in hopes of receiving special treatment and accommodations that theoretically could help a child do better.

Because this approach is rather popular in today's schools, and is basically required through existing education policy, millions of students are being diagnosed with ADHD, behavioral disorders, or other specific learning disorders or disabilities (and given IEPs or 504 designations). With a significant increase of special-needs kids in our classrooms nationwide, schools are supported through federal title monies in order to provide extra support for those diagnosed with special needs. Yes, believe it or not, school systems historically have received more money for getting more kids diagnosed with a disability. In fact, depending on whether students are performing at least two grade levels behind, a school district could receive upward of $1,000 per student per year.

Given that schools only receive monies as long as the child is performing at least two grade levels behind, and given that the use of ADHD medication has no real connection to actually improving academic performance, the picture starts to become clearer as to how the system we have is not designed to actually help the ADHD-diagnosed child improve academically. As many have learned, such approaches are not always beneficial for the child, parent, or school. This might be why some refer to IEPs as Individual Escape Plans. Others look at such behaviors related to ADHD through a different lens, a more positive lens, however, and ask for their child first to be tested for giftedness, or at the least ask the school to delay any rash decisions as they work together to fix the developmental or behavioral issues.

In other instances, teachers and educational administrators are the driving force behind such decisions being made, mainly due to education policy. Although there is great merit behind the much-needed efforts of the Individuals with Disabilities Education Act (IDEA), Section 504 of the Vocational Rehabilitation Act of 1973, and the more recent push for early childhood education to provide all children with early education and developmental support, the policy also has some limitations when it comes to the requirements the movements have brought along to "diagnose" all children at an ever-increasing earlier age. For starters, to label or diagnose at such early ages (when young children are acting even more like young children, displaying symptoms of ADHD) is not easy, necessarily accurate, or always recommended.

Furthermore, unfortunately, due to dwindling education budgets and practices that have stemmed from the standardized-testing focus, gifted programs are quite limited in size and scope for many schools. The more common practice seems to lean toward identifying such behaviors as problematic. Now for some schools, however, this just means their *problem-child classrooms* become even more overcrowded with kids who have received in-school suspensions or other behavioral reprimands. As many will attest, we have far too many such classrooms filled with students sleeping and not getting the education they desperately need. Therefore, it is not always a guarantee that this designation or diagnosis will lead to beneficial outcomes for kids or a better educational experience.

HOW SCHOOLS ARE JUGGLING WITH ONE ARM

It is quite possible that some of the challenges associated with behavior and academic issues, however, are also due to learning-environment issues. The problem in some cases might be the school or classroom and not necessarily the student. For example, bullying is still a major issue in schools, and we still are seeing close to a third of our students dropping out. Such issues suggest that the school climate in many circumstances is not always conducive to promoting optimal behavior or academic success.

Another example might relate to the issue we have with the number of kids in the average classroom growing out of control. Some schools' classrooms contain far too many kids for any one adult to handle or address. Some school districts are so strapped for cash and teachers that the classes have more than forty students to every teacher. A quick visit to your local zoo's ape or monkey house will give you an idea of how different beings adjust to being overcrowded, confined, and controlled. When students spend enough time in a chaotic learning environment, and a teacher is understandably showing signs of exhaustion and defeat, the students' behavior will begin to mirror or adapt to the chaos.

But even classrooms with what's considered to be a normal number of students are still a management challenge for most adults. For parents who don't believe this last statement, the next time you find yourself at your wits' end on a day when you are trying to communicate with your child, imagine being closed in one small room with twenty to twenty-five clones of your children. If one is able to drive you batty, imagine what twenty-plus can do together. Unfortunately, no matter the size of the classroom, many teachers—though not all—are not prepared, supported, or qualified enough to handle, let alone successfully educate, the diverse assortment of personalities, intelligence levels, learning styles, energy levels, and assorted challenges that some of our more, shall we say, *creative* students bring to the classroom. This is what educators call *differentiated instruction*, and it is no easy task for one or even two teachers to accomplish in a classroom.

But this is just the nature of the beast. When you have an underfunded education system you will always end up with overcrowded classrooms, their ensuing problems, and staffing issues. You will always end up with children being left behind.

As a result, instead of teachers having the luxury of asking their school boards, administrators, or peers for help, current policy directs educators to pursue legal guidelines established to label the *challenged* children (a.k.a. children who challenge their teachers) with ADHD, BD, or an assortment of learning disabilities. With a diagnosis in hand and an IEP or 504 in process, the challenged students can be put into a special-needs classroom, receive special accommodations, or, for two-thirds of children labeled with ADHD, be drugged as a means to control behavior. To exacerbate this problem, such labels are beneficial to schools under existing testing policies as well: the schools also get special accommodations when it comes to having special-needs kids take the standardized tests required in schools.

Many of the challenges with today's education policy and practices will be discussed in more detail in chapters 5 and 7. The foreshadowing point in this chapter concerning how extraterrestrial our education system seems at times is that part of the problem with diagnosing our children's apparently ever-increasing behavior and attention issues could very well be partially due to the education policy our schools are required to follow, a financial and testing incentive to diagnose more kids, and many other circumstances that originate in the home. Much of the problem in many instances, however, could be remedied via greater proactive collaboration and communication between parents and teachers.

The Rest of the Story

There are millions of parents and educators who long for the chance to actually work together more closely to help children catch up if they have developmental or academic issues, or improve if they are behaviorally challenged. These individuals and many more wish educators could have more funding, support, and flexibility in what and how they teach so that they can provide each student with the learning experience and personal attention needed, longed for, and deserved. Many parents and teachers would love to ditch the one-size-fits-all curricula required by current education policy for more individualized or flexible approaches to helping students (no matter the learning style) become their best and brightest selves.

Unfortunately, many educators have told me that there is often at least one teacher or administrator in the school who has drunk too much of the education-policy potion, what could be referred to these days as *Common Core Kool-Aid*. They believe that the curriculum and test scores emanating from the Common Core State Standards Initiative (our most recent education-policy attempt) are the most important, if not only, requirements for the job. Some of these educators are so overwhelmed by the testing-policy demands that they cannot focus on anything else, because keeping their job rests on the test scores. As a result, rather than collaborating with parents in order to help children develop the appropriate behaviors and habits needed to becoming more successful academically or understanding behavioral norms, some resort to pressuring a parent to medicate their child for ADHD.

Meanwhile, at the other not-so-rational end of the spectrum (or bell curve), you have parents who would rather blame educators for everything related to their child's behavior. Regardless of the fact that the parent has been responsible for the child's behavior since birth, some still feel empowered to blame everything on a teacher who has only worked with the student for a short time. As many teachers will tell you, there are many parents who won't even return a phone call or e-mail or agree to meet. And unfortunately, when the meetings actually do take place, they often are highly contentious.

As with many things in life, unfortunately ego often gets in the way of progress. Because parents are so overwhelmed, possibly acting defensive, and unsure about the right thing to do, and because educators are so overwhelmed and often pressured in many instances to do the wrong thing, and because supposed mental disorders and learning disabilities like ADHD are being touted as legitimate issues, students with issues related to ADHD are left between a rock and a hard place. At the end of the day in today's stressful worlds of education and parenting, sometimes it just seems that accepting the diagnosis of ADHD and medicating a child becomes the path of least resistance for both parties.

The fact that differing views exist between educators and parents within an education system in need of great repair begins to explain why the United States has an 11 percent average prevalence rate of ADHD. Such challenges begin to explain how the U.S. ADHD prevalence rate mysteriously increases annually while the rest of the world is holding steady at a 3 to 7 percent prevalence rate.

According to Centers for Disease Control and Prevention (CDC) data, nearly 6.4 million children in the United States between the ages of four and seventeen have been diagnosed with ADHD, and about two-thirds of them take ADHD medication. In some regions of the United States, such as the more poverty-ridden Southern states, about 23 percent of boys have been diagnosed with ADHD. Coincidentally, children covered by Medicaid have the highest rates of ADHD diagnoses: 14 percent according to the CDC data, about one-third higher than the rest of the population.

We must begin to realize (or at the least consider), with so many kids being diagnosed with a disorder that labels such normal childhood behavior as abnormal, the abnormal behavior of so many kids at some point starts to become the norm. At some point we must begin to consider that it could very well be the highly inattentive and impulsive education system that has ADHD rather than the students within the system. And with little hope of our leaders in Washington creating an education system in the near future that actually keeps the promise of leaving no child behind, we must begin to see the greater responsibility that rests on the shoulders of parents when it comes to addressing behaviors associated with ADHD.

SUMMARY

I am hoping your conscience is possibly at this point whispering a little louder in your ear, "Drugging kids because they are acting like kids is wrong." The intent of the embellished story about drugging da Vinci at the beginning of this chapter was to get you to begin thinking more about the what-ifs.

What if we are drugging our best and brightest students in the name of ADHD? What if those children might have one day become the next da Vinci, Lincoln, JFK, van Gogh, or Einstein? Well, maybe not van Gogh. There is a strong possibility he had numerous mental disorders. But what if the child wrongly diagnosed is your child or student? For that matter, what if we are drugging perfectly normal children because of the challenges of a family life they have little control over or an unforgiving, misguided education policy?

As you are about to read in chapter 2, most of the more mild behaviors associated with ADHD are evident in all children, and some of the more serious behaviors can be explained by the life circumstances many children face. Unfortunately, many adults have been told (or given flawed research from the powers that be—see chapter 6) that labeling kids with ADHD and medicating them is an ethical and legitimate approach to helping them. If the rest of this book does not convince you just how wrong this practice is, then I have failed in my goal to be the dissenting voice children deserve.

I can't end this section without further clarifying that I do not blame educators. In fact, I believe the educators (administrators, teachers, counselors, and support staff) serving on the front lines of our communities should receive the same level of respect we give our soldiers. I blame the system that educators have been forced to abide by. I blame the system for forcing education administrators to use any and all tools at their convenience to try to game the system so that their teachers, schools, and school systems are not punished for not making what they currently call in education adequate yearly progress (AYP) when it comes to test scores. As a result, many great educators and educational leaders have been put between a rock and a hard place themselves. And as a result, many of our best educators are leaving to pursue a different career or retire early.

As parents we must begin to accept that much of the reason for such behaviors related to ADHD, and the promise to overcome such behaviors, rests heavily on our shoulders. And if such responsibility rests in parents' hands, learning how best to navigate Planet ADHD is of major importance.

REFLECTION EXERCISE: IN YOUR CHILD'S SHOES

My ideas and opinions might seem extreme to some of you reading this book. This might be especially true if you have been on the ADHD Pharmaceutical Freight Train for a while now and as a result have come to the point of believing that the path you have taken was truly the best thing for your child. On the other side of the spectrum of opinions, others might see my viewpoints as a breath of fresh air and the justification they were looking for to just say no to drugs and ADHD altogether. No matter where you sit at this point of the process, I have a wonderful reframing exercise for you to try personally or to perhaps recommend to the concerned educators or doctors in your life. Reframing exercises are a great way to get a fresh or alternative view of a situation.

In mental health, *reframing* is often used to help clients put themselves in someone else's shoes, so to speak. It provides an opportunity to view our life (or, more specifically, the challenges we face that cause mental distress) through the eyes of another. When it comes to ADHD, I think I have an exercise that can help many adults see what kids are seeing (experiencing), which will explain why these kids act and behave in certain ways.

I once recommended this exercise to a teacher who was complaining about kids with ADHD in her classroom. She could not understand why they behaved the way they did. I suggested that she videotape a whole day of her instruction or even another teacher's efforts and then on Saturday, a day she wanted to be outside playing, put the video of her classroom on and sit attentively all day long, watching the video. I suggested she sit in the cushionless desks the kids are expected to sit in. I suggested she not daydream for one minute during that day. I suggested she remain quiet and diligently take notes while kids slowly answered questions the videotaped teacher asked. I suggested that she not fidget around in her seat.

Given the look she gave me after I recommended this exercise to her, I doubt she took my advice. But if you are a parent being forced to consider labeling your child with ADHD and possibly putting him or her on ADHD drugs, before you do, I suggest you ask if you could sit a whole day in your child's seat in their classroom. And while you are there, use the checklist of the symptoms for ADHD provided in chapter 2 so that you can check off each symptom as you slowly realize that spending seven or eight hours in today's extraterrestrial education will cause almost everyone to experience the feelings and behaviors used to label kids with ADHD.

2

DELUSIONAL DIAGNOSIS

REASON #2: There are no reliable or valid written, medical, biological, or neurological tests supported by conclusive scientific evidence that can actually distinguish between children who have or do not have ADHD; pro-ADHD experts have no way of identifying or measuring ADHD.

This chapter is focused on helping you understand how little it takes, according to today's standards, to be labeled with (wrongly diagnosed) ADHD and just how inappropriately the questionable diagnosis is being used. The chapter is also intended to help you get a better grasp on the historical roots and "evidence" used to justify the diagnosis.

Given that there is much controversy about the many financial conflicts of interest existing between the DSM creators and the pharmaceutical industry, I also want to explore some of the pros and cons of the DSM as well as the suggested differential diagnoses it proposes for ADHD. A *differential diagnosis* is the expectation for strong consideration of other disorders or conditions that may serve as a better explanation for the symptoms being exhibited. This process is essential so that the practitioner can clearly explain why the diagnosis offered is, without question, the most appropriate label for an individual's symptoms (*symptomotology*).

Since some of the suggested differential diagnoses provided in the DSM-5 for ADHD made me pause and sadly laugh, I thought I would end this chapter on a funny note and add a few of my own slightly humorous alternative explanations (differential diagnoses, if you will) that might better explain why children exhibit the all-too-common symptoms of ADHD. First, however, let's begin by considering an all-too-common experience many parents have encountered.

FOCUS ON THE FACTS

- ADHD is one of the most popular disorders listed in *The Diagnostic and Statistical Manual of Mental Disorders* (DSM) used to classify children and justify their medication.
- The DSM clearly states, however, there is no "test of attention" sensitive or specific enough to measure or identify ADHD.
- Even without a tool to assess ADHD, nearly 6.5 million kids in the United States are currently diagnosed with ADHD, and two-thirds of these children are medicated.
- The current diagnosis is based on using eighteen generic symptoms or behaviors kids exhibit.
- To be labeled *ADHD inattentive or hyperactive/impulsive* only requires that a child exhibit six of the symptoms outlined in the DSM-5; for those seventeen or older, only five symptoms must be observed.
- Frequency and severity of symptoms over six months across several settings and documented from the perspective of multiple observers is required; unfortunately, most kids are diagnosed during their first doctor's consultation in as little as ten to twenty minutes.
- To be labeled *ADHD not otherwise specified or unspecified*, however, only requires that a child exhibit a few to none of the symptoms outlined in the DSM-5.
- The history of the ADHD diagnosis follows a long and winding road from the early 1900s, when it was initially considered a defect of moral control and later believed to be due to an inflamed or minimal dysfunction of the brain, to today's persistent pattern of inattention and hyperactivity attributed to a host of "possible" causes lacking sound research and evidence.
- The DSM-5 (approximately a thousand pages long) is *the psychiatric Bible* mental-health practitioners in the United States are supposed to use to diagnose and assign a billing code to nearly four hundred mental disorders in order to prescribe medication and be paid by insurance companies; there were no billing codes and only 106 disorders when the first edition of the DSM was printed in 1952.
- Nearly half of the authors who defined and selected the psychiatric disorders included in the DSM-IV had financial relationships with the pharmaceutical industry at one time.
- One hundred percent of the panel members responsible for reviewing and approving what the authors submitted to the DSM-IV had financial ties with the pharmaceutical industry.

- Similar pharmaceutical-related conflicts of interest exist within the new edition, the DSM-5.
- Most recently the National Institute of Mental Health (NIMH) withdrew its support for the DSM-5.
- In fact, NIMH stated they will no longer fund research projects that rely exclusively on DSM criteria, due to "its lack of validity."

THE TEN-MINUTE DIAGNOSIS

For a large percentage of parents, their first not-so-pleasurable junket on Planet ADHD includes a trip to the family doctor's office or to the ADHD *expert* their school suggests they see. Let's see if we can capture how such a visit often goes.

After being encouraged to seek more professional input, a parent calls the pediatrician and sets the appointment. After a considerable amount of time in the waiting room, and then a similar forever moment spent in one of those sterile treatment rooms, the doctor enters. The doctor asks what the reason is for the visit today. The parent shares her short story of the school's concerns. The doctor begins to ask the child a few simple questions.

"Do you have trouble paying close attention to what they tell you in school? Are you making careless mistakes on your homework?"

He continues with his questioning of the six-year-old boy, who still has evidence of the peanut butter and jelly sandwich from lunch stuck on his face. "Are you reluctant to engage in tasks that require sustained mental effort?"

The boy answers, "Huh?" The doctor makes a note on his clipboard.

"Do you talk obsessively?" Boy remains silent as parent nods, vigorously affirming.

"Is he often on the go, like he is driven by a motor?"

"How did you know?" the parent asks.

"Your son has ADHD, ma'am. It is a serious neurodevelopmental disorder that is best treated with medication."

As he begins to write on the prescription pad, he explains that he is prescribing Vyvanse, a new stimulant made by the pharmaceutical company Shire that can help her child focus more and improve his behavior.

"Let's get your son started on this today, and you will be amazed at the improvements over the next few weeks. Here's a brochure on the medicine from the manufacturer that will answer a few questions you might have and make you see why this is the best thing to do for your child."

"Is there anything I should be worried about related to this drug?" asks the parent.

"There are some very rare side effects, such as decreased or dangerously high blood pressure, tremors, hallucinations, vomiting, anxiety, chest pains . . ." the doctor continues, his tone turning into a mumble as he lists more possible side effects . . . "But these are very rare. Just call my office if you have any concerns. But if you go fill this prescription, you should be good to go. Please set another appointment before you leave today for a follow-up next month to see if the medication is causing problems. This way we can test to see if it is affecting your son's heart or blood pressure or if he is losing too much weight. Oh—and to get a prescription for a refill."

"Are you sure there aren't any long-terms effects that can come from the medication?" the parent asks, trying to silence her conscience, which is screaming "Warning! Warning!" in the back of her brain.

"The pharmacist will give you a medication guide for the prescription, but there are no studies on children I am aware of confirming any long-term negative effects. Please see the nurse on your way out to schedule your next visit, and be sure to give her your most up-to-date insurance information to see what they cover related to ADHD. Have a great day, and let me know if your son's school needs any documentation."

This is how it starts far too often for far too many. One short ten- to twenty-minute consultation, and suddenly you're on your way to being a repeat customer for years to come. Of course there are more caring doctors who follow the flawed diagnosis requirements a bit more cautiously and actually put children before money.

For example, recently a mother shared that her family's pediatrician read the mental-health practitioner's report *confirming* her son had ADHD, but instead of writing a prescription the doctor suggested she spend a week or so thinking about and researching whether she really wanted her son to be medicated for ADHD. As suggested in the beginning of this book, this is the good news: there are caring doctors out there who won't rush to judgment or play a part in this game.

My above embellished yet factually accurate story, however, highlights three major problems associated with the DSM's diagnosis of ADHD. The first is that the symptoms describe how every young boy often behaves. For that matter, the symptoms describe how many young girls often behave. The second problem is that for a number of reasons (none of them good) the DSM diagnostic criteria are not being followed correctly by many who are licensed to write prescriptions for such drugs. The third problem, the linchpin, is that the many diagnostic criteria used to assess disorders covered in the DSM are lacking reliable, valid assessment tools (accurate tests) and definitive research essential to justifying the identification and existence of the disorders. And it is in this chapter that we focus on those main points.

To demonstrate further how problematic it is to misuse the DSM's existing diagnosis for ADHD and to overrely on those eighteen simple childhood behaviors as symptomatic evidence, let us now, without any further ado, take a look at the DSM-5's "test" used to label kids with ADHD.

Just Say Yes

The DSM basically proposes using eighteen symptoms to diagnose ADHD. According to the latest edition, the DSM-V, there are actually two sets of nine symptoms for two different categories of ADHD. The two categories are (1) inattention (this used to be considered the ADD part of the diagnosis in previous DSM editions) and (2) hyperactivity and impulsivity. Any person younger than seventeen years of age must have displayed or experienced six or more of the nine symptoms in one of the categories in order to be diagnosed with ADHD under today's standards. Any person seventeen or older, according to the new DSM-5, need only exhibit five symptoms.

According to the DSM-5, however, a child or adult demonstrating only a few of the five or six symptoms required can still be labeled ADHD. The DSM calls this "ADHD not otherwise specified." And if the patient does not have any of the symptoms but the professional doing the diagnosis still *feels* the patient has ADHD, the patient can still be labeled as having "ADHD unspecified." Yes, it is ridiculous, a person can be diagnosed with ADHD while showing few or even no ADHD symptoms.

But in my opinion, what pro-ADHD experts use to diagnose ADHD "correctly" is not much better. To show you how flawed the diagnosis is, the DSM-5 symptoms have been typed verbatim in the following (found in the manual on pages 59–60). As you are reading them and you think to yourself, "There is no way these descriptions could be what they use to diagnose ADHD—he made these up," rest assured . . . these are the symptoms they actually use.

There are a few more important details I'll share with you shortly, relating to how these symptoms should be used for diagnosing, but to start, as you read through each of the nine symptoms for diagnosing ADHD-inattentive, please *just say yes* to those that describe how you might have behaved when you were a kid—or quite possibly even today as an adult. Are you ready to be diagnosed with ADHD-inattentive? Are you ready to find out that you have or as a child might have had what some psychiatrists call a mental disorder? Then good luck. Here are the nine symptoms for diagnosing ADHD-inattention.

ADHD-INATTENTION SYMPTOM CHECKLIST

Directions: Put a check mark next to the symptoms that reflect behaviors associated with you or you as a child.

1. Often fails to give close attention to details or makes careless mistakes in schoolwork, work, or during other activities (e.g., overlooks or misses details, work is inaccurate). ____
2. Often has difficulty sustaining attention in tasks or play activities (e.g., has difficulty remaining focused during lectures, conversations, or lengthy reading). ____
3. Often does not seem to listen when spoken to directly (e.g., mind seems elsewhere, even in the absence of any obvious distraction). ____
4. Often does not follow through on instructions and fails to finish schoolwork, chores, or duties in the workplace (e.g., starts tasks but quickly loses focus and is easily distracted). ____
5. Often has difficulty organizing tasks and activities (e.g., difficulty managing sequential tasks; difficulty keeping materials and belongings in order, messy, disorganized work, has poor time management, fails to meet deadlines). ____
6. Often avoids, dislikes, or is reluctant to engage in tasks that require sustained mental effort (e.g., schoolwork or homework; for older adolescents and adults, preparing reports, completing forms, reviewing lengthy papers). ____
7. Often loses things necessary for task or activities (e.g., school materials, pencils, books, tools, wallets, keys, paperwork, eyeglasses, mobile telephones). ____
8. Is often easily distracted by extraneous stimuli (for older adolescents and adults, may include unrelated thoughts). ____
9. Is often forgetful in daily activities (e.g., doing chores, running errands; for older adolescents and adults, returning calls, paying bills, keeping appointments). ____

So, how did you do? How many of these nine symptoms did you say "yes" to? Remember, these were the nine symptoms for ADHD-inattentive, and if you are older than seventeen you only needed five to be declared ADHD-inattentive according to today's existing protocol. If you did feel that at least five or six of these relate or related to how you behave today or did as a child, you should not be surprised.

Beyond just describing how all kids behave while they are learning to be good students and responsible, polite adults, you might have noticed that the sentences describing the symptoms all seem to be quite similar or have been reworded basically to represent, in essence, the same thing. For example, if you said yes to "difficulty sustaining attention," you probably said yes to "distracted by extraneous stimuli" and "often avoids, dislikes, or is reluctant to engage in tasks that require sustained mental effort."

Also, did you find the DSM wording of these symptoms to be slightly vague or bothersome? For example, "reluctant to engage in tasks that require sustained mental effort"? Hello? We are talking about children. And even for adults . . . well, there is a reason why reality TV shows like *Real Housewives*, *American Idol*, *The Voice*, *Goldrush*, and *Finding Bigfoot* have huge viewership. Americans enjoy brainless downtime and watching from our couches as others pursue their dreams or delusions.

Distracted by extraneous stimuli? Uh, yes. Isn't this what extraneous stimuli are supposed to do—the definition of extraneous stimuli? And what exactly is meant by *often*? How many times a day, week, month, or year constitutes *often*? The use of such vague, subjective terms leave a great deal of room for interpretation, variance, and error when it comes to personal discretion on the part of a parent, medical professional, mental-health practitioner, and educator debating these symptoms' existence.

From a research-based child-development perspective, however, stating that a child *often* exhibits many if not all of the nine symptoms is perfectly normal for nearly all developmental levels, from infancy to adolescence. Many professor colleagues probably would confidently extend this to college-age adults as well. Furthermore, ask employers, and they will tell you that good help is hard to find because the majority of adults exhibit the nine symptoms used to diagnose ADHD-inattentive.

Now, it should be stated that using this list of nine symptoms as just a checklist and marking the symptoms you connect with is not the way the DSM suggests you do the diagnosis. What this exercise is asking you to do is basically follow the laymen's approach to diagnosing ADHD. What this exercise is getting you to do is simulate the way the DSM is being misused to misdiagnose the supposed ADHD disorder by far too many with a license to diagnose and medicate.

Other caveats concern the duration and the severity of the symptoms. Also, individuals using the DSM correctly are expected to rule out (that is, establish beyond doubt) that none of the sixteen other differential diagnoses consisting of specific disorders (e.g., bipolar) or categories of disorders (e.g., psychotic disorders) better explain or replace the ADHD diagnosis. You don't have to diagnose for a living to realize it would take longer than one short doctor's visit to rule out sixteen other disorders or categories of disorder.

But the eighteen symptoms are what they are, and they are being misused by far too many. There are even some people that want you to believe they have a test your child can take at school based on these eighteen common behaviors that can serve as an indicator of whether he or she has ADHD. But don't forget—many of the folks doing this at schools are not licensed to say whether or not someone has ADHD, and the DSM makes it very clear that no test exists for the diagnosis of ADHD.

More than 90 percent of those with whom I share the diagnosis for ADHD-inattentive during lectures on the topic (adults like you) keep their hands up as I read the symptoms, saying yes to nearly all of them. In other words, if this first set of nine simple descriptions defines what pro-ADHD experts want to call ADHD-inattention, we all basically are—or were as children—ADHD-inattentive. When you have diagnostic criteria or a test for a mental disorder that nearly encompasses the entire population—not to mention the fact that you do not have a test capable of discriminating between those who do and don't have a mental disorder—what you really have is a diagnosis of normal.

The symptoms of ADHD-inattentive are normal for so many of us and for kids as well. If you can't remember how you acted as a child, maybe take a moment to call one of your parents (preferably the more honest one). I have been told by grandparents on numerous occasions that their children acted the same as their grandchildren do today and that their kids (the parents of the grandchildren) turned out alright without being put on drugs. For those of us who answer honestly, it is probably harder to answer no to the symptoms comprising the DSM's ADHD-inattentive diagnostic criteria than it is to just say yes.

But the DSM also states that to be diagnosed as ADHD-inattentive, "six (or more) of the following symptoms [must] have persisted for at least six months to a degree that is *inconsistent with developmental level* and that *negatively impacts directly on social and academic/occupational activities.*" Of course, given the nonrigorous science and apparent lack of due diligence behind this diagnosis, a mental-health practitioner or medical doctor is not expected to take or allow for six months of exploring such behaviors in differing environments perceived by different individuals. Apparently being cautious about rushing into a diagnosis often requiring medication and looking for more evidence to confirm such a diagnosis is too time consuming.

Instead the clinical psychiatrist, mental-health practitioner, or medical doctor about ready to recruit a new customer is only expected to take the word of the people at school (individuals recommending a child be diagnosed due to perceived disruptive behavior) and possibly the word of a parent (a person not necessarily considered an expert in child development or capable of determining whether behaviors are inconsistent or maladaptive at specific developmental levels).

This happens despite the fact that the DSM-5 clearly states that "adult recall of childhood symptoms tends to be unreliable, and it is beneficial to obtain ancillary information." The word of these individuals—who may have preexisting personal agendas or, as parents, an inability to provide an objective, nonbiased view—is what is used to determine if the behaviors were displayed often by the children for six months or more. These individuals, some of whom have only known the child for a short time, also are expected to be able to determine whether such extreme behaviors existed before the ages of seven or eleven, another requirement or expectation of the existing DSM diagnostic criteria.

Most of us spend our lives trying to perfect or at least work on these not-so-perfect behaviors related to ADHD-inattentive that require us to be organized, detail oriented, attentive, polite, and responsible. These symptoms might be fine for trying to determine whether an adult could benefit from such a label and medication. For kids, however, the symptoms have set expectations for behavior that are far too high for the majority to achieve. This is why I suspect that nearly every child that is sent to be diagnosed by one of the *experts* energizing this ADHD movement leaves the practitioner's office labeled with ADHD.

But these first nine symptoms are used to diagnose ADHD-inattentive. What about diagnosing the ADHD–hyperactivity and impulsivity portion, you ask? Once again, there are nine highly generic symptoms, only five or six of which must be observable for you to be diagnosed ADHD–hyperactive/impulsive. For this set of symptoms I suggest that (if you don't have a female child that you are specifically concerned about) you read the symptoms and answer from the hypothetical perspective of a boy between the ages of 5-11. I suggest this exercise because a high percentage of kids diagnosed with ADHD are boys, and if you focus on this section's connection to the behavior of young boys you might see why this is the case.

In other words, imagine you are a young boy (or girl) who has to sit in school, fully focused on the one-size-fits-all curriculum, as sunny days or snow-covered fields call your name for months on end. Are you ready? Begin . . .

ADHD–HYPERACTIVITY AND IMPULSIVITY SYMPTOM CHECKLIST

Directions: Put a check mark next to the symptoms that reflect behaviors associated with you, your male child, or your young boy alter ego.

a. Often fidgets with or taps hands or feet or squirms in seat. ____
b. Often leaves seat in situations when remaining seated is expected (e.g., leaves his or her place in the classroom, in the office, or other workplace or in other situations that require remaining in place). ____
c. Often runs about or climbs in situations where it is inappropriate (Note: In adolescents or adults, may be limited to feeling restless). ____
d. Often unable to play or engage in leisure activities quietly. ____
e. Is often "on the go," acting as if "driven by a motor" (e.g., is unable to be or uncomfortable being still for extended time, as in restaurants, meetings; may be experienced by others as being restless or difficult to keep up with). ____
f. Often talks excessively. ____
g. Often blurts out the answer before a question has been completed (e.g., completes people's sentences; cannot wait turn in conversation). ____
h. Often has difficulty waiting his or her turn (e.g., while waiting in line). ____
i. Often interrupts or intrudes on others (e.g., butts into conversations, games, or activities; may start using other people's things without asking or receiving permission; for adolescents and adults, may intrude into or take over what others are doing). ____

So, how did it go on this one? Were you able to pay attention as a young boy long enough to read basic descriptions that describe how the majority of young boys behave? How many did you say yes to? Are you or your seven-year-old male alter ego ADHD–hyperactive and impulsive as well?

It is as if the individuals who wrote these symptoms have never been around kids before. It's as if they don't like kids—and most definitely little boys. Who in their right mind, besides a few old-school librarians and pastors protecting the sanctity of the quiet nature of their workplace, would expect children to play quietly? And who would associate "quiet play" as it relates to kids' leisure activity? For millions of kids, playing quite often encompasses, if not requires, one to run and scream. This is called "having fun" when you are young.

Regardless, just try sitting in one of those school desks made of hard plastic or particle board (void of any cushion or ergonomic design) for a whole day. The odds are quite great you will want to get up and walk around *often* yourself. To imagine that children—typically the more extroverted ones (by the way, extroversion is considered a positive trait linked to success in the business world)—would somehow choose not to talk excessively seems highly unlikely.

A few good reminder lessons for realizing nearly all kids talk excessively as well as display many of the other ADHD symptoms would be to volunteer one day at your child's school or a local youth organization. Or, better yet, load the kids up in the car for a road trip and drive eight hours somewhere without allowing them to watch videos or play with any smart phones or tablets. Or have your child invite five friends over for a sleepover.

As you will discover—or remember—from these simple lessons, kids seem to interrupt us all-knowing and wise adults all too often, and they are definitely driven by a motor. Why is it so surprising that they are still learning the social customs at the ripe and mature ages of five, seven, nine, thirteen, or fifteen? At some point children will learn to wait their turn (and develop the ability to be patient for that matter), but it takes time. If we are lucky, they will also stop fidgeting with their hands, tapping their feet, or squirming endlessly in their seats. We call it childhood for a reason; children act like children.

What we have is a game of semantics. The pro-ADHD experts call it "fidgety," "on the go," "driven by a motor," but it could also be called "energetic," "motivated," and "full of life." "Runs, plays, and doesn't remain seated" are signs kids like being active, which ought to be welcome with today's unheard-of levels of childhood obesity. They paint "not waiting your turn," "blurting out answers," or "interrupting" as a bad thing, but could it not be a sign of wanting to contribute with enthusiasm, which is much better than nonparticipation? "Doesn't follow instructions" or "engage in a series of tasks" and "avoids organization" are all signs of highly creative and possibly intelligent minds. "Doesn't pay close attention" and "provide sustained attention or listen" happens when we are thinking actively beyond what is being discussed. It just all depends on what side of the desk or prescription pad you sit. Once again, it is in the eye of the beholder.

It's That Easy

Yes, these are the eighteen symptoms you were warned about. The day I drove home from visiting the rural school that started my mission to help adults navigate Planet ADHD, I decided the first thing I would do when I arrived home was look in a copy of the DSM and see just exactly how they diagnose ADHD. I assumed the DSM would have some very specific symptoms they discovered through formal studies utilizing large random samples of children, which would accurately identify how we assess kids that suffered from this disorder. But instead of finding science-based measurements capable of teasing out those with ADHD from those without (what we call in quantitative research *using sound psychometrics*), I found the most pathetic eighteen symptoms used as a test, scale, or assessment tool I have ever come across.

There was little research documenting that these eighteen—or two sets of nine—similar behaviors (symptoms) were capable of measuring the same thing over and over again (what is called *reliability*). More importantly, there was no research documenting that these eighteen or nine symptoms measured what the pro-ADHD experts claim to measure (what is called *validity*). There was no evidence of predictive or discriminate validity. Instead, in the DSM-IV there were ten pages of outrageous claims and questionable causes void of peer-reviewed academic- or medical-journal references and definitive scientific or biological evidence.

This was surprising. Most of us in academia have spent our careers in higher education publishing conference papers, journal articles, and academic books that require references. Any credible studies we write up for publication in journals, or grant reports we complete for the government, require us to show that the surveys and scales used to measure the variables being investigated are reliable and valid.

Most colleagues in higher education would expect that the creators of the DSM would face the same requirements and that upon looking inside the DSM one would find some great research and scientifically based insights as to how pro-ADHD experts have determined ADHD is truly a mental disorder. Most would expect in today's technologically advanced medical world to find sound evidence cited in the DSM using brain scans, blood tests, or genetic markers showing that ADHD is truly a medical condition. But in the DSM-IV and DSM-5, one will only find suggestions of such links to such evidence.

Keeping Them Honest

Additionally, when I did the legwork independently and found the suggested so-called evidence in academic databases, I discovered the many shortcomings and limitations of the research—thus the reason pro-ADHD experts only hinted that research exists. This chapter and others to follow share the many studies, statistical shortcomings, and litany of limitations I have discovered.

In the latest DSM edition, the DSM-5—and, yes, they dropped the use of Roman numerals to show they are hip and with the times—they are even clearer that such evidence doesn't really exist. "No biological marker is diagnostic for ADHD," they state. The reason no blood or genetic test is claimed or possibly even exists is because the research suggesting that ADHD is inherited from our parents' bloodlines is weak when it comes to meeting the expectations of scientific and statistical-analysis.

The supporters of ADHD have historically supported a genetic link by showing that parents reported also having the same childhood behaviors used to diagnose ADHD or that twins behaved the same way. Basing a genetic link on research showing parents behaved (and most likely still behave) similarly to the child only further strengthens the argument that such behaviors are normal and quite possibly were nurtured (learned from their parents) and not inherited. We call this *learned behavior* in psychology. Suggesting that twins share similar behaviors is evidence of ADHD seems even more moronic.

But recent research published in 2010 and 2011 exploring the human genome (our genetic profiles) claims to have discovered that large and rare chromosomal deletions and duplications known as *copy number variants* (CNVs) have been implicated in contributing to neurodevelopmental disorders like ADHD. When you think of CNVs, just think of them as abnormalities in one's genetic fabric, serving as evidence of the fact one might be missing or duplicating important chromosomes (parts of the genome) that other individuals are not missing or do not duplicate.

Beyond using an unreliable and invalid tool (the DSM's eighteen symptoms) to determine if children used as the CNVs study's sample of participants actually had ADHD, they discovered that only 14 percent of the kids labeled with ADHD in the study actually had CNVs, and 7 percent of the participants not labeled with ADHD also had CNVs. But not letting weak numbers hold them back from getting airtime with Anderson Cooper, they then proceeded to claim that "our findings provide genetic evidence of an increased rate of large CNVs in individuals with ADHD and suggest that ADHD is not purely a social construct." Such scientific jargon sounds scary.

This is similar to claiming that if we did a study and discovered that 14 percent of kids with ADHD have red hair, then we could say that red hair is the genetic link explaining ADHD. A few of the original authors of this CNV ADHD study decided to dig further and do another study. This time they discovered that less than 14 percent of the study's young participants diagnosed with ADHD actually showed evidence of CNVs. Note that their study did not use a control or comparison sample of kids not diagnosed with ADHD.

The conclusion they came to from this study was that CNVs were less predictive of ADHD but more predictive of children with intellectual disabilities. This seems a more realistic conclusion to come to that does not overstep the merit of the study's findings. Kids with genetic abnormalities have challenges when it comes to intellectual abilities.

The bottom line is that if we are to find the genetic link that fully explains why kids exhibit qualities linked to ADHD, such abnormalities or unique anomalies would need to be present in the majority of kids diagnosed with ADHD. If it is only showing us a possible link to ADHD in 14 percent or fewer of the kids, then what is the genetic link to ADHD in the other 86 percent? But, as I will try to intentionally and repeatedly make very clear throughout this book, you cannot do a study and claim you have identified some sort of improvement or relationship to something (e.g., ADHD) if you do not have a reliable or valid way of measuring the very thing you claim to be studying. And no test—no reliable or valid way of measuring for ADHD—exists.

The DSM even states that tests of attention, executive function, or memory are not sensitive or specific enough to "serve as diagnostic indices." In other words, they honestly admit there are no real medical or written tests for ADHD that are supported by research as being accurate enough or capable of identifying such a disorder. Instead of using medical-based markers (like brain scans and genetic markers) or reliable and valid written tests, practitioners are instructed to use the eighteen symptoms as their guide to labeling a child with ADHD (an ill-informed, opinion-based diagnosis).

If practitioners continued to use the existing diagnostic criteria for ADHD, however, and also actually investigated a six-month span of behavior, paid attention to the severity of issues, utilized multiple observers, and took the time to rule out the sixteen other differential diagnoses, there is a good chance that the high level of ADHD prevalent in the United States would drop.

As to why medical doctors and mental-health practitioners are not allowing for the whole process of the diagnosis suggested in the DSM to be a part of the decision to label kids with ADHD one can only guess. Maybe it is because the DSM makes it too easy to diagnose far too many disorders. Maybe the practitioners haven't actually read the DSM or been trained in how to properly use it in assigning diagnoses.

Or maybe they were not trained sufficiently in the developmental stages, levels, or specifics of children, and they honestly do not know how children typically behave at different stages of development. Maybe it is because they were not trained in how to collect reliable and valid information and through sheer ignorance assume that the folks at the children's school reporting such behaviors provide a representative, generalizable, and nonbiased sample capable of documenting how the children act elsewhere. Or just maybe they have bought into the popular label of ADHD and the practice of medicating children for acting like children and don't really care what the evidence says or doesn't say.

Which brings us to the next point: what exactly is ADHD if the DSM's eighteen-symptom diagnostic criteria don't provide enough science or structure to identify it accurately or don't offer sufficient detail to separate supposed ADHD symptoms from normal childhood behavior? To explore this question, let us take a look at the roots of the research used to justify ADHD as a real disorder.

A BRIEF HISTORY OF THE ADHD DIAGNOSIS

The Grateful Dead song "What a Long Strange Trip It's Been" provides a good theme for the evolution of today's ADHD diagnosis. In piecing together literature and research, the efforts of the supporters of ADHD have definitely taken liberty to stop at several strange viewpoints along the way. As I began to research just when or where this so-called mental disorder originated, I kept coming across the same claims of historical developments and medical discoveries believed to represent the existence and evolution of today's ADHD diagnosis. The following is a synopsis of the abbreviated time line you will find if you do the same research.

It would appear part of what you will find in the DSM has been influenced by medical and fictional literature from the eighteenth and nineteenth centuries. Yes, make-believe literature was used to document a supposed medical condition. Based on this literature, some in psychiatry would like you to believe that the diagnosis has been around in some form or another for several centuries.

The works forming the basis for this belief are a couple of books mentioning some symptoms related to inattention and distractibility—one written in 1778 by Dr. Sir Alexander Crichton, discussing studies on a small sample of his mentally ill patients, and the other a German children's book, *Zappelphilipp (Fidgety Phil)*, written by German physician Dr. Heinrich Hoffmann. These two literary works conveniently provide similar descriptions of the ADHD symptoms listed today in the DSM.

In one of his books, Crichton wrote a chapter "On Attention and Its Diseases." In his writings he defined attention, explored the "sensibility of the nerves" (whatever that might be), and talked about how symptoms similar to his mental patients' could be seen early on in kids who had trouble paying attention in school. Please note that Crichton believed these symptoms would diminish with age around or after puberty for many youth, which was a common notion up until the early 1900s, when the supply of common sense began to wane in the psychiatric world.

Hoffman's work was a fictional account of a kid being fidgety at the dinner table. Given that he wrote that Fidgety Phil "wriggled and giggled and then, I declare, swung backward and forward and tilted his chair," I wouldn't be surprised if Hoffman did indeed inspire the first symptom for ADHD—"Often fidgets with or taps hands or feet or squirms in seat." I can only assume it was either Dr. Hoffman or Dr. Seuss.

As to how a book written in the late 1700s based on a few clinical observations of a very small sample of Crichton's mentally ill patients and an illustrated fictional children's book written in the mid-1800s by a German physician describing how a bad boy acts at dinner might serve as the foundation for the most popular diagnosis used today to label and medicate children, one can only imagine. But when no real research exists to hitch your wagon to, folks begin to reach for straws.

Moving onward and upward from the literary evidence at the bottom—or what some might call the foundation—of the case for ADHD, let's now briefly examine the commonly touted medical side of the historical ADHD-evolution research. According to the *experts*, the history goes back as far as 1902, when a British doctor, Sir George Frederic Still, documented a disorder relating to impulsiveness, called *defect of moral control*. He believed that if kids were not "mentally retarded" or suffering from disease, and if they had an average IQ, the only reason explaining why they would act so imorally, showing so little concern for others, was because they had a "defect of moral control."

Dr. Still believed that the defect was probably a mix of nature (genetics) and nurture (family upbringing) and was most definitely beyond the control of the afflicted. His sample for this study's conclusion was mainly focused on case studies of a meager twenty troubled kids (e.g., picture twenty of the young cast members from the musical *Oliver*). Although most of the symptoms that Dr. Still related to a moral deficit are not associated with the whole view of today's ADHD, ADHD supporters cite his work today because parts of his research tend to mirror some of their beliefs about ADHD.

Mainly, Still suggested that the delay for gratification is a major challenge for some children and is related to impulsivity. Exploring the developmental work of Piaget and Vygotsky, which we'll review more thoroughly in chapter 7, will help us form a different perspective as to how delay of gratification and impulsivity are related to developmental stages. Dr. Still's work, tied to what he believed to be immoral or bad behavior, however, begins to document how impulsivity and the need for instant gratification are tied to the supposedly problematic behaviors associated with ADHD today.

Skipping twenty years into the future, in 1922 some symptoms we might associate with ADHD today were named *postencephalitic behavior disorder. Encephalitic* refers to the inflammation of the brain. It turns out that many of the affected children who survived the encephalitis lethargica epidemic, which spread around the world from 1917 to 1928 and affected approximately twenty million people, showed remarkably abnormal behavior, including significant changes in personality, emotional instability, cognitive deficits, learning difficulties, sleep reversals, tics, depression, and poor motor control.

These kids were described as hyperactive, disruptive, distractible, antisocial, unruly, and unmanageable in school. Similar to Dr. Still's work, this assumption of a connection between brain damage and hyperactivity/impulsiveness (disruptive abnormal behavior) is important to some experts in further conceptualizing today's ADHD. As for others, we might wonder how connecting the horrible side effects (from a devastating disease resulting from one of the worst epidemics in the twentieth century) relates to today's ADHD. We might wonder, because ADHD is not linked to any disease and has little supporting research related to birth defects.

In 1932, however, Kramer and Pollnow (more German physicians) decided that studying and naming the effects of brain damage and hyperactivity linked to the residual effects of the encephalitis lethargica epidemic was not enough. And so they determined that a disorder was needed to reflect the "hyperkinetic disease of infancy," or, as they called it *"Über eine hyperkinetische Erkrankung im Kindesalter"* (which, when translated into German, for some reason sounds even scarier).

Yes, these two trailblazers wanted to distinguish a disorder separate from others that described how infants once able to crawl and walk cannot stay still for a second. As their publication on the disorder describes, they wanted to name a disorder that described how children (yes, even toddlers) run up and down a room, climb about, preferring high furniture in particular, and are displeased when deterred from acting out their motor impulses.

As crazy as this sounds—diagnosing infants with mental disorders— can you see the commonalities between what they coined and described for how those horribly ill-mannered infants behaved and the current symptoms used for ADHD? "Often leaves seat in situations when remaining seated is expected," "often runs about or climbs in situations where it is inappropriate," and "acts as if driven by a motor" are three ADHD symptoms possibly inspired by Kramer and Pollnow.

Not that we should believe that any of this research actually substantiates the existence or legitimacy of ADHD as a mental disorder, but you have to admit that if we were to name any of these earlier researchers the founding father(s) of ADHD, Kramer and Pollnow ought to get our vote. It shouldn't be surprising that their brave efforts to stigmatize the abnormal behavior of children starting during infancy as a mental disorder was quite deserving of accolades when Adolf Hitler took power in 1933.

The next event in the history of ADHD, in 1937, however, steals the show. This was when Dr. Charles Bradley stumbled onto the use of stimulants to treat children who were hyperactive. You see, Bradley was a medical director at a hospital in Rhode Island founded by his great-uncle George, which specialized in treating neurologically impaired children. As part of Bradley's research to *help* kids and further explore structural brain abnormalities, he apparently performed pneumoencephalograms (sometimes referred to as PEGs) on many of the children at his hospital.

Pneumoencephalography was a popular medical procedure in the early twentieth century in which most of the cerebrospinal fluid was drained from around the brain and replaced with air, oxygen, or helium to allow the structure of the brain to show up more clearly on an X-ray image. Yes, just imagine something similar to that part in the movie *Frankenstein* where the monster gets a brain replacement, with lightning flashing and thunder crashing in the background, and then replace the monster with a poor, sick child. This procedure would have often left the children with severe headaches, due to their significant loss of spinal fluid. It also would have caused severe vomiting and been incredibly painful, and it would have taken each child two to three months to naturally recover the fluids lost through the procedure. "Gee, thanks, Doc! That really helped."

To further help these children with the extreme headaches, Dr. Frankenstein—I mean, *Dr. Bradley*—decided it would be a good idea to arouse the choroid plexus of the children's already tortured brains with the most potent stimulant available at the time, Benzedrine. He discovered that while Benzedrine had hardly any effect on the headaches, in some children it provided a great improvement in behavior and school performance. Wait—do you mean that children lying around with no cerebrospinal fluid in their brains actually appeared more energetic once they were shot full of the most potent stimulant? *Really?*

Regardless of the merit of serendipitous medical miracles, after stumbling onto this discovery, Bradley decided to do a trial study using Benzadrine on thirty other lucky children. What he discovered was that it gave some kids (the less-hyper ones) extra energy to focus and work more quickly and accurately, while others (the more hyper ones) "became emotionally subdued without, however, losing interest in their surroundings." Such research is somewhat similar to what we discovered on numerous occasions decades ago and still find today: stimulants have nearly the same effect in regard to increased focus on non-ADHD kids as they do on ADHD kids.

As reliance on psychoanalysis (talk therapy) to treat mental disorders fell out of fashion, the interest in pharmaceuticals grew, and, as you probably have guessed by now, Dr. Bradley's research led to the practice of treating hyperactive or hyperkinetic children with stimulants (over-stimulation). In 1956, Ritalin was introduced as the drug of choice. As a result, by the 1960s stimulants were used by a wider population, which is miniscule when compared to today, however.

The only symptom at this point really documented as having been "effectively" treated by the stimulants, however, was hyperactivity. Yet in the early 1960s, when technology was not so great for studying the brain, a new disorder called *minimal brain dysfunction* was discovered. According to pro-ADHD researchers, this discovery further builds the case for ADHD and provides evidence ADHD was or is actually related to brain dysfunction. But by the end of the decade, that whole brain-dysfunction vocabulary was dropped and the name of the disorder was changed to *hyperkinetic disorder of childhood*.

In relation to today's ADHD, new symptoms were tacked on to the disorder. Along with hyperactivity, lack of focus associated with impulsiveness was added, among other symptoms. Impulsiveness now included verbal, cognitive, and motor impulsiveness. In 1980, the disorder was given the name of *attention deficit disorder* (ADD), with or without hyperactivity. This was documented in the DSM-III. Until 1987, ADD and ADHD were two different diagnoses, at which point ADD was changed to attention deficit/hyperactivity disorder. The American Psychiatric Association further noted that ADHD was a medical diagnosis and not purely psychological. They also noted that ADHD could *cause* behavioral issues.

Please note that when I teach research methods, there are two words that I tell my students they should never use—the P word and the C word, *prove* and *cause*. I choose to not use these words because if science has taught us anything it is that we can rarely state that one thing is solely responsible for *causing* another and that once we think we have *proven* something we are soon thereafter proven wrong ourselves. As a wise mentor once suggested, if you read research that uses such words you should place it in the circular file.

This brief review of the historical roots of today's ADHD diagnosis, however, shows us that behaviors related to ADHD have varied in causation from moral deficit to an enflamed brain to a brain dysfunction to hyperactivity or behavior issues treatable with stimulants. The disorder has gone from a psychological diagnosis to a medical diagnosis void of any medical tests. And what previously was used to treat a very small percentage of *people* with highly abnormal behavior is now being applied to millions of *children* behaving like children worldwide who are not old enough to sometimes know better.

But what's truly sad about all of this research is that even with our technological advances we are still unable to document—provide evidence to support—that such behavior associated with ADHD is due to any type of preexisting brain malfunction or defect in our DNA. In other words, all of this so-called research (evidence, if you want to give it that much credit) is based on unsubstantiated and quickly abandoned scientific hypotheses suggesting that the ADHD disorder is due to something being wrong with our brains or DNA. In other words, the powers behind the DSM and the few pharmaceutical companies drugging our children have no real substantial or indisputable research to stand behind. If such research did exist, doctors would perform a blood or DNA test or an MRI instead of asking eighteen stupid questions related to common normal behaviors all kids exhibit.

A BRIEF HISTORY OF THE DSM

Before we end this chapter with a bit of humor and discuss the need for differential diagnosis or, more aptly, more honest explanations for such ADHD-like behavior, let's further discuss the valuable but often-misused reference book for mental-health practitioners. In theory, the DSM is a good idea; heck, it's a great idea. Every field should have at convenient reference some sort of all-encompassing manual summarizing everything experts should know. But somewhere on the road to creating a useful tool for psychiatry, in my opinion the wheels fell off the bus, or, more accurately, the carpool's navigators took a wrong turn at Albuquerque. Although the DSM started out as an admirable undertaking, it has slowly turned into a book that many are finding to be problematic.

If you don't believe or possibly agree that the DSM has turned down the wrong road, take a moment to explore what the other APA—the American Psychological Association, not the American Psychiatric Association—has to say about the DSM. Take a look online at what European mental-health professionals and medical doctors have to say about it. For that matter, read about what the people who were responsible for writing its third and fourth editions have to say about what it has done. You will find that the great majority of psychologists, counselors, and therapists play no role in the development of the DSM. Furthermore, given that many psychologists, counselors, and therapists typically do not believe in or practice prescribing medication, large percentages are harsh critics of the most recent DSM editions.

But if a mass lack of belief in the DSM weren't already a problem, most recently the National Institute of Mental Health (NIMH) withdrew its support from the latest edition, the DSM-5. In fact, NIMH stated that they will no longer fund research projects that rely exclusively on DSM criteria, due to "its lack of validity." It was once such a useful tool that held great potential for doing good. So, where did things go so wrong?

The need for a DSM-type manual began in the late 1800s and early 1900s. During the project's infancy, the goal was to combine systems that collected census data, statistics from psychiatric hospitals, and information pertaining to the U.S. Army. In 1917, a committee from the American Psychiatric Association (APA—then known as the American Medico-Psychological Association) along with the National Commission of Mental Hygiene, developed a new guide called the *Statistical Manual for the Use of Institutions for the Insane*, which included twenty-two diagnoses. This document was revised numerous times before much of it became a subsection of the U.S. medical guide and from that point forth was known as the *Standard*.

As World War II resulted in an enormous number of soldiers returning home in great need of care, psychiatrists in the United States found themselves involved on a large scale. This took the focus of traditional psychiatry away from mental institutions and traditional clinical approaches. These events led to a new classification scheme in 1943 called *Medical 203*, as well as to further publications that encompassed mental disorders with other diseases. Many of these efforts were intended to help the United States and divisions of the armed forces treat our soldiers and resulted in the APA's publication of the first volume of the *Diagnostic and Statistical Manual of Mental Disorders* in 1952. The first manual was 130 pages long and listed 106 mental disorders.

Since that time, the DSM has been reprinted and updated nearly a dozen times. The reprints and revisions have been mainly due to how the ever-evolving field of psychiatry's views changed in relation to theoretical approaches and the use of terms such as *neurosis* and *psychosis*. Also, it has changed due to how the field views the disorders' relationships to sociological and biological factors, as well as the constantly moving boundary between normality and abnormality. In other words, a great amount of second-guessing has taken place basically every decade as to the correctitude and accuracy of views for diagnosing disorders.

In 1968, with the first printing of the DSM-II, the manual grew to 182 disorders (134 pages). After a decade of further debate, in 1980, the DSM-III grew to 265 diagnostic categories and 494 pages. With the DSM-III came the introduction of the multiaxial system (a supposedly better way to categorize the disorders). The DSM-III led to abandoning the long-standing acceptance of the psychodynamic view (that is, that behavior is directed by forces within one's personality but is usually hidden in the subconscious) or physiologic view (that is, something normal, due neither to anything pathologic nor significant in terms of causing illness) in favor of a regulatory and legislative model.

Basically, they went from theory-supported approaches focused on finding the best ways to *treat* those suffering from mental disorders (before jumping the gun and claiming they were mentally ill) to a more *efficient* means of *categorizing* people. Robert Spitzer, chairman of the DSM-III task force, later criticized his own work on this volume, saying it led to the *medicalization* of 20 to 30 percent of the population who may not have had any serious mental problems.

The next decade brought even more debate and revisions as the APA prepared to publish the DSM-IV. Disorders such as premenstrual dysphoric disorder and masochistic personality disorder were removed, while other disorders were being lobbied for and slated to be added in. Homosexuality and sexual-orientation disturbance (disorders for labeling gay people) were also removed but then subsumed (renamed, if you will) with titles such as *sexual disorder not otherwise specified* or *hypersexual disorder*. You might note that prior to 1973 the disorder tied to homosexuality was called *sociopathic personality disorder*. In 1994 the DSM-IV was published, and after another revision in 2000, the great big book of everything wrong with us grew to more than 365 disorders and close to a thousand pages.

Most recently, with the printing of the DSM-5, also nearly a thousand pages long, more disorders such as Asperger's syndrome were removed or subsumed under a different label. In fact, Asperger's was added to the autism spectrum disorder, and, believe it or not, at one point autism spectrum disorders were thought to be a type of childhood schizophrenia. Also with the DSM-5 the multiaxial system was dropped for what they now believe to be a new and improved trait-specific diagnostic method. Are you beginning to see how they could be wrong when it comes to the ADHD diagnosis? History strongly suggests it would not be the first time.

They have added on new disorders in the DSM-5 too, such as excoriation disorder (skin picking) and hoarding disorder (Thanks, cable TV!). Senior moments of forgetfulness can now be labeled *mild neurocognitive disorder* so that grandma's Medicare can foot the bill for some mind-enhancing pills. You can even get labeled with a mental disorder if you suffer from temporary circumstance-induced grief after having lost a loved one (depression) and as a result receive a prescription. Beyond the diagnosis for depression, they have lightened the requirements for other disorders, meaning it is no longer as difficult to be diagnosed.

For example, along with the number of symptoms being reduced for an ADHD diagnosis, the diagnostic threshold for generalized anxiety disorder (GAD) was lowered. In previous versions, GAD had been defined as having any three of six symptoms (such as restlessness, a sense of dread, and feeling constantly on edge) for at least three months. In DSM-5, this has been revised to having just one to four symptoms for at least one month. Critics suggest that this lowering of requirements could lead to people with everyday problems being misdiagnosed and needlessly treated. This makes complete sense, given that most working parents and adults experience such a month of dread or anxiety prior to the holidays or tax season.

Meanwhile, the DSM still includes disorders that lack enough evidence to realistically be listed as disorders. For example, disruptive mood dysregulation disorder (DMDD) is defined by the DSM-5 as severe and recurrent temper outbursts (three or more times a week) that are grossly out of proportion in intensity or duration in children up to the age of eighteen—once again, a subjective call to make. The definition for (or existence of) this disorder is said to be based on a single piece of research. Professor Allen Frances, MD, *professor* emeritus at Duke University and former chair of its department of psychiatry, as well as the chair of the DSM-IV task force, points out that this diagnosis may "exacerbate, not relieve, the already excessive and inappropriate use of medication in young children."

There is a good reason a large part of the rest of the world diagnoses mental-health conditions not with the DSM but with the World Health Organization's system—ICD-10 (International Classification of Diseases). According to far too many mental-health experts, the DSM just keeps getting worse. Rather than labeling the DSM-5 the "Psychiatric Bible," it may be better to view it as a basic travel guide to a land we have barely begun to explore. These changes, additions, and ignored flaws are part of the reason critics of the DSM say the American Psychiatric Association is out of control, labeling common human problems as mental illness and thus contributing to our "pop-a-pill" culture.

This should come as no surprise, given that the American Psychiatric Association has approximately thirty-four thousand psychiatrists as members, doctors who treat mental illness. And unlike many of their colleagues in psychology, counseling, and therapy—those who have little to no say about what goes into the DSM—psychiatrists can and often do prescribe medication. To add insult to injury, a great number of pediatricians, with little to no prior clinical training in mental disorders, have begun using this manual as a reference and justification to diagnose and also medicate children.

All in all, most of the revisions of the DSM over six decades have been largely based on differences in semantics as to how to label things, theoretical perspectives (how to approach treating these labeled things), and usage (how to connect the diagnosis to medical practices—like billing insurance). But as with all things, political and media influences have played a large role in the revisions as the APA continually tries to keep their critics at bay. It is worth noting that in comparison to years past, today insurance companies pay for very little talk therapy. But nearly all will pay a larger portion or all of the costs associated with drug therapy. As a result, and related to other conflicts of interest to be clarified a bit more in the chapters to follow, much of this change can be connected to the pharmaceutical powers.

Unfortunately, what has been ignored historically during the many revisions of the DSM is a focus on research to better support and guide mental-health practitioners in actually helping people get better. Dr. Nick Craddock, professor of psychiatry at Cardiff University, and director of the National Centre for Mental Health in Wales, said the DSM-5 is flawed because definitions of disorders were sometimes changed on the basis of insufficient fresh scientific evidence.

For example (and to be clarified more in chapter 6), the pro-ADHD experts want us to believe that disorders such as ADHD and bipolar are genetic or biological (we inherited them from our bloodline, parents), but the research behind such claims is sparse, and what evidence does exist is weak and at the very least suspicious. As Dr. Lydia Furman's 2008 research determined, "evidence for a genetic or neuroanatomic cause of ADHD is insufficient. ADHD is unlikely to exist as an identifiable disease." The bottom line is that the DSM keeps getting bigger and bigger, making it easier to label more individuals with more disorders treated by a long list of pharmaceuticals that continues to grow endlessly.

It Gets Even More Fishy

It is worth noting that beyond the points of concern related to the many revisions and the underreliance on sound research supporting the DSM, there are also numerous conflicts of interest that further damage its credibility. First, the DSM has earned over $100 million for the American Psychiatric Association. Although this is a large number, it pales to the amount of money being made annually by pharmaceutical and insurance companies as well as medical doctors because of the DSM. But it does show you that profit is one of the motives involved. Profit, however, is not solely related to DSM book sales.

Of the authors who selected and defined the DSM-IV psychiatric disorders, roughly half had financial relationships with the pharmaceutical industry at one time. Of the panel members responsible for reviewing what the authors submitted to the DSM-IV, 100 percent had financial ties with the pharmaceutical industry. And according to Dr. Lisa Cosgrove, from the Edmond J. Safra Center for Ethics at Harvard University, and Dr. Sheldon Krimsky, from the department of Public Health and Community Medicine at Tufts University, it has not gotten much better when it comes to those behind the DSM-5; seven in ten DSM-5 task force members have drug-company ties.

Although the APA would like you to think they have lowered the risk related to financial conflicts of interest (for example, DSM authors and reviewers who were once paid by the pharmaceutical industry are now claiming they are no longer taking or have not taken any more money in recent months or years), Cosgrove and Krimsky point out that it is not considered a reportable conflict of interest to be paid by pharmaceutical companies to give speeches for the pharmaceutical companies, which in reality, at $2,500 or more per speech, can quickly add up to a major financial conflict.

To make matters worse, in the publication *Nature* Heidi Ledford clarifies that "the committees with the highest number of industrial links are those evaluating conditions for which drugs are the first-line treatment." Was this happening with those overseeing the latest ADHD revisions?

We could go on, seemingly forever, about the DSM's flaws, but it's already clear that the DSM, this very important scientific manual doctors often cite to make you feel better about accepting that the diagnosis for ADHD is real and supported by science, is riddled with controversy and limitations.

ALTERNATIVE EXPLANATIONS

In the world of mental health, when a disorder is lacking unique systems, symptoms, or signs (components essential for a very accurate medical diagnosis), the need for a differential diagnosis should be explored. A differential diagnosis allows the mental-health provider, client, and caregivers to consider alternative explanations or additional disorders as to why the client might be behaving in a certain way. According to the DSM-5, a long list of sixteen common differential diagnoses is associated with ADHD.

Typically many of these differential diagnoses have common symptoms; this is why they often overlap or can be mistakenly overlooked. It is possible that a client has several disorders at the same time; this is called *comorbidity*. The differential diagnoses supposedly associated with ADHD include anxiety disorders, depressive disorders, psychotic disorders, autism-spectrum disorder, intellectual disability, specific learning disorder, bipolar disorder, and on and on.

Given that the DSM-5 defines attention as "the ability to focus in a sustained manner on a particular stimulus or activity," some of these differential diagnoses make complete common sense. One can easily understand how feelings of anxiety and depression and the manic mood swings associated with the popular up-and-coming disorder of choice known as bipolar might lead to an inability to pay attention. Having a specific learning disorder or challenged intellect might also explain such attention deficits.

A few other differential diagnoses that I found interesting or novel were operational defiant disorder and intermittent explosive disorder. My interest was aroused when I gave them the acronyms of ODD and IED for my notes, which struck me as odd and explosive. These were two disorders I had heard of but never read about in depth in the DSM before writing this chapter.

According to the DSM-5, operational defiant disorder (ODD) represents a slightly stronger resistance to the demands of school characterized by negativity, hostility, and defiance. Intermittent explosive disorder (IED) is similar to ADHD in relation to high levels of impulsivity but also unlike ADHD, because IED is associated more with serious aggression toward others and not with problems sustaining attention. With the existence of such differential diagnoses documenting other disorders representing those with extreme ADHD-related behaviors, it makes me think we could easily get rid of ADHD all together and just diagnose children with extreme symptoms.

Strangely enough though, beyond a few unique caveats, ADHD and the many differential diagnoses are very similar. When you read about the other disorders that have been named in the DSM-5 as differential diagnoses for ADHD, you will notice that nearly all of them share very similar if not the same differential diagnoses lists. So when trying to figure out what a person is possibly suffering from, it truly comes down to the opinion of the mental-health practitioner. But as the autism spectrum disorder shows us, whether we christen it a disorder or a gift truly depends on the severity and combination of these symptoms. Maybe this is why you will not find definitions in the DSM-5's glossary for *disorder*, *mental disorder*, or *gift*; maybe they don't actually know themselves what the difference is between a disorder and a gift.

As I once overheard a doctor explain, autism spectrum disorder covers a wide swath of people. She explained that on one side of the spectrum you basically have talented employees in Silicon Valley and on the other far side you have a group of people so communicatively challenged they cannot function in social, occupational, or academic settings no matter how much assistance is provided. Meanwhile, in the middle we have amazing individuals that are still as brilliant as the Silicon Valley wizards but possibly can only communicate their thoughts by typing them out. This explains why some people suggest that there is not just *autism* (a disorder that is automatically bad) but more like a variety of autisms.

In other words, along the autism spectrum we have what some might want to call a disorder but what is in reality a gift. Along the spectrum we have a group of what might be described as incredibly intelligent socially challenged people who are leading the world in technology. Along the spectrum we have people who, despite being severely socially challenged, should not be dismissed and medicated because we—society—can gain and learn so much from them.

Please note that these incredibly creative and intelligent people typically are not being medicated in most circumstances and that these strange behaviors (symptoms) associated with the broadly interpreted autism spectrum disorder are exactly what make them amazing. Sure, some of them might not be able to communicate quite so easily with the barista at their favorite coffee shop in Silicon Valley, specifying what type of soy, skinny mocha-choca latte they want that morning, or maybe they can't mingle comfortably at business get-togethers. But these communicative challenges allow them to harness their intellectual abilities elsewhere.

There is considerable literature and debate as to whether the autism spectrum disorder is focused too wide and is actually capturing people that in decades past would have just been described as extremely introverted or even nerdy. But at least, compared with ADHD, the autism spectrum disorder allows for some folks to receive a much leaner and lighter diagnosis—a less harsh verdict and sentencing, if you will. It holds a place and provides a label for those among us that just don't fit in.

Autism allows for a little more common sense to be practiced when it comes to diagnosis. Instead of just prescribing drugs, experts in autism focus on many socially based interventions (like behavioral-modification programs) to help diagnosed kids and their families navigate the childrens' communication challenges. And this is similar to what differential diagnoses should do. Before placing harsh judgments on children for their inability to show interest or concern for the mundane societal and institutional rules and expectations placed on them, how about we just tell parents what the problem really might be? How about we close the DSM-5 book, put it on the shelf, and just talk about what *really* might be the problem?

So, enough with the serious stuff; let's have some fun, if that is possible when it comes to the label of ADHD. Let's take a light-hearted look at what they call *differential diagnoses*. If ADHD is so hard to actually identify and the creators have changed the definition at least half a dozen times on the road to Wellville, then what else might explain what kids are suffering from in today's world?

To start helping mental-health practitioners—and the moonlighting pediatricians and family physicians playing the role of mental-health practitioner—be a bit less clinical and a little more honest, let's add a few differential diagnoses that might better explain why kids are behaving the way they do at school. To be clear, I am making these up.

Similar to a few differential diagnoses Dr. Peter Breggin recommended more than a decade ago, such as DADD (dad attention deficit disorder—kids need more attention from adult males) and TADD (teacher attention deficit disorder—kids want more attention from their teachers), the differential diagnoses to follow are fictional disorders. But from what I have discovered about the lack of scientific rigor needed to justify a disorder, I might be closer to getting these into the next DSM than I think I am. To follow are nine new disorders that could more sensibly explain what is truly affecting the 6.5 million children labeled ADHD.

- *Chronic boredom-induced behavior (CBIB, also known as the boredom disorder)*. This category applies to the presentation of symptoms illustrating a pattern of you-lost-me-hours-ago behavior. Symptoms include (but are not limited to): (1) nonverbal communication suggesting the child would rather have a root canal instead of sitting through one more minute of instruction; (2) utterances similar to "I am bored" and "I hate math"; and (3) the constant asking of questions such as "When is lunch?" "Why can't we go outside for recess?" and "Why do we only have music, art, and gym class once a week but have to read silently three hours a day?"
- *Sudden irrepressible creativity kinetic operations inattention tantrums (SICK-O-IT)*. This condition arises when children are no longer allowed to think for themselves or be creative in any way. With recess, physical education, art, and music having been replaced by multiple-choice-based testing curricula, the number of cases reported has escalated. Lack of project-based learning and discovery learning has further contributed to the cause. Research suggests there might be a strong correlation between the demand to focus for six hours a day and the limitation of a developing child's brain's inability to focus for more than five to twenty-five minutes.
- *Sedentary academic disorder (SAD)*. Known to be a common differential diagnosis of CBIB, SICK-O-IT, and others, SAD typically is first apparent after summer ends and several weeks or months of standards-based curriculum have been administered. Due to exposure of close to 180 days a year of such academics, symptoms also include fidgeting in seat and sadly playing at lunch with starchy structures and today's mystery meat.
- *Gifted disorder (GD)*. Sometimes confused with CBIB and SICK-O-IT, gifted disorder is different and often due to the fact that some kids are smarter and more advanced than others in the class. As a result, they want to be challenged more and actually taught something they do not already know, in a fashion that connects with their learning style.

- *Lethargic state–based development (LSD).* Removal of physical education and lack of time for exercise has led to a large spike in reported
cases of LSD symptoms. Characteristics are associated with rising
childhood-obesity rates and a lack of interest in doing anything
physical or healthy. Overuse of video games and extended periods
of sustained instruction have been linked to hallucinations of actually exercising and running freely through nature.
- *Nonexistent guardian parental systems (NO-GPS).* This disorder is
typically related to children living in homes with working parents
or single parents who have been unable to find or position sufficient
quality time with their children. The symptoms of NO-GPS further
illuminate conditions arising from lack of structure and routines
essential to raising children who better understand how to adapt
and act in public settings. NO-GPS helps explain why kids do not
behave the way the adults in their life hope they would behave.
- *Dysfunctional unidimensional dietary state (DUDS).* This disorder is
often associated with kids who have been programmed to eat only
one source of food, such as fried unidentifiable chicken parts (sometimes referred to as *chicken fingers*). Lack of a balanced diet leads to
nutritionally challenged brain development and the fuel needed to
energize cognition.
- *Numerous other reasons for maladaptive levels (NORML).* This disorder
serves as a category to explain and identify that not all children
develop at the same rate. Some children will be developmentally
delayed for numerous reasons and as a result exhibit many normal
behaviors associated with said developmental levels. NORML also
provides a trait-based indicator to group the many behaviors all
children exhibit at some point in time.
- *Infant attention-deficit disorder (IADD).* This disorder explains why
infants are unable to pay attention . . . Oh, wait . . . Those imaginative
German physicians, Kramer and Pollnow, beat me to this one.

In other words, our children are reacting to education and life the way
any normal child would because

1. they are bored, sick, and sad from doing the same old thing every
day
2. they are gifted and want more from their education
3. they need more love, structure, and attention from their parents
4. they long for more time to play and be creative
5. they lack exercise and good nutrition, and
6. so many more things that common sense would tell us need to
become a part of the education and child-rearing process.

Dr. Jerome Kagan, a Harvard professor named the twenty-second-most eminent psychologist of the twentieth century, recently stated that "[ADHD] is an invention. Every child who's not doing well in school is sent to see a pediatrician, and the pediatrician says, 'It's ADHD; here's Ritalin.' In fact, 90 percent of these 5.4 million kids don't have an abnormal dopamine metabolism. The problem is, if a drug is available to doctors, they'll make the corresponding diagnosis."

SUMMARY

I should note again that there is a large consensus that kids diagnosed with ADHD are quite capable of sustaining attention if given the opportunity to pay attention to what they are interested in or motivated to do (like computers, video games, outdoor activities, etc.). In fact, pro-ADHD researchers would like you to believe that when kids diagnosed with ADHD focus intensely on things such as video games, it ought to be called *hyperfocus*; in other words, their ability to maintain attention has become something else to view negatively and be highly concerned about. But in the real world, for experts working in science, medicine, or even law the ability to hyperfocus is essential to success. The ability to pay close attention to what you think is important and ignore the trivial information you feel is not worthy of distraction is a skill. The point is that kids with ADHD don't have attention problems; they have interest and motivation problems. They have opinions.

Whether or not you still feel that ADHD is a real mental disorder after reading this chapter, most of you would have to admit that the symptoms used to diagnose children for ADHD and other diagnostic criteria provided in the DSM have numerous limitations. The symptoms have far too high expectations for children to not *often* exhibit such behaviors. The symptoms are so common that they catch and justify medicating individuals displaying behaviors similar to Leonardo da Vinci's. The symptoms are just part of a semantics game being played at the expense of children.

The diagnosis of ADHD has been justified by reaching for straws and trying to connect unrelated past discoveries when it comes to the historical research in mental health. There are far too many conflicts of interest related to the DSM to assume that the intentions of such a diagnosis are the opposite of a moral deficit. And there are so many other reasons (that do not need to be considered a disorder) that would completely explain why some kids act the way they do—the main reason being that they are kids.

Plus, the creators of the DSM have removed disorders before. In other words, they have decided on numerous occasions that they had been wrong for previously suggesting a disorder was real. Let's also not forget that this same field of study at one time regularly used electroshock therapy void of general anesthesia to rid sad, desperate people of depression. Of course, today their practice is to at least *knock people out* before performing the therapy (also known today as electroconvulsive therapy).

As I was researching other strange medical and psychiatric beliefs that, luckily for us, have mostly gone by the wayside, I became aware of how for centuries doctors used genital massage on women to rid them of anxiety, insomnia, irritability, nervousness, and (as cazy a it sounds) wetness between the legs. They said such symptoms were due to a disorder known as *hysteria*, which today is known as *sexual frustration*. I use this example to point out two things: One, watch the old movie *The Road to Wellville* with Matthew Broderick and Anthony Hopkins (or read the book) to see how when we look back in time at what was once believed to be state-of-the-art medicine we realize in hindsight that such practices and beliefs were just borderline if not outright ludicrous. The second reason I have included this slightly silly, unrelated reference to hysteria is to share that from fanatical medical beliefs and practices good things can develop. According to a host of publications and websites, luckily—due to extreme chronic hand fatigue on the part of the doctors treating hysteria—one of the greatest inventions known to womankind was created: the electric vibrator. I can only hope that good things come from the foolish time period we are living in, where we have decided to medicate children for acting like children.

At the very least I hope that this chapter has alerted you to the fact that basically eighteen very generic and similar symptoms are the main if not only thing being used today to diagnose kids with ADHD. The science that pro-ADHD experts claim supports this diagnosis is incapable of producing or justifying any other means for identifying or testing for ADHD. I hope you are beginning to see that although they want you to believe that ADHD is a genetic condition or caused by an abnormal brain dysfunction, the nonexistence of any types of tests should serve as evidence that it is all hearsay at this point in time.

The way they test for ADHD is just a diagnosis of normality that basically confirms that all children exhibit such behavior *often*. The current test for ADHD is not much better than the popular so-called IQ test that you might find at your local Cracker Barrel Restaurant, which consists of a triangular Peg-Board made of wood and filled with holes for golf tees to be removed systematically. The number of golf tees you leave on the Peg-Board determines how smart you really are, supposedly. Sadly enough, removing golf tees from a simple triangular Peg-Board made of wood is probably more capable of ascertaining a normal distribution of skill levels (intelligence) than are the eighteen symptoms used to determine a normal distribution of ADHD symptoms—or, more importantly, used to identify those who exhibit abnormal levels of ADHD symptoms.

I realize that words have consequences. And the words I am sharing with you might provoke some to publically disagree with me or scorn me for sharing such supposed heresy. I am fully aware of the consequences. To me, actions speak louder than words, and together we must take action to be quite skeptical of anything that pro-ADHD experts tell us about this seemingly unsubstantiated mental disorder. In the next two chapters, we will further delve into the lack of evidence at the basis of the diagnosis for which so many children are medicated.

REFLECTION EXERCISE: DIAGNOSING NORMAL

In the appendix of this book I have provided the eighteen-symptom ADHD checklist to use in diagnosing the symptoms of ADHD. For a reframing exercise based on the diagnosis, I thought it might be helpful if you were to make a few copies of these assessment tools and spend some time playing the role of a mental-health practitioner during the next few weeks. Once you have made a few copies of the checklist, keep them handy.

As time and opportunity allows, pull them out and either openly or secretly diagnose some of the adults and children in your life. Sit down with friends, family members, coworkers . . . anyone you feel comfortable with. Maybe explain to them that you are reading this book and are in the midst of debating whether you want to accept or reject ADHD as a solid, scientific diagnosis. If need be, ask them if you can ask a few questions related to themselves or their children. Then use the sheets provided to determine whether they or possibly their children meet the diagnostic criteria loosely interpreted as it is normally used, and see what percentage of people in your life would actually be diagnosed with ADHD.

Don't forget that, for not otherwise specified or unspecified categories of ADHD, "patients" don't need to report five or even six symptoms. If you approach this exercise with an open mind, and an unbiased heart, I suspect you will find that nearly everyone you diagnose will report the same thing: yes, we all have ADHD . . . we are all *normal*.

3

MEDICATED MYTHOLOGY

REASON #3: Despite the fact that manufacturers of ADHD drugs readily admit to not knowing what their products actually do to children's brains or development, an abundance of research documents the drugs' contribution to harmful, irreversible neurological and developmental conditions in children.

In this chapter we will explore

1. how ADHD drugs are intended to work
2. research into the real effects ADHD drugs have on physical and neurological (brain) development
3. a few more myths related to ADHD medications, and their debunking, and
4. just how wrong and dangerous ADHD drugs really are for children.

PICK A PILL, ANY PILL

There are far too many ADHD medications currently on the market for us to cover all of them individually in this chapter, but for the most part they share a great deal in common. Therefore, this chapter covers the basic nuts and bolts related to ADHD medications commonly prescribed to children. Here you will find the tools needed to determine whether you need to research the specifics related to particular ADHD medications.

As the focus on the facts states, there are two main types of ADHD medication: stimulants and nonstimulants. The majority of this chapter will focus on the stimulants, since they represent a much higher percentage of ADHD medications prescribed. Typically, nonstimulants are only

FOCUS ON THE FACTS

- There are two main types of ADHD medication: stimulants and nonstimulants.
- Typically nonstimulants are only prescribed if side effects from the initial stimulant medication prove to be *too* troublesome for the child.
- Close to 90 percent of children in the United States taking ADHD drugs are prescribed stimulants.
- The first red flag warning us that ADHD medications are dangerous is the fact that a backup medication is necessary for curbing the side effects of stimulants that are too much for kids to handle.
- Despite the continued controversies associated with the many side effects of ADHD drugs, on Planet ADHD it would seem that nearly every advance in ADHD medication is somehow linked to making stronger pills that last longer, ignoring developments that might reduce side effects.
- When a person takes ADHD stimulant medications, one of the things the medication is hypothesized to do is increase the normal levels of dopamine and norepinephrine.
- Dopamine and norepinephrine are two neurochemicals—already existing naturally in our brains—that help us focus and pay attention (not get distracted).
- Some want you to believe that taking ADHD medication helps a brain focus and a child behave better, but what you are really seeing is the outcome of a brain being deprived of oxygen and nutrition, taken over by an unnatural level of neurochemicals and exhibiting signs of a brain malfunction.
- Drugging kids to experience brain malfunction on a daily basis might explain why the use of ADHD drugs fails in the long run to help children make more rational decisions.
- Preliminary evidence suggests that during the past fifteen years, in nearly all mass shootings in schools, the shooter was either currently taking or suffering withdrawal from a prescribed psychiatric drug (often ADHD drugs).
- This chapter will share more research documenting the detrimental effects and shortcomings of having children spend their lives diagnosed with and medicated for ADHD.

prescribed if side effects from the initial stimulant medication prove to be too troublesome for the child. This might explain why numbers suggest that close to 90 percent of children in the United States are prescribed stimulants to treat their ADHD, which is a troublesome statistic. Another reason this chapter will not spend as much time discussing nonstimulants is because typically they are considered less effective in treating the behaviors associated with ADHD.

Stimulate Me

Under the stimulant category, a few of the more popular medications are Ritalin, Focalin (or Focalin XR), Adderall (or Adderall XR), and, the latest and greatest, Vyvanse. The *XR* stands for "extended release," and these pills contain two to four times more of the active ingredient to prevent the patient's having to take multiple pills throughout the day. These medications' main ingredients consist of methylphenidate and amphetamine. On the nonstimulant side of the coin, you have another endless list of medications that all seem to have their own active ingredients.

As a side note, I should mention that when I am in a store with a pharmacy, I often take the time to ask the pharmacist questions about what is being prescribed for kids with ADHD. What you might find surprising is that many pharmacists do not find the practice of medicating youth for ADHD to be a good thing. Another thing I was surprised to learn is that Ritalin, historically probably the best-selling stimulant for kids, is not prescribed as often these days in many parts of the country.

As some of the following research will illustrate in greater detail, for close to four or five decades a great deal of scrutiny has been given to, and not-so-supportive or -positive research published on, the evils of Ritalin. Beyond advances in technology that allow the pharmaceutical manufacturers to create time-released medication (providing a vehicle for prescribing stronger medication doses that last longer—not necessarily a good thing), the negative evidence-based stigma might be why the makers of Ritalin, a megacorporation called Novartis, are also the makers of Focalin. Not only did they learn from the marketing mistakes of Sedersi Zitto e Si Concentrano (Sit Down, Shut Up, and Focus) and create a much snappier name, but they also were able to leave behind some of the baggage that Ritalin brought to the party by adopting a new name.

Vyvanse adds an extra compound to the chemical mix, called *lysine*, which connects itself to the active ingredient (amphetamine), causing the body to have to take an extra step to cut off the effects of the drug. This results in a pill that lasts up to fourteen hours. It's possible you have taken medication that has an extended time-release component. Whether the extended time release of the medication is accomplished through using several hard coatings or a more-advanced compound-chemical beading structure, the goal is the same: pack more of the active stimulant ingredient into the pill so that it can last from breakfast to bedtime.

These new stronger and longer pills were created supposedly because of the new demands placed on children to focus on longer school days and finish their homework—expectations that didn't exist back when many of today's parents were kids. Maybe this is why many refer to ADHD medication as study drugs. At one point, doctors operated under the assumption that ADHD was a Monday-through-Friday disease. At one point, ADHD even took summers off.

When stimulants first started being prescribed to kids, the dosing directions often suggested only using the drugs during the school day. There was supposedly no need for kids to take drugs at night when they were home or during the summer when they were not in school. This is evidence that in the beginning such drugs were not prescribed to treat a disorder (or a disease, if you want to believe such claims). They were prescribed to drug kids into acceptable behavior—that hypothetically addressed the behavioral and academic demands of school.

This is why in decades past the vast majority of pills treating ADHD only lasted for three to four hours and often the kids took them before school and at lunch time. But as the critics pointed out, you can't claim kids have a disease or disorder if that disorder only exists while the kids are in school. And so the DSM stepped up its game: Suddenly, with a growing awareness that the prescription advice contradicted the diagnosis, the DSM decided to declare ADHD a real medical-based mental disorder. Soon after, pharmaceutical companies followed suit.

It would appear that nearly every *major* advance in ADHD medication has somehow been linked to making stronger pills that release more slowly, thus creating a medication that lasts longer and packs a bigger punch. With this slow-motion, stiffer sucker punch came other challenges. As you will read in the next chapter, nearly every stimulant comes with a disclaimer that long-term use of stimulants can result in addiction. The question still remains unanswered whether building stronger and longer ADHD pills has escalated this risk. The potential for increased addiction is supported when you consider the fact that once kids start taking the ADHD drugs they cannot quit them instantly. They have to titrate down the level—reducing the dosage little by little, instead of quitting cold turkey—to avoid suffering extreme withdrawal effects. If this isn't a sign of addiction, what is?

HOW MEDICATIONS ARE
INTENDED TO TREAT ADHD

In essence, our brains are run by, or at least are heavily reliant on, what is called the *prefrontal cortex* of the brain. Residing just behind the forehead, this part of the brain serves as a command center. In simple terms, the prefrontal cortex is where thoughts and emotions go to be addressed, organized, and then put into action. When it comes to children and teens, however, the prefrontal cortex is rather underdeveloped. This somewhat noodle-like part of kids' brains, in charge of determining how they behave, still has much maturing to do before being capable of making rational, adult-like decisions. We'll discuss the prefrontal cortex at greater length in chapter 7.

To begin to understand how ADHD medications are *believed* to actually impact the behaviors associated with an ADHD diagnosis, we need to understand the function of two specific chemicals—or *neurochemicals* or *neurotransmitters*, to be more specific. Dopamine and norepinephrine are two neurochemicals that help comprise the cerebral cocktail our brains crave, and they are essential to stimulating and regulating the brain's prefrontal cortex. Both of these neurochemicals exist naturally in the brain, and both are important to any person's ability to focus and pay attention.

Dopamine and norepinephrine are critical to the prefrontal cortex's operations. Dopamine is responsible for decreasing signals from external stimuli—life's many distractions—and helps prevent our becoming too distracted and overwhelmed by everything we encounter in our day-to-day activities. Norepinephrine, on the other hand, is responsible for improving the attention we're giving to whatever it is we're trying to focus on. When dopamine and norepinephrine are at their best possible levels in our brains, we can be fairly focused and calm. But sort of like when visitors to our homes overstay their welcomes, too much dopamine and norepinephrine send our brains into a panic—or just shut them down.

The overarching theory on Planet ADHD is that the brains of kids diagnosed with ADHD need an increase or balance in dopamine and norepinephrine levels. Some want you to believe that kids diagnosed with ADHD behave differently from their peers because they suffer a type of chemical imbalance—that a shortage of dopamine results in these kids' inability to filter out life's distractions, rendering them uncommonly inattentive. Please understand, this is just a theory.

This chemical-imbalance theory is weakened by a great deal of conflicting research. Although the propaganda provided by the clairvoyant ADHD drug-pusher gurus insists that kids demonstrating the normal childhood behaviors associated with ADHD suffer from chemical imbalances or deficiencies, don't forget that pharmaceutical companies readily admit they have no conclusive evidence explaining what really happens when ADHD drugs are used. But one thing they think they *do* know—despite a glaring failure to provide supporting evidence—is that when a person takes ADHD stimulant medications, the medication brings up or balances the normal levels of dopamine and norepinephrine through the magic of chemistry. Contradictory research, however, disputes any claim that the brains of kids diagnosed with ADHD have different levels of neurochemicals.

Although most Planet ADHD experts still concede that no lab or medical test exists to diagnose ADHD, other experts claim that an assortment of lab tests (e.g., blood and urine tests) can help identify the levels of neurotransmitters active in a person's brain. So, then, why isn't the medical community routinely using these lab tests to improve diagnoses, or at least to further study the effect of ADHD drugs on dopamine and norepinephrine levels? We can only guess. Maybe pro-ADHD experts know through secret experimentation that the lab tests are actually fairly accurate and don't want others to know. Or maybe they don't want to know if such tests are accurate or what such tests might tell us; ignorance is bliss.

What ADHD Medications Might Actually Do

Even with only the limited evidence we do have, it is apparent that the process of increasing dopamine in a child's brain has a few other not-so-wonderful effects. The jury's still out on the specifics, a verdict not having yet been reached due to conflicting interpretations of the results.

To better understand what pro-ADHD experts are *not* sure about, let's start by identifying what we *do* know. Decades of research confirm that we have billions of brain cells that, when nurtured, stimulated, and fed correctly, help us think more efficiently and connect the bits of information they store. Brain cells, or *neurons*, are comprised, in part, of *synapses* and *dendrites*, which basically serve as the two ends of the neuron, complementing the natural transporter system by using neurochemicals to communicate and connect with other neurons. (See figure 3.1.)

In simple terms, our prefrontal cortex is able to *think*, make decisions, because neurochemicals like dopamine and norepinephrine connect the neurons' dendrites and synapses. In order for our brains to complete simple tasks or accomplish higher-level thinking (for example, to not be distracted by a sunny day outside, instead focusing on our history lesson), we must be able to connect many neurons that store different pieces of information and knowledge. We'll talk about them in greater detail in chapter 7, but to understand them better still, I urge you to visit YouTube to explore the many uploads on neurons, synapses, and dendrites; it's fascinating stuff.

Now, the pro-ADHD powers that be want you to believe that in order for kids with ADHD to think more *normally* and lessen distractions, their

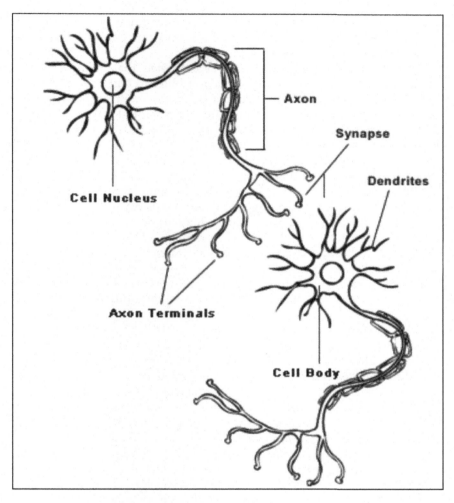

FIGURE 3.1 Components and Connections of a Neuron

brains need more dopamine. Research has suggested, however, that stimulants used to increase dopamine levels coincidently to some degree also block the brain's natural transporter system from removing dopamine. The theory behind this view suggests that when you overload a brain's synapses with stimulants, producing higher levels of neurochemicals, like dopamine, that brain is then fooled into thinking it must increase the *muscle* of the transporter. This extra exertion results in the brain's vigorously trying to overcome the stimulant effects. Regardless of what time and future research will tell—whether or not the theory is 100 percent correct—many can attest that building stronger unnatural or abnormal muscles through the practice of infusing foreign, unnatural chemicals into our bodies normally does not equate to a healthy outcome. Consider what we now know about steroids.

More recent research, however, has suggested that taking pills that produce more dopamine in the brain contributes to higher density levels of dopamine transporters. One role of the dopamine transporters in the brain is to clear the dopamine out after the chemical has been sent. In fact, the more dopamine transporters present and accounted for means the more quickly the dopamine team works to clear the dopamine out of the brain; and this quickness increases when kids don't take their ADHD drugs. To create a drug that punishes the patient for not taking the drug might be good business for the ADHD drug manufacturers, but it is not good for the patient. According to Dr. Gene-Jack Wang, this medication practice "could result in more severe inattention and need for higher doses of medication."

In other words, based on inconclusive evidence we are being told our kids' brains lack dopamine. As a result we are giving them ADHD drugs to increase dopamine, but these drugs are designed to increase the removal of dopamine. At the very least, the process is nonintuitive, at the worst, dangerous.

Much of the research reliant on scanning the brains of children diagnosed with ADHD uses this dopamine theory as the basis for their claim that kids with ADHD have different brain structures. To be honest, the limited studies have been so divergently interpreted (or misinterpreted) by so many people that it gets a little confusing even for the seasoned researcher to follow. Speculative research, however, also suggests kids diagnosed with ADHD have smaller or slower-developing brains. But there is also research suggesting that some kids with the biggest brains can suffer from ADHD symptoms that are just as severe. Further research still suggests that a smaller brain does not always equate to lower intelligence and that sometimes those with smaller brains who display ADHD symptoms may actually have parts of the brain that are much larger than others' with bigger brains. At this point, we can only say that there are no definitive answers.

These brain-scan studies basically only suggest that it is *possible* that ADHD kids have challenged chemical-transporter levels or structures. But what many people do not know is that a large percentage of kids historically used in these studies have at some point been on ADHD stimulant medication. And once a child takes ADHD drugs, a deformity is created—an unnatural dopamine transporter muscle or chemical abnormality—which often does not go away quickly, if ever. Therefore, many of the brain-scan studies are merely showing us what the brains of kids who have taken ADHD drugs look like. They provide us the after picture and not necessarily the before picture.

But for all the current confusion, brain-scan research is actually starting to produce some interesting findings. Most likely, in the not-so-distant future neuropsychologists, armed with some amazing technology, will provide more definitive answers as to how our brains work, and as a result we may learn why some kids behave the way they do. For example, the FDA recently approved the first medical scan—called the NEBA system, or Neuropsychiatric EEG–Based Assessment Aid—to attempt to confirm diagnoses of ADHD by measuring brain waves.

Supposedly doctors can use the NEBA system to help confirm an ADHD diagnosis (which is still based on the flawed DSM criteria) or to determine whether more testing is needed (even though no other tests exist). But let's not get too excited; it is rumored that this test, which hasn't yet been released to the public, is based on *one* study of 275 patients who *had* attention or behavioral issues. Typically, vague descriptions of the study's patients mean that the participants have taken stimulants in the past, and conveniently the good folks at NEBA Health have not bothered to clarify this point in their study's summary. Given that very few ADHD brain studies use investigative methods that limit the shortcomings of past studies—like definitively studying kids with ADHD symptoms rather than kids who have previously taken ADHD drugs—it will take quite some time to study a sufficiently large and diverse sample of children before we can explain why some children behave one way and others another.

Regardless, we should look forward to the day when brain scans can tell us why kids diagnosed with ADHD are different. It will probably confirm not only that before these kids are medicated their brains function differently but also that their brains operate more efficiently and possibly at a much higher capacity than the mere 10 percent usage of most human brains.

Unfortunately, these future studies will possibly also confirm that the currently available research has been improperly applied. At some point we must stop allowing the powers that be to use every piece of new information to justify medicating children for acting like children. Brain-scan research at this point in time is only confirming that some kids who are more energetic, creative, and communicative think differently than do some of their peers, which seems like a no-brainer.

Now given that currently most doctors licensed to medicate are not going to test kids' levels of dopamine and norepinephrine, nor are brain or PET scans presently capable of telling us anything definitive, the science of medicating children with intentions to find optimal levels of dopamine and norepinephrine is more similar to a not-so-accurate art form. In other words, often doctors are just guessing on the dosage of ADHD drugs that their child patients need. And when a child takes too much, the brain and body are significantly stressed, which in turn only worsens the behaviors associated with ADHD.

By the way, if a child doesn't respond well to a methylphenidate-based stimulant medication (Ritalin, Focalin, or others), doctors will often try an amphetamine-based stimulant medication (Adderall or Vyvanse) before trying nonstimulant medication. The same goes for kids who try amphetamine-based medications first with minimal response or overwhelming side effects. They will be given a methylphenidate-based medication before they are given nonstimulant medication. Such guesswork can last up to several months, causing major stress and additional health risks to the child, not to mention many expensive doctor's visits.

How Are Nonstimulants Different?

The obvious difference between stimulant and nonstimulant medications is quite simple: nonstimulants do not contain the stimulant (amphetamine, for example). These drugs are used because for some kids more stimulants result in higher aggression or more substantially bitter mood swings.

Another difference between the two medication types is that while stimulants are believed to directly affect dopamine and norepinephrine, nonstimulants often focus mainly on controlling norepinephrine. By ignoring dopamine, the nonstimulants (once again, through the magic of chemistry) seem to better avoid the side effects associated with stimulants—like greater agitation. But these nonstimulant drugs come with a list of additional not-so-wonderful side effects that their stimulant cousins don't offer. You should also note that some of the other drugs that fall in the alternative or nonstimulant group of medications are drugs originally intended to lower blood pressure.

Beyond scientists trying to make pills hypothesized to increase levels of neurochemicals in the brain, there is little science publicly available explaining what these pills really do to a child's brain. Neither is there much science directing how best to prescribe the right pill or right dosage. The process is a trial and error that resembles a large lab-animal experiment, and it's taking place in clinicians' and doctors' offices across the country. Our kids are being placed at the bottom of the food chain when it comes to the ADHD-medication movement. It should raise another red flag for you that medication and dosage guesswork often span months for every child diagnosed with ADHD.

Kids Are Not Guinea Pigs

Maybe you assume that the science behind increasing attention and lowering distraction through ADHD medication is sound, maybe even amazing. But what you may not have realized before now is that when we use ADHD drugs to maximize focus and reduce impulsivity, we are basically causing a malfunction of the brain—it only appears externally that we're helping anything. Drug-inducing daily brain malfunctions likely sacrifices a valuable element of a child's development—the natural, essential process of forming good character and determining common-sense solutions.

As Dr. Peter Breggin puts it, "the kind of 'attention' produced through stimulant drugs does not involve the making of rational choices or acts of will." It is, as he says, more of an *enforced obsessive-compulsive attention to rote activities.* In other words, kids on ADHD drugs don't really have to think because their brains have been medicated to just react and malfunction automatically. Like rats in cages, kids are medicated into coexistence (or, more aptly, compliance) within environments that are probably not conducive to their learning styles, interests, or developmental levels. Like rats in cages, they are medicated into obediently navigating a maze (or the expectations of our education system) in order to be rewarded for not deviating from the expected path.

When children are on stimulant medication they may become more obedient, but what is sacrificed is much of the learning and development process essential to becoming self-motivated and capable of creative, rational, or socially acceptable behavior. When we force children to spend their developmental years making choices while on medication, they unfortunately lose part of the natural learning process essential to helping them become capable of making nonmedicated rational decisions later in life. Research indicates that kids on ADHD drugs still have the same if not worse behavior problems years later when taken off of ADHD drugs. In other words, the drugs have not fixed the problem.

One anecdotal yet potentially powerful piece of evidence to consider in relation to the impact ADHD psychotropic drugs have on kids' development and ability to make good decisions is the connection between these drugs and the individuals who have committed mass shootings in schools and public places. A good amount of data readily available online (just search "school shootings ADHD") begins to document how during the past fifteen years in nearly all school shootings the shooter was either currently taking or suffering withdrawal from a prescribed psychiatric drug for ADHD, depression, or other conditions. Is this evidence that all kids being medicated for ADHD, depression, or other disorders, such as bipolar, will become mass killers? Of course not. But it at least suggests that we might place equal if not more blame on the pharmaceutical industry than on only the gun industry when it comes to figuring out why we've suffered so many horrible mass shootings over the past two decades. The possibility also exists that the kids taking these prescribed drugs and mercilessly killing were extremely unstable to begin with and providing medication might have made the situation worse.

The reason kids taking ADHD medication miss the critical opportunity to fully develop the ability to think rationally is because stimulant use, especially long-term stimulant use, is harmful to the developing brain. When we drug the brain to not think as actively and to focus on fewer stimuli, many brain cells that had the potential to be stimulated and connected are, unfortunately, pruned from our personal trees of thought. From the time the first pill is taken, stimulants cause malfunctions in the brain. Similar to illegal stimulants like cocaine, Ritalin and other legal stimulants given to regulate ADHD reduce blood flow in all areas of the brain (a 23 to 30 percent reduction according to some studies). The frontal lobe (prefrontal cortex) is included in this brain drain. When blood flow is reduced, it results in less oxygen and nutrition, causing brain malfunction.

When a child takes a pill for ADHD, you ostensibly see them quiet down and supposedly behave better. But what you are really seeing is the outcome of a brain being taken over by an unnatural level of neurochemicals, which are depriving it of oxygen and nutrition. With the brain functioning more slowly—malfunctioning, really—a child certainly would appear less spontaneous and disruptive. Maybe since the ADHD-medicated brain is only able to focus on one thing the child appears more focused, but this is not actually the case.

An Important Reminder

Before we discuss some of the interesting studies on the effects or efficacy of ADHD medication, we must remember something very important that I brought up in the last chapter. As of the printing of this book, and most likely for decades to follow, there is no reliable or valid measurement or written test that can identify ADHD. There are no biological markers, blood tests, or DNA tests that can identify ADHD. Brain scans at this point cannot accurately diagnose or identify kids with ADHD but instead provide a very good picture of what kids' brains look like when they have taken ADHD medication. Quite simply put, there is no test for diagnosing ADHD.

Why is this important? Because in research if we are going to say that some sort of medication, intervention, or therapy reduced the severity of a disorder like ADHD or "cured" it, if you will, then there needs to be a reliable and valid assessment tool that is actually capable of identifying the disorder and, more importantly, capable of measuring the level or severity of the disorder. You can't claim to have treated something effectively if you can't show or measure what that something was in the first place or measure accurately whether it actually changed. Think about it for a second.

Imagine, as a thought exercise, that you are told by your realtor that the new house you have just purchased is haunted and full of ghosts. Maybe you believe in ghosts, maybe you don't. Maybe you're open to believing, present real proof. But to be safe, just in case they're real, you contact an expert to rid your house of these ghosts before you move in.

The expert comes in and spreads his sage smoke up and down the hallways of your new home. Holding some spiritual artifact in hand, he speaks in tongues. Maybe you hired him because he was connected to other leading experts in ghostbusting; maybe he even borrowed a proton pack from doctors Egon Spengler and Ray Stantz at the local university, much to the disagreement of their partner, Dr. Peter Venkman. In the end, Spengler and Stantz *say* they have caught the ghosts and leave your house torn up and covered in green slime—what they call *ectoplasm*. But how could you have ever tested whether the ghosts were there to begin with if no test exists to determine the presence of ghosts? And how would you confirm whether the ghosts were gone absent this test? How can you determine where the ectoplasm came from or what it even really is? Who might you call?

No offense to the world-renowned parapsychologist trio, the *Ghostbusters*, but does this silly example as it relates to ADHD diagnosis and medication make sense? No test exists to scientifically determine—in medical or psychological terms—whether a child actually has the chronic neurologically based disease or mental or neurobiological disorder they insist he has (more on this in chapter 6). No test exists to show to what extent a medication or therapy helped reduce or rid a child of the symptoms associated with this supposed disorder or disease.

Brain scans and other medical images are riddled with methodological flaws and are unable to show visual evidence of ADHD's existence. Therefore, the medical and pharmacological communities' claims rest on the word of a few people who insist that children evidencing those eighteen behaviors have ADHD. But as research supports, such claims that the medication "works" to treat ADHD are only based on observations quite possibly documenting the outcomes of brain malfunction.

If no reliable or valid tests exist to identify or measure the treatment of a disease, any study completed claiming the existence of the disease and touting the efficacy of a treatment is scientifically unsound. Thus, most people who understand the basic requirements of scientific research—and who have not been paid off by the pharmaceutical industry or aren't drinking the ADHD-epidemic Kool-Aid—easily understand why it is critical to dismiss any research on medications given to children claiming that we are actually capable of treating ADHD.

You must fully understand that since a test does not exist, most of these flawed studies on ADHD-medication efficacy use educator or parent opinion—not real research-assessment tools—as evidence of a child's improved behavior and lessening of behaviors associated with ADHD. Given what we have already learned about how ADHD symptoms are not representative of a real mental disorder and how one or two people are not a representative or large enough unbiased sample of witnesses to the changes in a child's behavior, we should not assume anything, then, based on these observations. It is quite possible that they are misguided, biased, and misinterpreting a drug-induced brain malfunction to be improved behavior.

So even though you can access many academic- and medical-journal articles making claims regarding the efficacy of ADHD treatment, you should take these studies with a grain of salt. First, these supposedly peer-reviewed, "unbiased" articles are published by journals that often rely heavily on advertising dollars from the pharmaceutical industry. Also, the DSM and pharmaceutical medication guides make it very clear how little research exists.

In the next chapter we'll see how pharmaceutical companies' legal documents reveal that the companies rarely assert that their claims are research-based. Why? Because they know that without a tool or test to identify and measure ADHD we are left to subjectively interpret what is taking place in a child's brain. Also, pro-ADHD experts are aware that a significant amount of additional research contradicts what the biased research is claiming.

RESEARCH ON THE
EFFECTIVENESS OF ADHD MEDS

Stimulants have been prescribed to children since 1956 when Ritalin was created. To date, there are very few studies that have looked at the effectiveness after a year or more of stimulant use on kids who've been diagnosed with ADHD. Most studies only investigate drug effectiveness over the first few months of treatment. This should be of great concern, considering that many kids start taking these drugs in preschool and don't stop (if they ever stop) until adulthood. Basically, what this means is that research into ADHD drug treatment effectiveness is limited to a very few studies following medicated kids for more than a year and to a bunch of shorter studies that focus on documenting the reduction of ADHD symptoms but lack the scientific rigor that could justify pro-ADHD claims. The full extent of the real long-term *and* short-term effects of ADHD drug use on kids is simply unknown.

As of 2003, only a few marginally soundly-designed studies looked at ADHD-drug effects on kids for more than a fourteen-month span. I say "marginally" because the studies didn't have a reliable or valid measurement to perform the study with and because they ignore the possibility that the behavior they are observing is a manifestation of brain malfunction. In a 2003 analysis of the existent studies on ADHD drugs, Dr. Lily Hechtman, pro-ADHD researcher at the Montreal Children's Hospital, admitted that "little is known about the impact of such extended long-term use." Since 2003 no other long-term studies of great value or positive findings supporting the use of ADHD drugs have been produced.

Some pro-ADHD advocates, such as Children and Adults with ADHD, who as of 2009 received 30 percent of their funding from drug companies, will argue that the more recent National Institute of Mental Health–funded multimodal-treatment study on ADHD (referred to as the MTA study) legitimates ADHD drug use. On the surface the MTA looks to have used a decent scientific design, since its researchers actually tracked differing groups of participants—such as kids with ADHD on drugs, kids with ADHD not on drugs but receiving behavioral modification interventions, and kids not diagnosed with ADHD—and also followed the kids for eight years.

According to the 2009 MTA results, however, the kids on ADHD drugs experienced a reduction in the severity of ADHD symptoms that was similar to the reduction of those same symptoms observed in kids who had received only behavioral modification and no ADHD drugs. To be crystal clear, the drugs did not provide any better results than did old-fashioned talk therapy plus a dose of behavioral modification. To Dr. Hechtman's credit, and the credit of other MTA researchers trying to produce long-term studies supporting the position that ADHD drugs are good for kids, at least they finally took the time to do a fairly sound longitudinal study. But as with other studies prior to 2003, however, theirs took the same flawed approach to evidence gathering.

The MTA didn't have an assessment tool to scientifically measure the outcomes (reduced ADHD symptoms) with sound psychometrics, they used small samples of a few hundred kids to justify a diagnosis that labels 6.5 million annually, and they ignored the fact that the reduction in symptoms might have been due to permanent brain damage from the ADHD drugs. Furthermore, as of this writing, no other studies replicate the MTA's findings. One study using flawed measurements cannot serve as definitive proof of anything. In fact, were someone to attempt to replicate the MTA studies' results, they likely wouldn't have even been able to find adequate funding, given NIMH's decision to not fund research using DSM criteria for disorders like ADHD.

Also of great concern is the fact that a high percentage of the researchers contributing to the MTA study were paid personally by the pharmaceutical industry, or their research centers or universities were reliant on its support. Dr. Hechtman, for example, is paid to research, give speeches, and serve on advisory boards for Eli Lilly, GlaxoSmithKline, Janssen-Ortho, Purdue Pharma, and Shire. Just follow the link to the full text article in the references section at the end of the book to see all of the financial disclosures reported by the MTA study's "unbiased" researchers. If their research was truly definitive, significant, well designed, and unbiased, however, the drug companies wouldn't be downplaying their involvement.

The 2009 MTA study had been intended to build on the findings of the 1999 MTA study, which had claimed that ADHD drugs were more effective than behavioral therapy in the first fourteen months of use. But the 2009 report found that the medication and behavioral-therapy groups experienced similar outcomes. Additionally, the later study found that the drugs' effectiveness might dissipate after fourteen months of use and that the drug-treatment advantage is gone completely after three years of use.

According to the *Journal of the American Academy of Child and Adolescent Psychiatry*, the 2009 MTA study found that children still being given ADHD drugs by their parents six and eight years later "fared no better than their nonmedicated counterparts, despite a 41 percent increase in the average total daily dose, failing to support continued medication treatment as salutary."

The 2009 MTA also found that after three years children taking ADHD drugs grew an average of .79 inches less than did nonmedicated ADHD kids. And despite the efforts of many pro-ADHD groups and individuals to simplify and paint the study's outcomes as evidence supporting ADHD drug use, the 2009 MTA study "fail[ed] to find better outcomes associated with continued medication treatment." Though the lion's share of the MTA cooperative's researchers were funded by numerous pharmaceutical companies, at least they honestly reported the study's findings.

Pro-ADHD folks will also want to tout a study done on preschoolers diagnosed with ADHD—the preschool-ADHD-treatment study, or PATS study, but the idea of diagnosing preschoolers with ADHD and drugging them for it is idiotic, so let's not even give this misguided research a place at the discussion table. But we should pay close attention to a few points from these few multimodal longitudinal studies. Both medication and psychosocial treatments made a significant difference during the fourteen months in which the drugs were being administered in a controlled way. And if psychosocial treatments—traditional therapy and counseling approaches—worked just as well as medication, we should strongly consider not adopting drugs that have so many negative outcomes and far too many unknowns.

Lack of Evidence for Long-Term Effects

Of the more-recent research attempting to support ADHD medication use, Dr. Hechtman's 2003 analysis of existing ADHD research was interesting for several reasons. First, she readily admitted that she had received research support from several pharmaceutical companies, including Shire, the maker of Adderall and Vyvanse. Second, she held back very few punches. In the article Dr. Hechtman and her colleague, Dr. Greenfield, shared research that suggested ADHD drugs might reduce ADHD symptoms over the short term while also clarifying that studies capable of showing the benefits of long-term use were inconclusive.

In other words, prior to 2003 no research existed that showed stimulants were effective for more than a few months. But what is truly astonishing is that in her article Dr. Hechtman also admirably reported on some of the studies that have raised great questions about ADHD-medicating practices.

For example, in 1997 Gillberg and colleagues conducted a study to investigate the effectiveness of amphetamine medication on kids. Over the course of three months the researchers gave amphetamines to sixty-two children who had been diagnosed with ADHD. Then, for the next twelve months, thirty of the children were given a placebo—a sugar pill—while thirty-two continued on the amphetamines. The study claimed to have shown that most patients benefited from stimulants for fifteen months before having to drop out of the study; and by "benefited" they mean that according to a few people close to the children the stimulants effectively reduced the severity of the ADHD symptoms. But the study also found that 29 percent of the kids taking the placebo did not deteriorate during the course of the study.

In other words, the 29 percent of kids taking the placebo were just fine taking a fake pill. Meanwhile, 71 percent of the kids taking the placebo dropped out (for reasons unexplained by the study). Maybe they discovered the same thing the other 29 percent had reported. One other note worth mentioning is that 29 percent of the kids taking amphetamines also dropped out. In the rational scientific world, if 50 percent of a study's participants dropped out and a third of the control group taking a fake pill did just as well as the stimulant-pill-popping kids, then the study would be precluded from claiming that stimulants work for up to fifteen months. Please note that there is an abundance of research on the efficacy of placebos in the treatment of ADHD and other disorders, like depression.

In other studies conducted prior to 2003, researchers found that having a well-functioning family was more predictive of better academics, lower levels of delinquency, and positive emotional adjustment than was medication. These studies show that having or improving supportive family resources (that is, improving parental engagement) is more effective than pills. Note that numerous studies have found that stimulant-drug treatment has no dramatic effect on academic achievement.

Many studies have also shown that long-term stimulant use by children cannot predict less hyperactivity in adolescents; the initial short-term benefits of stimulant drugs cited by so many flawed studies do not translate into positive outcomes later in life. Some studies have even found that longer use equates to even more-severe ADHD symptoms and behavior. Longer stimulant use has been associated with more-serious arrests, institutionalization for delinquency, higher levels of substance abuse, lower education completion, and poorer adolescent and adult outcomes.

Recall our thought exercise about Leonardo da Vinci and his many challenges, had he been evaluated for ADHD. It is clear that most children sent for ADHD evaluation, beyond being all but guaranteed to leave with an ADHD diagnosis, also have multiple preexisting and ongoing challenges. They have challenges with academics often linked to the instruction they are receiving and the learning climate they sit in. They have social and family challenges. All of these multiply their personal problems. Why anyone would think a label and a pill could cure all of this is beyond understanding. And by the time we've worked through the next chapter on disclaimers, you will see that ADHD drugs should play no part in this farce of a diagnosis.

Much more research exists beyond what I can cover in this short chapter, and someone will undoubtedly want to bring it up for debate; of course additional research has been completed since 2003. But at the end of the day when the assessment for ADHD symptoms is flawed from the get-go and no medical diagnostic exists, there is no sense in even discussing the endless studies that try to show that stimulants reduce ADHD symptoms over a few months or maybe even years.

Additional Limitations Related to Research
on the Effectiveness of ADHD Medications

Please note that for every study completed by unbiased researchers unconnected to the pharmaceutical industry contradicting the current popular opinion that drugs are effective for treating ADHD, there are dozens of studies completed by researchers in the pocket of the pharmaceutical industry that, not surprisingly, advocate ADHD drug use.

The pharmaceutical industry has put their profits into flooding search engines and research databases with their results. But even many studies published by authors being paid by the pharmaceutical companies making the drugs they are studying (e.g., Lerner and Wigal 2008) point out that ADHD studies have "major methodological deficiencies [that] are compounded by their restriction to school-age children, relatively short follow-ups, and few data on adverse effects."

One of the other major flaws in research comes down to the inadequate sample of participants selected for the average ADHD study. In most studies published, you typically see a sample size of about thirty to one hundred kids being studied. But when it comes to sampling techniques, a well-designed study must select a representative and generalizable group of participants. By "generalizable" we typically mean that the study must be performed on a sample of randomly selected kids from a population large and representative enough to allow the findings to be generalized to the whole population.

Basically, for the past decade or so we have seen the annual average number of kids diagnosed with ADHD go from 2 million to 6.5 million. When you have annual numbers this large, the total number of kids diagnosed with ADHD over the course of the prior ten years probably numbers in the twenty- to thirty millions. Given that the strongest pro-ADHD studies in existence that support the pharmaceutical companies' agenda have an average of thirty to one hundred kids participating (at the high end a few studies utilize six hundred kids), we ought to seriously question how their findings can possibly be generalized to the whole population of people (kids) labeled with ADHD. Beyond not having reliable or valid mechanisms to gauge or measure ADHD, pro-ADHD experts have not studied enough kids to even make the claims they make. In nonscientific terms, they haven't found diddly-squat.

What Else Do We Know?

If the studies on children taking ADHD drugs are flawed and provide conflicting findings, then how will we ever know the whole truth? Well, sadly, some real solid answers can come from the animal kingdom. Very few like the fact that we use lab animals to test how products might affect humans, but, unfortunately, it's our best and only option. The difference between testing stimulant medication on children and lab rats comes down to the fact that we can do much more medical testing (using tiny electrodes, for example, to measure the activity of brain cells) and even autopsies on the animals.

For example, earlier I cited a study showing how cocaine and stimulants both reduce blood flow down to 23 to 30 percent in all areas of the brain. How do we know this? In 1987 NIMH-funded researchers found that in animals Ritalin reduced the metabolic rate throughout many portions of the brain. In other words, the brain stopped functioning normally on Ritalin. They also found that these changes brought about by the pharmaceutical drug would occur in any animal or human regardless of whether they were diagnosed with ADHD or not. As a side note, the NIMH also funded a study in 1993 that determined that half of children treated with stimulants develop signs of drug-induced obsessive-compulsive disorder (OCD).

These studies, though troubling, are interesting on several levels. And once we finish giggling over the image of a lab rat lying on a chaise lounge, one can only guess as to how NIMH researchers tested lab animals for or diagnosed them with ADHD. But such rudimentary rodent-diagnostic approaches can't be any less accurate than what we use today to diagnose children. More importantly, having had knowledge of the horrible side effects of these drugs for several decades, how could NIMH have allowed their researchers to ignore findings in the more recently funded MTA study?

How can they fund studies on children identifying OCD as a result of ADHD drugs or studies on lab animals that show stimulant-induced brain malfunctions explain the reduction of ADHD symptoms, and then several decades later fund an eight-year-long study on stimulant use with kids, and allow the researchers to claim that stimulants improved behavior related to the symptoms? If they would consider, connect, and stop ignoring the previous research they funded, they might discover that the multimodal study serves as further evidence that the stimulants caused mass brain malfunctions across the sample of kids.

There is an abundance of research on animals related to stimulant use. Duke University's Everett Ellinwood, MD, an experienced researcher and professor, stated that the "drug levels in children on a[n] mg/kg basis are sometimes as high as those reported to produce chronic CNS [central nervous system] changes in animal studies." Other research has described these CNS changes as damaging to blood vessels in the brain, causing brain-cell loss and microhemorrhaging (blood loss).

While the pharmaceutical industry wants you to believe that stimulants are fast acting and basically do their job before flushing out of the child's system, other research exploring gene expression in animals has found that potential exists for the stimulants to cause long-lasting changes in brain-cell structure and function. Something to keep in mind is that most of this research on lab animals used the shorter-acting stimulant medication prescribed a decade ago, efficacious for three to four hours at a pop. Imagine what studies today would tell us about the use of stimulants lasting fourteen to twenty-four hours.

Tests showed that when given small doses of stimulants, chimpanzees, our animal cousins with whom we share 99 percent of our DNA, became more compulsive, obsessively picked at their skin, repeatedly fiddled with things, paced aimlessly, became increasingly submissive, stared off into space, withdrew socially, and exhibited inappropriate responses to imaginary stimuli. What an appropriate response to imaginary stimuli is might be debatable, but the chimps' behavior was similar to that of kids given stimulants.

Instead of acting out spontaneously, sometimes causing disruption to the class, many kids on ADHD drugs withdraw into their own little worlds. While drugged chimp perhaps worried over the skin of its armpit, a drugged kid is given a worksheet. And though at one point this very same worksheet was a boring, tedious, repetitive assignment, tiring the child, the ADHD drugs make it seem novel and very, very interesting. Some think, however, that such compliance obtained through the magic of chemistry is improving behavior and developmental progress.

Basically, all drug development begins with animal testing. That we can't easily find an extensive amount of children's ADHD-drug testing performed on animals raises additional red flags. It's quite possible that the pharmaceutical powers dabbling in the world of drugging children have seen exactly what the long-term effects of the drugs are in their studies on lab animals. And it's quite possible they don't want you to know what these effects are. So perhaps instead of spreading lies and increasing liability, they merely remain silent, play ignorant, and try to distract you with other research, repeating over and over that stimulants and other ADHD drugs effectively reduce the symptoms associated with ADHD, a disease or disorder we have no means of measuring.

Paying the Price

In 2008, congressional investigators found that pro-ADHD researcher Dr. Joseph Biederman had taken something like $1.6 million from the pharmaceutical industry, including ADHD- and bipolar-drug manufacturers.

In an interview with Katie Couric, Biederman, a medical doctor and professor of psychiatry at Harvard University, acknowledged having a professional relationship with the pharmaceutical companies Janssen, Eli Lilly, Bristol-Myers Squibb, AstraZeneca, and Pfizer, makers of atypical antipsychotics. "I have a professional relationship with dozens of manufacturers," he said. Once considered one of the leading researchers on and proponents of medicating youth for ADHD, Biederman had earned around $1.6 million from drug companies but failed to report at least $1.4 million of it to Harvard. Why? Because doing research—while acting like it is legitimate and unbiased—and taking monies from beneficiaries of the studies' positive findings is a conflict of interest and extremely unethical.

This is just one example of how through sheer power and greed pharmaceutical companies are winning the battle to convince parents and educators to become complicit in drugging children. Most parents, educators, and even mental-health practitioners reading research from a respected Harvard professor would instantly think, "Harvard! Well, this *must* be true and accurate." But Biederman regularly gave workshops and told people it was fine to drug children three years of age. This is the guy who now wants you to believe that some children as young as three are bipolar. But as most parents have learned, the terrible twos can extend even to three years of age, and as a result extreme mood swings are not uncommon, abnormal, or even developmentally inappropriate.

SUMMARY

I know most of you reading this book are not experts in statistical analysis or research methods, and as a result you might find the research discussions a bit tedious. Believe it or not, this chapter could have been much longer if I'd bothered to discuss the copious *bad* research out there. The research I have discussed, however, provides a good picture of what is out there and of the limitations and conflicts of interest that exist. It is of great importance that we understand the basic major flaws of the research that is being touted as *proof* and is being used to support the ADHD-medication trend. It is no less important that we understand that many researchers in the ADHD world have numerous financial ties to the pharmaceutical industry.

I have colleagues from Harvard whom I deeply admire and love. They are intelligent and caring individuals, and Harvard is a great institution. But any person who wants to look at the behavior of a three-year-old, or even a five-year-old, and call it bipolar (a diagnosis often associated with major mood swings and manic episodes, leading to sleepless nights—a somewhat common experience with that age group) is either stupid or unethical. Given that Dr. Biederman was able to get $1.6 million to support his agenda, I will let you determine his motives.

The bottom line is this: The research out there being used to support the pharmaceutical industry's efforts to drug kids is just plain horrible. I can't imagine that the research experts the pharmaceutical industry has recruited are that bad at research. I suspect they are just having troubles trying to turn straw into gold. And when you are trying to accomplish the impossible—namely, convince the masses that drugging children for acting like children is scientifically sound and safe—you'll settle for anything you can squeeze out.

To be honest, I feel sorry for many of the experts who have fallen prey to the pharmaceutical industry. I am sure that before they became desperate for money they had ethics and a love of children. Maybe some honestly thought the pharmaceutical-company money would allow them to do real and honest research. But instead of thoroughly researching the real effects of ADHD drugs, the pharmaceutical companies are strong-arming researchers to push product daily on more than 4.5 million kids in the United States alone. They sponsor and coerce once-respected doctors, scientists, and researchers into producing endless similarly flawed studies that supposedly document how their drugs effectively treat ADHD symptoms.

Once you dig past all of their scientific jargon and the numbers they spew as proof, these same pharmaceutically funded researchers time and time again provide us with the one basic fact we need to know: *there is little known about the impact of extended use of ADHD medication.* And many go so far as to say we desperately need to know more. Given that kids rarely are prescribed these drugs on a short-term basis, isn't this all we really needed to know? If they don't know or, even worse, don't want to admit what the long-term use of these medications will lead to—and this six decades into ADHD-related drugging—don't you think this is reason enough to steer clear and maybe first focus on improving the support systems at home, which research shows us is much more effective than medication at treating symptoms associated with ADHD?

REFLECTION EXERCISE: MAKING A LIST

There is a pamphlet for Vyvanse from its manufacturer, Shire, that shows a parent looking at her son and saying, "I want to do all I can to help him succeed." But let's set aside the obvious attempt by the drug manufacturer to make a parent feel guilty or to play on their fears, and for a moment think about that statement. If we truly want to do all we can to help our children succeed in school and life, what else beyond medication might we want to focus on providing that has no negative short-term or long-term side effects?

Maybe this list would include putting more time toward helping our kids with homework every night. Maybe this list would include meeting with teachers more often to better understand how we can help with our kids' academic needs.

Maybe the list would include exercising more regularly or getting them more involved in youth sports or clubs. Maybe we could add to the list sending our kids to art, theater, or music lessons, which would allow them to express and nurture their creativity. Maybe we'd take a close look at our kids' home diet and make an effort to reduce processed foods that possibly contain pesticides or food coloring with links to increasing ADHD-like behaviors. Maybe, just maybe, our list would include a bunch of things you can do as a family to make home seem more like home. Maybe it would include seeing a family therapist to work on family dynamics.

You may have already made a list of your child's possible challenges associated with ADHD, or maybe you have done something like this as part of a New Year's resolution. If you have, then you know that the main obstacle to accomplishing these and similar goals is fitting these new routines into your schedule. So after you have created a list and edited it down to the three to five most important priorities, try to create a weekly schedule that allows you to fit these important components into your busy schedule.

If you have picked this book up because you are just embarking on your maiden voyage to Planet ADHD, maybe you could spend the next few nights as you read this book adding to the list. Maybe you could spend the next few months focusing first on just trying to improve the things on your list before you even think of agreeing to medicating your child. Maybe if you are already months or years into this pleasure cruise, you could put thirty hard days of work into accomplishing what is on this list and then reevaluate at the end of the month whether it's worth possibly seeing your doctor to wean your child off medication as you continue with your other more holistic efforts on the list.

The point is that we know these drugs are not good for kids. And if we can reframe the approach from medicating the child to possibly engaging in therapy or a more family-focused effort to help the whole household, we just might be able to see the many, many things impacting your child's behaviors associated with ADHD symptoms. Nearly every parent I have ever spoken to who was successful in raising academically successful children has told me that they worked just as hard if not harder than the teachers in assisting and guiding their children with school work.

4

DISCOMBOBULATED
DISCLAIMERS

REASON #4: With the possible health risks and side effects of ADHD drugs ranging from seizures and long-term growth suppression to even death, the minimal supposed benefits of ADHD drugs related to increased focus and behavior improvements in school do not justify blindly experimenting with a child's life and future.

We spend most of our lives seeing warning signs. Sometimes we even pay attention to them and actually read them. We typically won't buy milk if it is past the sell-by date. Some won't select food unless it's labeled "zero trans fat," "no GMO," or "certified organic." We won't use the allergy medicine sitting on our bathroom shelf from last year's sneezing season if the use-by date has passed. Most of us, who have lived long enough to learn, heed the advice of the *Danger: High Voltage* signs. And nearly everyone of driving age has seen and paid attention to signs on the road warning of forthcoming dangerous obstacles—bump in road, slippery when wet, ice on bridge, sharp turn, falling rocks, and railroad crossing.

If we typically read and heed such warning signs in our daily lives, then why are so many of us on Planet ADHD not reading and heeding the warnings related to ADHD drugs? One can only assume most are not reading the disclaimers printed in the ADHD-drug medication guides because most people who have seriously considered all of the health risks and side effects associated with these drugs cannot understand how anyone would ever consider giving them to kids, innocent lab animals, or even their worst enemies. And so in this chapter I'm giving you the CliffsNotes version of ADHD-drug medication guides.

FOCUS ON THE FACTS

- Although the Food and Drug Administration (FDA) requires relatively minimal evidence or review time to approve ADHD drugs to be sold to children, when you actually read the medication guides you will find that at least the review process is pretty honest when it comes to informing consumers.
- ADHD drug manufacturers all have medication guides readily accessible in which they admit the drugs they're selling are associated with many dangers.
- The dangers of ADHD drugs range from sudden death related to heart problems to the development of more serious mental problems.
- The dangers of ADHD drugs include side effects that are similar to symptoms associated with diagnosing depression and bipolar disorders.
- The medication guides admit the pharmaceutical companies don't know exactly how the stimulants interact in the brain to reduce the behaviors associated with ADHD symptoms or how stimulants impact a child's central nervous system.
- The medication guides admit the pharmaceutical companies don't know all of the drugs' long-term effects.
- The medication guides admit the pharmaceutical companies know that ADHD stimulant medications can be addictive.
- The medication guides admit the pharmaceutical companies know that taking ADHD drugs can lead to long-term growth suppression, seizures, and blurring of eyesight.
- And the medication guides clearly and honestly share about a dozen other serious side effects from ADHD drugs that no child should be exposed to for a short-term *fix* of behaviors.

This chapter will be short but not so sweet. It will be short because most of you don't have the time to read everything posted on a host of pharmaceutical and watchdog websites, printed in academic- and medical-journal databases, and available at your local pharmacy. I could write a whole book listing only the warnings and disclaimers pertaining to ADHD-drug side effects. And this chapter will not be sweet because none of these disclaimers and side effects is sweet—not in any sense of the word. So in the following I hope to make the warnings that the drug companies readily share in the ADHD-drugs medication guides a little more interesting and brief enough for you to want to read about and easy enough to understand.

THE DEVIL IS IN THE DETAILS

Just in case you don't watch a lot of TV, be advised that there are an alarming number of pharmaceutical commercials aired that promise to treat an array of illnesses, mental disorders, pains, or age-related challenges. At the same time that they promise amazing results, however, they do their utmost to downplay the uncomfortable parts of the medication process and make everything seem more manageable.

Have you ever noticed how the health-challenged people in these commercials—usually paid, rather pretty actors—are always smiling, dressed well, driving nice cars, and the sun is always shining on their beautiful homes? It is as if anyone suffering from herpes, erectile dysfunction, or depression can be rendered carefree via a pill. But what is most amazing is the end of the commercials.

They turn up the brightness of the picture, play the happy, feel-good music a little bit louder, and then proceed to show you footage of flowers, butterflies, and ponies as they narrate, in a much softer voice, what could go *wrong* if you take these medications. They often read the disclaimer so quickly that only a covert operative trained in cryptic language decoding could understand. And some commercials aren't even this forthcoming—in the smallest font known to humankind they flash their disclaimer quickly at the bottom of the screen so that only anyone armed with a DVR and a magnifying glass can read it.

It's no coincidence that these commercials become more distracting and deceptive when we should actually be tuning in and listening most closely. Because rarely will you hear them list a side effect that would make you really want to take the medication or to give or recommend it to kids, friends, or family members.

For some reason, however, you don't see a whole lot of advertisements on TV for ADHD medications that are marketed for children. Maybe the pharmaceutical companies are afraid that if their advertisement brands their pharmaceutical name on your brain, they might also—due to advertising laws—brand the many side effects onto your brain. And just maybe they are worried that your subconscious will eventually tell you that something is wrong with this advertisement.

Or maybe they have come to the conclusion they don't need to advertise on TV because the system is working just fine for them and their stockholders: having schools direct families to doctors serviced weekly by pharmaceutical sales reps has already recruited 4.5 million customers for them, after all.

Regardless, one commercial that sticks out among the many pharmaceutical mini-infomercials is for a depression medication called Abilify. In the advertisement the makers of the drug explain that a great number of people suffer from depression. This is true, and depression is a normal part of life. They then explain that drugs prescribed to treat depression often do not work well enough, which is most likely true as well. Therefore, they continue, if you, the casual viewer, are depressed and on depression drugs already, maybe you should try taking their drug in addition to the other drug you are already taking. They are selling a depression medicine to help those already on depression medicine who are still suffering from depression.

This commercial sticks out because it screams to our subconscious mind that drugs are *not* the answer. Forget about allowing for enough time to get over the loss of a loved one. Forget exercising, finding a new job, making new friends, finding a new soul mate, or creating a new lifestyle or daily routine that gets you out of the doldrums that have brought you to this point. Forget about maybe moving to some place different to start a new life. Just take another pill . . . Trust us . . . And, oh, by the way, taking this pill might result in thoughts of suicide, new or worse symptoms of depression, panic attacks, acting on dangerous impulses, seizures, uncontrollable facial movements, vomiting, insomnia . . . the list goes on. But you get the picture.

Why is it that we pay attention to warning signs like *Danger: High Voltage* and yet ignore disclaimers from drug companies? They are easy to find. The health risks and side effects for each of the popular ADHD drugs marketed are provided in the pharmaceutical companies' medication guides, and if you want to find the one specific to your medication of choice, just perform an Internet search for *medication guide* and the name of the drug.

Although it might take you some time initially to look up a few medical terms that are new to you, it won't take you long to read through these medical guides, because nearly all of them are strangely quite similar. In fact, you will find Novartis's Ritalin and Focalin medication guides to be nearly identical; Shire's Adderall and Vyvanse medication guides are also incredibly similar. In fact, these drugs have a number of health risks, disclaimers, and side effects in common.

Honesty *Is Such a Lonely Word*

Although the Food and Drug Administration requires relatively minimal evidence or review time to approve ADHD drugs to be sold to children (as short as a few months to review research produced and provided by the drug manufacturer), when you actually read the medication guides you will find that the process for informing consumers appears to be pretty honest. In their medication guides, manufacturers of ADHD drugs readily admit to a great deal of the information I've already presented you so far in this book. But given how popular these drugs are despite what their makers admit they do, makes it obvious that most consumers do not read the disclaimers.

Maybe you haven't read the medication guidelines because you think you'll need a dictionary or an MD to understand many of the medical and scientific terms used to detail the pills' dangers. Maybe you've been discouraged from more fully informing yourself because there are no familiar road signs to warn you of the oncoming danger. Maybe you are so desperate to fix the problem that you're willing to try anything, regardless of the known risks. Whatever your reason for avoiding the drug disclosures, I'm going to help you see clearly what lies ahead as you navigate Planet ADHD. Let us start by looking at a few of the warning signs that have been publicly disclosed for quite some time about the granddaddy of stimulants, Ritalin.

Ritalin was created six decades ago, and yet even today its medication guide generalizes that "the mode of action in man is not completely understood, but Ritalin presumably activates the brain-stem arousal system and cortex to produce its stimulant effect." *Mode of action in man? Presumably activates the brain-stem arousal system? Presumably?* What does this all mean?

This means that even after more than sixty years of drugging children for acting like children, Ritalin's manufacturer, Novartis Pharmaceuticals Corporation, has still evidently not done sufficient research to understand how the product it's peddling even works, let alone how it affects our brains. Their medication guide divulges that "there is neither specific evidence [that] clearly establishes the mechanism whereby Ritalin produces its mental and behavioral effects in children nor conclusive evidence regarding how these effects relate to the condition of the central nervous system." *Conclusive* is the key word here.

Some researchers of ADHD drugs act like they know how stimulants similar to Ritalin increase the levels of neurochemicals in the brain and assert that it can in no way cause permanent brain damage. And yet the makers of the pill themselves admit in their own medication guide—which is available on the FDA website as well—that they have no conclusive evidence about how it works or affects a child's brain. Given that Focalin, Metadate, Concerta, and other ADHD drugs use the same active ingredient, methylphenidate, you can be assured that their makers don't know why their product works either. So what else can we say that pro-ADHD experts conclusively know that they do not know?

In Ritalin's medication guide, Novartis specifies that their disclaimers also apply to their newer ADHD drug, Focalin. They say that "specific etiology [cause] of this syndrome is unknown, and there is no single diagnostic test." They admit there is no test or way to identify the cause of this supposed disorder. It is strange that they can sell a pill for a disorder that has no documentable cause or measurable existance.

Hearing Voices

So, skipping over the rest of what all pro-ADHD experts are confident they know they do not know, let's take a look at what they *do* know. This list is very long and includes a number of drug side effects, which have been disclosed in almost every single medication guide created for an ADHD drug. Whether you are considering having your child take methylphenidate or amphetamine stimulants or a nonstimulant, or even if your child is already on one of these drugs, know that your child is at increased risk for almost every side effect I list in the following.

The first one that nearly all of the guides hit you with is heart-related problems. Yes, be forewarned that children on these medications have experienced "sudden death" due to heart failure. They may also suffer increased blood pressure and heart rate. Decreased or lowered blood pressure could also result, which itself can lead to Raynaud's phenomenon—hands, fingertips, or toes may discolor when insufficient blood reaches their extremities.

Maybe you've read this far in the book and still aren't convinced that your child should not take ADHD medication. At the very least, demand that your doctor run an extensive battery of tests to make sure your child does not have any preexisting heart conditions before starting with these medications. Not all heart conditions can be diagnosed by simply checking blood pressure and heart rate on any random day during a brief doctor's appointment, so concerned parents should ask that more in-depth procedures be completed to determine whether a child's heart is healthy before starting ADHD medications. But also be forewarned that ADHD drug-prescribing doctors use regular checkups to monitor your child's heart to keep you coming back.

For many of you, putting your child at risk for hypertension, low blood pressure, or a heart attack from ADHD drugs is reason enough to look into more holistic treatment alternatives—like counseling. But others of you may need a little more convincing. Well, mental problems, the medication guides disclose, are also an increased risk for children taking ADHD drugs. As if being told your child has a mental disorder isn't enough to begin with, yes, medicating them for that diagnosis may increase the likelihood they'll suffer from additional and often more serious mental problems like manic episodes—extended periods of anger, sadness, or happiness, and extreme moods swings—which are very similar to the symptoms used to diagnose bipolar disorder.

Now, some people will insist that using ADHD drugs hasn't caused a new disorder but merely uncovered a preexisting condition in your child. It's as if the drug worked magic in the brain and somehow was able to discover that the child was not ADHD but instead bipolar—or maybe both. But since the manufacturers of these drugs supposedly have no idea how their drugs affect a child's brain, it is equally if not more probable that the drugs created—or caused, if you will—the bipolar symptoms. It's like a baker's dozen: you agree to twelve months of drugs and get a bonus disorder for free!

A large percentage of kids taking ADHD drugs also develop symptoms of obsessive-compulsive disorder (OCD). ADHD drugs can also increase aggressive behavior, hostility, and agitation. And they have been known to increase thought problems that sometimes result in behavior symptoms commensurate with a depression diagnosis. Some who have taken ADHD medications have experienced depression so extreme it led to suicidal thoughts. And, catastrophically, kids have committed suicide possibly as a result of being unable to handle the side effects of ADHD drugs.

Taking ADHD drugs has led to some kids developing serious psychotic symptoms such as hearing imaginary voices, being suspicious or paranoid that others are out to get them, or being more susceptible to believing untruthful things that other kids tell them. But just because you've been told your child is now depressed and bipolar, don't go rushing back to the drug store for treatment: the medication guide specifies that mixing drugs prescribed for these various disorders is very dangerous.

OTHER SERIOUS OR COMMON SIDE EFFECTS

Nearly all ADHD medication guides report that children who take these drugs experience slowed growth (height and weight), seizures, and blurring of eyesight. None of these side effects is conducive to health or academic success. Some of the guides even admit they have no evidence that the drug-related growth loss can be recovered. Pro-ADHD experts call this *long-term suppression of growth*. And, once again, regular checkups to the doctor are often required of children taking ADHD drugs to monitor for growth suppression.

If you have been able to stomach these more extreme side effects, then maybe the rest of our list won't seem so bad. Decreased appetite, headaches, stomach aches, trouble sleeping, nervousness, anxiety, panic attacks, dizziness, dry mouth, tics (facial spasms), impairment of fertility (mainly in males), hallucination, nausea, vomiting, diarrhea, dark urine, problems passing urine, itching, yellowing of skin, and flu-like symptoms can all occur in children who take ADHD medications. Oh, but the list doesn't stop here: there may also be tiredness, irritability, and serious allergic reactions (difficulty breathing, swelling of the face, neck, and throat, rashes, hives, and fever). And one side effect listed in the medication guide for the nonstimulant Strattera deserves attention: *priapism*—a male erection lasting more than four hours—can lead to serious physical problems.

Putting your child at risk for any or many of these side effects sounds much worse to me than talking with your child's teacher—or more holistic-focused doctors or mental-health practitioners—and hashing out a plan to work together to help your child.

Risks of Withdrawal and Toxicity

Medication guides also warn that children taking their ADHD medications must never cease taking the drugs without first consulting their doctor. As with antidepression medicines—or any addictive narcotic—quitting ADHD meds cold turkey will most assuredly result in severe withdrawal symptoms. But why is this? The stimulant medication guides explain that long-term stimulant use can lead to addiction. Even the evil Dr. Frankenstein we met earlier who drained children's brains of their cerebrospinal fluids admitted this seventy years ago. Basically, then, a doctor must gradually wean the addicted child off ADHD medication by lowering the dosage slowly over a few months.

This withdrawal process, which is a definitive sign of addiction, might explain why research has shown that kids who take stimulants over the long term are more likely to abuse drugs and alcohol in adulthood. In fact, the FDA requires that each manufacturer specify on their packaging that the ADHD drug "is a federally controlled substance because it can be abused or lead to dependence."

Consider the Adderall medication guide, similar to other ADHD medication guides, that warns, "If you or your child takes too much Adderall XR or overdoses, call your doctor or poison-control center right away, or get emergency treatment." If that isn't jarring enough, consider that an estimated 30 percent of these addictive stimulant medications are being given or illegally sold to people not diagnosed with ADHD.

There is nothing healthy about these drugs. As we'll see in chapter 6, research suggests that food dyes may contribute to an increase in behaviors associated with ADHD. And guess what! The lovely folks at your favorite ADHD pharmaceutical company have been kind enough to put food dyes in all of the new drugs they manufacture! FD&C Blue No. 1 and No. 2, FD&C Yellow No. 6, and FD&C Red No. 3 are just a few you will find. The Strattera medication guide warns that you should "avoid touching a broken Strattera capsule. Wash hands and surfaces that touched an open Strattera capsule. If any of the powder gets in your eyes or your child's eyes, rinse them with water right away and call your doctor."

I don't have to be a chemist to understand that it seems pretty unhealthy to take something that can be so toxic externally and ingest it daily for years to come. Maybe it is the "edible black ink" they have listed as one of the inactive ingredients in Strattera that we should avoid putting in our eyes. Or the yellow iron oxide. Or red iron oxide. Or . . .

It's Not Right . . . for You

The last thing I want to point out from the ADHD medication guides falls under a headline usually titled something like "Who should not take [insert drug name here]?" The lists normally start with the obvious candidates. Of course, given the side effects we've just learned about, if your child has a heart condition, tics, seizures, or an eye condition, the drug companies suggest your child avoid these drugs. If your child has a history of drug abuse, do not give him or her more addictive drugs, of course. If your child suffers from liver, thyroid, or kidney problems, they recommend telling your doctor before you start the medication. But how many kids have been tested during their ADHD visit to see if they have liver, thyroid, or kidney problems?

Many of these are obvious warnings any smart drug manufacturer would include in their literature just to avoid more lawsuits. But some of their warnings raise particular concern. For example, they suggest that if your child shows signs of mental problems as a result of taking ADHD drugs, including psychosis, mania, bipolar, or depression, you should tell your doctor.

Well, isn't the fact that you are already medicating your child for ADHD, considered a mental disorder, a sign of mental problems? So, is ADHD a mental problem or not? If by *psychosis* they are suggesting that a child might hear voices, isn't it a common thing for many children from three to even seven years of age to have imaginary friends they play with? My guess, given the private conversations children often have with their imaginary friends, is that those imaginary friends have voices.

Recall Dr. Biederman who took $1.6 million from pharmaceutical companies while recommending that children as young as three years of age could be diagnosed with bipolar disorder. Most parents would likely agree that the symptoms related to bipolar are fairly similar to typical toddler or young child behavior, depending on the direction of the wind on any given day. The medication guidelines even say that if your child shows preexisting signs of anxiousness, tenseness or stress, or agitation they should not take the ADHD drugs. And then they often say that children under six should not take the medication. To most, the list of who should not take the pills basically excludes anyone displaying behaviors associated with the ADHD symptoms to begin with. But the declaration that children under six should not take the pills is where we must draw the line.

First of all, we've finally found something we can all agree on: children under six should not be drugged. But how is a child of six years of age that different from a child of seven, eight, or nine years of age? The developmental theory and research we'll cover in chapter 7 reveals that there is often not much difference.

So, these drug manufacturers know nothing about how their drugs affect the adult brain, and they even wish to avoid acknowledging the animal research that one can be fairly confident they discovered themselves. And of course they have no understanding of how it affects a child's brain. Then how are they so sure that the age of six is where we draw the line? And why are some doctors medicating kids younger than six when nearly every single medication warns them not to? There are no answers to these questions because the movement to diagnose kids with ADHD—and to drug them for exhibiting normal childhood behaviors—is by definition delusional.

SUMMARY

I had the opportunity to sit with a friend and finally hear the story of how her son went from being diagnosed at a young age with autism-spectrum disorder to later in grade school being labeled with ADHD. I had heard part of her son's story before, but I hadn't realized that along the way her son had been medicated to help him with his behavior.

My friend told me she wished she'd had someone—a resource or book—to help her better understand how the diagnoses were determined, how the drugs really worked, and how to choose the right path for her son. Instead, after years of arguing with his teachers, threatening to find a different school, actually moving to a new school district, and going through a half dozen different doctors and even more medications, she told the doctor one day that she was done with medicating her son. And she told me it was the best decision she ever made.

I understand why it takes so long for many to come to the conclusion my friend did. I understand why so many people don't want to believe that they have been misled about the ADHD diagnosis and drug treatment. Like it was for my friend, it's incredibly painful to think they might have done the wrong thing and that, just maybe, allowing their children to take medication has contributed to causing permanent brain damage.

How do you about-face and tell your child they no longer have ADHD or that it never existed in the first place? If you haven't yet been pulled on board the ADHD bandwagon, it would be much, much easier to just say that the evidence is telling you to just try harder and avoid the whole label and drug scene. But for those of you already in the ADHD trenches, it's hard to climb out. Please don't think I don't understand.

When we go to doctors, we expect to be given good advice, diagnosis, and treatment. But unfortunately, out of ignorance or plain deception, too many doctors' and mental-health providers' offices are not giving us and, more importantly, our children what we need or want. We expect the same out of manufacturers of drugs—good, safe, effective treatment. They are making drugs you might want to call medicine, but much of it bears little of the promise of penicillin or antibiotics. Plus, the pharmaceutical industry has a few rotten eggs responsible for a long history of selling bogus pills.

Paxil manufacturer GlaxoSmithKline suppressed data on their antidepressant medicine and allowed far too many to suffer through suicidal thoughts and even go as far as drowning their own children. This is what we are dealing with when profit concerns enter the health industry. According to *Bloomberg*, however, GlaxoSmithKline's greed led to a billion dollars in lawsuit settlements. Merck, the makers of the recalled painkiller Vioxx, were similarly financially hit when it was learned that they had attempted to cover up studies showing that users of their drug were possibly suffering heart attacks as a result. It's rumored that the coverup may have been aided by the FDA.

By taking the Hippocratic Oath, doctors used to vow to "first (above all else) do no harm." But when they prescribe drugs without adequate concern for the unknown, have they not forgotten this promise?

A deception and lack of transparency is everywhere we look. It's even in our grocery stores where genetically modified produce is labeled organic and all-natural. Recently I discovered that according to *Consumer Reports* the protein powder I had been drinking daily is packed with unsafe levels of arsenic and lead. Somehow the product manufacturers had been able to skirt FDA regulations. I couldn't believe it. I'd been drinking it for several years. So I went to GNC, the vitamin and health store where I'd bought the powder, and asked the friendly staff if they'd known about this. The guy at the counter read the *Consumer Reports* printout I gave him, looked at me, and asked, "How can we be selling this stuff?" Good question, I replied. I e-mailed GNC's headquarters and got no reply. A month later I noticed the same product on a display case at a Dick's Sporting Goods. I asked the manager this time, and he basically dismissed me and walked away.

Some companies unconscionably sell dangerous products, and other companies sometimes irresponsibly sell them. So when it comes to choosing products for our children, we need to be especially aware. How many toys, baby seats, and cradles have been pulled off the shelf over the past decades?

You may remember that stores used to sell a game called Jarts, a lawn game equipped with six massive darts made of metal (with a pointy end) that you threw in the air, aiming for the plastic circle near where your opponent stood—kind of like horseshoes, but sharper. One of my brothers learned just how unsafe this game was when, one day, my sister threw her metal lawn dart high in the air and, as his attention was distracted elsewhere, it came down and stuck in one of his thighs. Talk about a lesson in paying attention. Large metal projectile lawn darts? Who would have thought *those* would be unsafe??

I don't think the craziness of selling oversize lawn darts is much different from giving stimulants to kids. Ask any grandparent over sixty-five, and the majority of them will tell you the idea of drugging children for misbehavior is just *plain crazy*. Back in their day maybe 1 to 2 percent of the kids were on *some* sort of behavior medicine. Today as many as 11 percent of our boys are being drugged to treat an ADHD diagnosis. In some parts of the country it's over 20 percent.

In some extreme cases, certain kids might actually need drugs to protect them from themselves or prevent their hurting others. By all means, get these children a diagnosis, and get them help. But do not give your child dangerous drugs because they are bored, disruptive, or distracted in school. There are so many other effective and safe alternatives available to you.

I hope looking at discombobulating disclaimers has helped you see just how risky medicating kids for ADHD really is. As we've seen, ADHD drug manufacturers offer a flurry of product disclaimers and warnings and a startling number of admissions that they don't know how or why their product works. We should be very aware of and concerned about that. In fact, their list of health risks and side effects are so numerous they run for pages and pages. If that doesn't make a person wary of exposing their child to the product then maybe it is not the child who should seek mental counseling.

If drug companies actually had evidence or even claimed to know that their drugs were not harmful to kids, I might be inclined to be more forgiving and overlook some of the side effects. But they don't, and I am not. And neither should you.

REFLECTION EXERCISE: IT'S A SAFETY DANCE

I am big believer in to-do lists. So for the next few days or weeks I would like to add something to your to-do list: make a list of products you have in your home, on your deck or patio, and in your car that you have purchased because a competitor's product had a warning sign or disclaimer that led you to look for an alternative.

Maybe you still have a child young enough to require a car seat or booster. Maybe you buy organic milk to avoid all of the chemicals sold in nonorganic milk. Maybe you bought a mattress touted as much better than the rest. Maybe you have DVDs or Blu-ray discs that are rated safe for kids. Do you see what I mean? What have you bought as a result of doing your research on the competing products or learning about the not-so-healthy attributes of the competing products?

As part of this exercise, also keep notes on products you buy during the week as a result of looking at the labels or disclaimers. And while you are constructing this list, get online and download the medication guides for prescriptions your child is taking or being encouraged to take. At the end of the week, review your list, and reflect on the reasons that led you to not buy other products, big or small. Compare these reasons to the warnings and disclaimers you found in the medication guide. And ask yourself if the warnings and disclaimers on the medication guide are as important or more important to pay attention to as the other products you have not bought.

5

EXTRATERRESTRIAL
EDUCATION

REASON #5: American education policy is extremely focused on increasing standards-based test scores, meaning that our educators are being strong-armed into following procedures that have drastically increased the misdiagnosis and overdiagnosis of ADHD.

In this chapter we'll largely build off of what we learned in chapter 1 about the role education plays in the ADHD movement. By learning more about the standards-based-testing policy by which schools are measured today, we'll better understand the role it plays in the rise of ADHD diagnoses in the United States.

Specifically, we will see how U.S. education policy is threatening an admirable education system trying to help those truly special-needs children. Unfortunately children displaying marginally annoying behaviors are also being labeled special needs. As a result, the system is flooded with far too many, millions of kids, who need just a little more attention in order to learn and mature. This takes resources away from kids who have more serious—real—mental disorders and learning disabilities.

Parents and concerned adults, this chapter is intended to help you better understand why existing policy is contributing to increased ADHD diagnoses. Educators, this chapter is intended to help others understand what you are up against when it comes to juggling what you want to do (inspire young minds to greatness) and what instead many are being forced to do (reduce the educational experience down to a sole focus on academics, higher standards, and increased testing). For all readers, this chapter is intended to help you better understand how our education system is

FOCUS ON THE FACTS

- Most recent education policy in the United States—first No Child Left Behind (NCLB) and now the Common Core State Standards Initiative—has focused heavily on, if not been obsessed with, standardized-achievement test scores.
- These test scores are typically based on assessing the student body's proficiency in reading, math, science, and history.
- Public schools in all states are required to use these test scores to guide as well as evaluate the effectiveness of their work if they wish to receive or even be eligible for federal monies.
- For the majority of states, however, scores on the achievement tests failed to indicate the adequate yearly student progress or proficiency that NCLB legislation required.
- In fact, using the tests to help our students better prepare or better perform on international achievement tests has not panned out as expected.
- The international achievement test Programme for International Student Assessment (PISA), used to rank education systems globally, has shown a steady decline in U.S. test scores since the adoption of No Child Left Behind.
- The 2009 PISA scores ranked the United States as average in reading skills and science, at fourteenth and seventeenth out of thirty-four places, respectively, and below-average in mathematics, at twenty-fifth place; 2012 PISA scores show continued mediocrity.
- Since focusing so strictly on testing we have only managed to force more teachers to teach to the test or, at the very least, prepare for the test, thus leaving even less classroom time for teachers to focus on inspiring individual students to become better academics and future citizens.
- The pressure of testing-focused education policy has created a learning atmosphere where diagnosing behavior-challenged kids with ADHD or some other learning disability is preferable to providing the time and support to help each child flourish and develop.

alienating kids and how we can take steps to fix its shortcomings and help kids exhibiting ADHD-associated behaviors understand that education is their means to achieving everything they want out of life.

WHAT'S NOT TO LIKE ABOUT SCHOOL?

But before we delve into the details of how alien or alienating our education system has become for many students, as well as parents and educators, let's start by finding common ground and admitting the obvious: *school has never been loved by all students at any time in history.* This is an important point to begin with, because we all must realize that helping kids embrace a well-rounded education is not an easy task for parents or educators.

We know it is important for all kids to become fluent readers, proficient in math, and knowledgeable of science and history, not to mention explore many other important subject areas like art, music, physical education, and myriad vocational studies. Despite our priorities, we've always had trouble retaining a level playing field for all kids in today's classrooms and schools, and, for a number of reasons, we seem to have a hard time explaining to our kids the importance of school and all the benefits of receiving a solid education. There are just too few kids who like school or, more importantly, realize how important the academic side of education is to their future.

As an adult, you don't doubt the importance of education. Our communities are filled with unemployed and underemployed white- and blue-collar workers who wish they would have received a better education or at least had taken their education more seriously when they were younger. Even those members of the workforce who are considered to be highly educated or skilled, and are lucky enough to be fully employed, often wish they would have pursued a higher level or different route of educational success needed to achieve a more promising degree, technical training, or trade. We're, of course, looking at all of this in hindsight, from which vantage point it's easier to equate missed educational opportunities with later life challenges. But how can we adults convince more kids that education is the vehicle to achieving a more financially fruitful career experience and personally fulfilling life?

Convincing kids to double down, so to speak, on getting the education we know they need—and will be quite grateful for later in life—remains a challenge solvable by no algorithm. Far too many children are stuck in a cycle of *learned helplessness,* unable to see that quality education is obtainable to them and can help them achieve even their wildest dreams. Part of our challenge is to provide children with the role models and support systems they need to awaken their inner learner and then keep them on track during the long years of institutionalized learning. It's a tall order, and to some extent the odds are stacked against us.

Being responsible for ending summer every year is reason enough for school to be held in suspicion by a majority of kids. Then, once there, school tells them day after day to stay seated, stay quiet, pay attention, listen to information related to something that's probably uninteresting to a lot of them, and, oh yeah, do those mountains of assigned homework and worksheets because the big test is coming . . . Well, let's just say it isn't completely inexplicable that so many kids dislike school.

So let's start by focusing on that unfortunate and far-too-widespread dislike many students have for school: doing so challenges us to figure out how to make school more likeable for students. Research shows that motivation to learn and the feelings a student has for school (or, more specifically, the feelings a student has for the teachers or subject matter) are quite predictive of that student's educational success. To get our kids to more deeply appreciate academics and learn to like going to school, we also must realize that education is much, much more than just learning subject matter.

For many kids, it is all about the social side of education. Schools are, after all, important social incubators that prepare kids for the test of life and not just a life of tests. It has been shown that academic success is predicated at least in half on kids actually enjoying being at school with other kids.

The social side of school is the highlight of many kids' day; it's the reason they want to go to school. For some students, there is nothing more enjoyable than spending time with friends and caring mentors. And yet for others who have not yet mastered or embraced certain social skills, the social side of education is one of their greatest challenges—something we parents and educators must understand. The point at which a child begins to struggle to fit in socially is the point at which those behaviors associated with ADHD can begin to emerge. And, sadly, with newer and crueler methods of bullying and the threat of devastating violence and sometimes even mass murder taking place in our schools, figuring out how to help our kids navigate these social challenges becomes even more critical—for both our kids' sakes and society at large.

Research documents how social development and support is paramount to increasing achievement scores. My colleagues and I call this *prosocial education*. Once considered foundational to our U.S. education system, prosocial education today is, unfortunately, receiving less—or less valuable—attention in many of our schools. We'll discuss this in greater detail in chapter 8. The current obsession we have with testing makes it hard for schools and educators to balance academics with nurturing good people, good citizens. The testing focus and the policy behind it is unfortunately taking teachers away from building the supportive relationships and learning environments essential to kids who struggle with behaviors associated with ADHD, which often contributes to an increase in these behaviors.

In the following we'll look at just how unreal, how out of this world, the current focus and expectations of education have become for kids, parents, and teachers by looking at

1. what our current education policy is focused on
2. the reasoning behind this focus
3. the measurement behind this focus
4. what it means to schools and educators
5. changing enough to say we've changed and setting common standards and
6. what it ultimately means to children possibly given an ADHD label.

OUR CURRENT EDUCATION-POLICY FOCUS

As you are probably well aware, our most recent and current education policies have mainly focused on increasing test scores. Over the past three decades, we have adopted a great number of tests that we use to assess our education system's success. Some have been around longer than others. The National Assessment of Education Progress (NAEP—what many call our "nation's report card") has been around since the early 1990s and provides us with the longest view of how we are doing when it comes to getting all kids proficient in the core academic subjects.

Under No Child Left Behind (NCLB) each state was allowed to create standardized tests to measure what the government calls adequate yearly progress (AYP); more on this shortly. And then we have a whole host of other international tests, such as the Third International Mathematics and Science Study (TIMSS) and the Programme for International Student Assessment (PISA). This last one, PISA, is considered the important one, drawing much of our attention. This test of fifteen-year-olds worldwide ranks education globally among industrialized nations.

Quite honestly, the NAEP is a hard test, and many states feel it is unforgiving and too difficult for kids to master. These opinions are mainly born of the fact that some states created extremely easy state achievement tests that didn't paint the same picture as NAEP scores. For example, a state's standardized test might show that 83 percent of students are reading at a proficient rate, but the NAEP shows that only 23 percent of the same students are reading at a proficient rate. It sounds crazy, but such variance in scores holds true for about a third of states, which gives you a good idea of the problems associated with tests used to assess NCLB. But it really doesn't matter what test you look at.

For close to two decades, whether we look at test scores using the National Assessment of Education Progress or AYP assessments based on individual state standardized achievement tests, the U.S. education system has made little to no progress in its efforts to raise academic-achievement scores.

For example, in 2011 the Center on Education Policy found, based on NCLB states' standardized test scores, that "an estimated 38 percent of the nation's public schools did not make AYP in 2011. This marks an increase from 33 percent in 2010 and is the highest percentage since NCLB took effect." In other words, even using each state's standardized achievement tests (that they were allowed to create and set the level of proficiency for) did not yield adequate yearly progress. Even after allowing states to "renorm" or "improve" their tests (i.e., create new, possibly easier, tests), many states failed to improve. The bottom line here is that we are not seeing the progress that the billion-dollar testing policies were meant to achieve.

The recent strong focus on testing has also failed to help the United States perform better academically internationally. The United States has fallen to average or below average in reading and math. As noted by Harvard University's Pathways to Prosperity Project, "Unfortunately, the United States' performance on the four rounds of PISA over the past decade has been uniformly mediocre." The 2009 PISA scores ranked the U.S. average at fourteenth out of thirty-four for reading skills, seventeenth for science, and a below-average twenty-fifth for mathematics. Furthermore, as President Obama stated in his January 2011 State of the Union address, "America has fallen to ninth in the proportion of young people with a college degree"; the United States was once number one. We now have the highest college-dropout rate in the industrialized world. In the 1970s we were first in high school graduation and are now thirteenth. Furthermore, the most recent 2012 PISA scores showed no meaningful improvement.

In fact, nearly a quarter to a third of our students are still dropping out of school. And we are losing many of our best teachers and not retaining new teachers. To put it bluntly, since our current testing focus is *neither* contributing to higher tests scores nor facilitating progress in a number of other areas, it's time our education system got its priorities straight.

Playing with Priorities

At this point in time, our schools are facing massive challenges. We have the highest level of childhood obesity our nation has ever seen. For the first time in history it is quite possible that parents will live longer than their children, since so many kids are developing diabetes and other medical risks related to obesity. Yet we have cut physical education, recess, and play time in our schools to make room for more instructional minutes.

We have witnessed some of the worst violence ever in schools in recent years. And even after far too many school shootings and unimaginable acts of violence, we fail to successfully prioritize creating safe, caring, and supportive school environments. Although in an effort to better support all students we have focused more than ever before on identifying kids with mental disorders and learning disabilities, we are still not paying close enough attention to kids with serious mental disorders that unfortunately have contributed to violence.

Although we are increasingly focused on turning out a more technologically advanced workforce to help our nation remain a leader in the global economy, we can't forget that our communities need all types of workers. Yet we continue to drop vocational-education offerings in many schools. Instead of preparing our students for a multitude of different careers—white collar and blue collar—we have settled on a one-size-fits-all approach to education in hopes of creating better scientists and engineers. It is as if we think all students will be good test takers and that everyone must approach school with an aim to going to college.

Meanwhile, we need to address an aging, dilapidated educational infrastructure, creating better and newer schools. We need to update technology in our classrooms. We need to better train and support school administrators. We need to hire more and better teachers. We need to figure out how to retain our best teachers and support their efforts to work more closely with parents to nurture, develop, and educate our future citizens. Our list of needs is staggering. And even in the face of these pressing priorities, and many more I haven't even listed here, we still somehow think that test scores ought to remain our educational focus. But even for all of these needs, our country only allots approximately 2.6 percent of the national budget to education, with far too many billions of those dollars paying for testing.

THE REASONING BEHIND THIS FOCUS

For many decades if not a century, the education system in the United States was considered one of the best in the world. At one point we were one of the few effective education systems providing all kids in our country with a well-rounded, free education (compulsory education) that successfully helped them become the knowledgeable, contributing, and caring citizens we needed for our communities and workforce. But at different points in history we began questioning whether we were falling behind other countries and if we should change what we were doing to make sure we didn't. This has been a concern of our lawmakers for many decades, because, as the logic goes, if we fall behind when it comes to education we jeopardize America's economic and industrial standing in the world.

On April 26, 1983, the concern for low-performing schools and their connection to test scores escalated when the Reagan administration released a report on the status of America's schools, titled *A Nation at Risk*. This criticism of the public-education system, which basically blamed teachers and schools for the decline in student performance, was prepared by a prestigious committee, given the endorsement of the secretary of education (William Bennett), and warned that this decline would be the demise of America's industrial clout.

Through the power of the media (with a lot of help from the agenda-setting gurus working in our nation's capital under the Reagan administration) the idea was branded. To some degree it was even accepted as fact that America's future business prominence would only be as strong as the student test scores being produced in America's public schools. To many, this was the tipping point—when the movement toward a competitive testing environment gained great momentum.

The arguments put forth in the mid-1980s (or specifically those made during the Cold War), however, were not that different from the claims made prior to enacting No Child Left Behind. The arguments were no different from the rhetoric associated with today's Common Core State Standards Initiative and the call for a new Common Core standards–based national test. The reoccurring declaration is that our test scores and greater need to improve our focus on STEM subjects (science, technology, engineering, and math) are the fulcrum on which our ability to continue to compete globally in science, technology, and industry rests.

Such claims are somewhat true and at the same time scary. That's probably why they have had so much success in redirecting education policy's focus from an effort to help all kids experience a productive childhood and become outstanding adult citizens to trying to help all kids do well on standardized tests. The quality of our education system most definitely will be one of the deciding factors as to whether our country will remain a world leader. But the test scores we are putting so much value on will not necessarily be the most reliable or valid indicators of the extent of our success or failure. In fact, research shows that the achievement tests, similar to tests for ADHD, have little validity to support what they claim to measure.

For the sake and future of our education system, let's hope the test scores are not an accurate measurement of our success, because our standardized-test scores have not looked very promising during the past two decades. So, in an effort to expedite this historical synopsis and fast-forward to the lessons-learned part of this brief chronological overview, let's move forward from the 1980s and parachute pants to the year 2014 and skinny jeans, where we find standards-based standardized tests to be the latest fashion.

THE MEASUREMENT BEHIND THIS FOCUS (HOW WE USE TEST SCORES)

Basically, the way our current system operates is that in order to monitor the education efforts taking place nationwide as a means of justifying individual states' eligibility for federal education funding, school systems are held accountable through an annual test each state is required to administer to its students. Though schools are required to do a whole lot more to make sure a quality education and safe, caring learning environment are provided, this test we use to assess the total effectiveness of schools focuses only on testing the subject matter taught in reading (or English and the language arts), math, science, and history (or social studies). If states show steady progress in improving test scores in these four core subjects—what the federal government currently calls *adequate yearly progress* (AYP)—then the schools continue to be eligible for and possibly receive federal funding.

This is what is called a *compliance model*. If the school systems of America are complying by giving the mandated standardized achievement tests, and showing AYP, then they get to ask for and possibly receive monetary support from the federal government. So each state's department of education, often monitored by their governor's office, passes down the details expected from this federal-compliance model and orders all of its local education agencies to plan and prepare for the test. They often explain to the local education agencies that if schools within their district do not meet AYP then the schools will receive several warnings, and that if they do not improve then the state will take over the school. This is sometimes done by allowing a charter-school organization to acquire the school for a nominal fee to try to "save" it.

To some degree, this approach sounds like a feasible model for monitoring the effectiveness of education in our nation. The fact that we have some sort of monitoring system is a good place to start. But the efficacy of this system rests on the quality of the tests given and how they are used to help schools improve.

Unfortunately, previously during the implementation of No Child Left Behind, each state had been allowed to create a collection of specific grade-level *standard* tests for all kids to use. *Standardized tests*, as we have come to call them, were supposed to be written to measure challenging state educational *standards*, which explains our use of the similar term *standards-based tests*. A standard in education is not that different from a standard a business puts in place to operate by. For example, your favorite restaurant's standard might be that they will settle for nothing less than providing good food and good service. An education standard, then, might be committing to ensuring that all students become proficient in math by learning all specified grade-level goals.

In some states this might mean that a standard for kindergarten is that the kids will learn to count proficiently. In first grade they will learn to add, in second grade they will learn to subtract, and so on. (In part II of this book we'll explore how knowing the grade-level expectations in advance can be a huge help to parents.) But when you allow each state to choose their standards and create a set of standards-based tests, you end up with fifty-plus sets of standards and fifty-plus sets of different tests that are hard to compare at the federal level.

Another problem is that the tests are only designed to test a few subject areas and are only given to students in certain grades. As a result, in the end the tests only tell us how well the subject matter is being learned in those few subject areas at a few grade levels. The current model for most school districts does not allow us to effectively track how individual kids are progressing from year to year.

With the present system we are unable to determine how well all teachers are teaching, since some of the teachers don't teach the tested core subjects related to reading, math, science, and history, or do not teach the grade levels being tested. For example, we have no idea how well a second-grade math teacher or ninth-grade physical-education teacher is doing since most states don't start testing until third or fourth grade and we don't test physical education.

Furthermore, this model of testing does essentially very little to monitor the quality of school administration, school climate, or learning environment. And it doesn't come close to assessing how much work and preparation teachers put into teaching and supporting individual student needs. But it gets worse.

Pure Genius

Ideally standards-based tests can at least tell us how well teachers are teaching specified subject matter within specified grade levels, but the way we use the test scores is flawed. Instead of using them to see how each student progresses in a specific year under the guidance of a specific teacher, we combine the scores of the class together and create a percentage score to tell us how many classrooms within a school have kids that are performing at a *proficient* level. We use the proficiency score of a teacher's specific class for this year and compare it to the score of the teacher's specific class from last year. And if a teacher has a class that does better than the year before, then they have possibly showed adequate yearly progress and get to keep their job.

There are several problems with the process's logic. First, it is radically unfair to expect a teacher to pull this off year after year. As many teachers can attest, some years you are assigned a fairly smart and motivated class while other years you are assigned more challenged classes. Another reason this use or expectation of the test scores is unfair is that we don't use them to track the academic progress of individual students.

If we don't compare Tommy's sixth-grade reading test score with the seventh-grade reading test score he achieved in Mrs. Jackson's class, then we really can't tell if Mrs. Jackson has helped Tommy improve. But one of the biggest problems the Mrs. Jacksons of the education world have is that Tommy and his fellow students are not held accountable for their test scores. And if you don't put some sort of responsibility on the student to try harder, to improve, common sense says the student will not try very hard to do well on the achievement tests. Where there's no accountability for doing badly, there's little motivation to improve. More on this shortly.

Also, as previously noted, a good part—if not all—of the test is based on reading, math, and the critical-thinking skills needed to understand science or history—more or less what an IQ test uses to measure intelligence. As we saw in chapter 1, however, research on IQ testing has found that intelligence is normally distributed and that often we cannot increase IQ scores more than fifteen points over the lifespan of an individual.

But more recent education policy has ignored these findings, instead demanding that schools perform modern miracles and take every student to a statistically significant higher level of intelligence year after year. This was the rationale behind No Child Left Behind—for all schools to be at 100 percent proficiency by the year 2014. Basically, the hope was that if year after year, starting around 2002, students in first grade were able to significantly increase their intelligence, by the time they reached twelfth grade they would be scoring off the charts on standardized tests.

But as we have found, improving standardized-achievement test scores is just as hard as increasing IQ. Flip back to figure 1.1 for a moment. Recall that most people, as the figure shows, are of normal intelligence, designated by the dark gray zone, and most will never move out of that zone. In other words, year after year most students will perform nearly the same as they did the year before when tested on the new grade-level information they have been taught.

Why do we think a system so focused on academics can fly in the face of historical research telling us that intelligence is somewhat innate, inherited from nature, and for the most part not nurture dependent or changeable? Perhaps you think comparing IQ tests to standardized tests is problematic. Well, think of it this way: doesn't it seem odd to say that intelligence plays no role in predicting standardized test scores heavily reliant on reading, math, and supposedly critical-thinking skills?

In fact, according to the 2007 study *National IQs Predict Differences in Scholastic Achievement in 67 Countries*, in an analysis of a standardized test used internationally and an IQ test, the IQ scores accounted for—or predicted, if you will—79 percent of the student math scores and 74 percent of science scores. What this shows us is that we are spending billions on increasing standardized test scores that are basically reflective annually of a normal distribution of students' IQ scores. Decades of research show us IQ scores rarely change significantly, which confirms that our present education policy, high-minded and well-meaning, is misguided and even futile. Research shows that we are forcing our educators to focus heavily on unachievable goals at the expense of helping our kids develop into the ethical and driven citizens we need.

At best the current test-driven approach—which in the statistical world is called a *cross-sectional analysis*—only assesses how smart this year's kids are compared to last year's kids at the end of the school year. And if the research into normal distributions of intelligence provides us with a bell curve, historically showing that when assessed by an IQ test (heavily reliant on reading and math skills) a great majority of individuals (68 percent) falls within one standard deviation of the norm (one hundred-point IQ), shouldn't we assume that each year will provide a normal distribution of intelligence in our classes? And if our standardized tests are also heavily reliant on reading, math, and critical-thinking skills (just like the IQ tests), shouldn't we also expect a normal distribution of standardized achievement scores each year?

Why do lawmakers continue to think educators can move more and more test scores year after year from the left of the normal distribution curve (and the middle) to the far right, turning a bell curve of scores into a graph resembling a tsunami? It is as if they're saying intelligence has nothing to do with the ability to think critically when it comes to scientific inquiry, how well we can read and comprehend, how well we can do mathematical analysis, or how well we can recall history correctly and comprehend how historical events play a role in shaping our society. If standardized tests don't measure intelligence, then what are they measuring?

The Reflection of Test Scores

To play devil's advocate, it is quite possible that in some instances test scores do not solely reflect intelligence. A great number of intelligent students do poorly on standardized tests. I know this for a fact because I was a student who didn't take standardized testing seriously.

The Iowa Test of Basic Skills was a standardized test given to my generation in ninth grade to determine how smart we were and help us determine what career we should pursue. When told my Iowa Test scores would not impact my grades or my ability to move on to become a sophomore, I proceeded to fill in the letter C (for *Corrigan*) for a majority of answers on the bubble sheet in order to complete the test more efficiently. Let's just say my tests scores were not good. But since I took the more fun part of the Iowa Test measuring my hand and eye skills more seriously, my counselor informed me that I should seriously consider becoming a carpenter or janitor and drop the college-prep courses (where I was earning straight A's) for more technical, trade-oriented courses the next semester.

This was short-sighted advice on two fronts: One, my counselor did not believe me when I told her I hadn't really taken the test. And two, she was speaking as if technical trades required no or little intelligence.

Standardized tests (in addition to measuring one's intelligence and subject-matter knowledge or lack thereof) also reflect motivation to learn, intrinsic motivation, and work ethic (or lack thereof). Standardized-test scores also reflect whether a student is actually interested in taking the test or even cares about a test score. Beyond my personal experience, research backs up this assumption.

In 2011, a decade-long longitudinal experiment led by the University of Pennsylvania's Dr. Duckworth was published. Researchers observed video footage of adolescent boys taking a standard IQ test to rate their motivation and IQ. Then over the course of a decade the study measured how well the boys fared in terms of criminal record, job status, and educational attainment. According to Duckworth, a student's motivation to take a test and the IQ scores were nearly equally predictive of the adult outcomes concerning years of education attained, employment status, and criminal record. "What we were really interested in finding out was when you statistically control for motivation, what happens to the predictive power of the IQ tests? What we found is that the predictive power goes down significantly," Duckworth said.

In other words, the motivation to take the test accounted for a good part of the IQ score and students' future success. Low test scores are not necessarily a reflection of a lack of intelligence (or lower reading and math ability) but quite possibly a reflection of a lack of motivation. Given that our children have grown tired of the current testing focus, it should come as no surprise that many students have little interest in doing well on standardized tests. If we do not hold students accountable for their performance on these test scores, then motivation will continue to be an issue hampering standards-based tests results in schools.

A great number of students from elementary to high school admit they know that their scores will not influence whether they move on to the next grade. They admit that they know their scores won't affect their grade-point averages. And a few have even admitted that they know the only person these test scores will impact is the teacher. From the devilish smiles I have seen on the faces of a few of the students telling me this, my guess is that some of them didn't try that hard because they didn't like their teacher.

If we want test scores to have any chance of improving, then we must begin to create tests that help us to measure the progress of individual students and use these tests to better guide us in helping individuals improve. If we want kids to value the test scores, then we must make the testing focus interesting to students who have grown bored with taking these tests that hold so little personal consequence. We also must be willing to accept the fact that some students are performing at the level they will perform at for decades to come and halt our futile pursuit of 100 percent proficiency.

But most of all we must allow educators the luxury of focusing more quality time on building relationships with students. As the old education saying goes, "They don't care how much you know until they know how much you care." And to show students how much they care, teachers and parents must focus on the social side of education, which in turn will help students become academically successful.

The problem is that current policy holds educators accountable for an unfair number that tells us very little. Now, test scores are important; they do tell us whether students are learning new information being taught. But we should not expect students to do better than the class ahead of them every year; at some point we will hit a ceiling. Plus, one test score measuring proficiency is not enough to measure what a great education system, school, teacher, or classroom is truly providing or should be doing to improve.

WHAT DOES THIS MEAN TO
SCHOOLS AND EDUCATORS?

Unfortunately, due to our present obsession with testing, once-inspired school systems focused on developing good citizens and a well-rounded community workforce have begun voting to cut many other creative outlets to make more time for the testing focus. According to the Center on Education Policy, among the consequences of overtesting are the prioritizing of a few content areas and the thinning of the curriculum. This has resulted in the loss of music and art courses, recess and other play time, and various other nonacademic time, meaning that opportunities for artistic, creative expression, and play are diminished.

Can you understand how this can affect kids? Can you recognize how purging what actually makes school more enjoyable—or at least bearable—is contributing to kids displaying behaviors associated with ADHD? Can you see how it might contribute to students' dislike of school? As a teacher once lamented to me, "We can't even use the F word anymore in school—*fun!*"

Unfortunately, current policy is forcing many schools to turn what could be an inspiring and enjoyable educational experience into a narrow, accountability-driven school culture that is alienating students and parents and demoralizing and driving good teachers away from the profession. Under these regulations, teachers are being forced to abandon what their experience, education, heart, and instinct tell them to do. As I mentioned in chapter 1, instead of being provided the luxury of slowing down when it comes to instruction or spending more time with a child who appears to need more help or attention due to academic struggles or behavioral issues (as teachers had been able to do for decades back when our education system was the best in the world), educators are now basically forced to report these students at the first sign of trouble.

Instead of giving a child a chance to overcome what is quite possibly a temporary obstacle, educators are forced by the legal system accompanying current policy to recommend assigning the child an Individual Education Plan (IEP), 504 Plan, or what is called a Response to Intervention (RTI). When these designations are assigned, children are normally required to be diagnosed formally with a mental disorder or learning disability. And once children have gone through the whole legal process schools now are forced to abide by, labels that may have been temporary become lifelong designations, requiring accommodations. To fuel this flawed mandate, school systems receive more monies for every child diagnosed.

The testing focus has created a system in which a kid must be diagnosed in order to get extra help. Teachers could be fired if it turns out they failed to follow procedure if they knew a student had academic challenges. While the system is theoretically designed to help kids in need, it is mainly focused on reducing disruptions in class so that teachers have more time to teach what will be on the test. As a result teachers and parents essentially must have a legal agreement in place before they can work together for the betterment of the child.

As Dr. Maurice Elias at Rutgers University explains, too many schools are being forced to "prepare students for a life of tests and not the tests of life." Given that this inadequate and ineffective testing model costs billions of dollars annually, school systems are short on cash and as a result too often cut valuable programs like vocational training for kids who want to learn a trade rather than obtain a college degree. The policy takes away so many things that make school actually bearable and meaningful for kids. It hampers parents' and teachers' ability to work together to take holistic steps to nurture children's academic and social development, a process research shows can actually increase academic achievement.

Although No Child Left Behind had its good points—like encouraging educators to focus on developing the character of a student and getting communities and parents more involved—many educators realized there was too much to focus on and decided instead to limit their focus to making sure they did what they needed to do to get the federal monies offered through NCLB. They focused on the tests. But one thing the policy and many educators failed to realize was that a lot of intelligent, knowledgeable students are not good test takers. NCLB and educators failed to account for the many students who do not plan to go to college and that high test scores designed to measure math, reading, history, and science knowledge are not necessarily as relevant to students who would rather learn a trade than get a diploma.

The policy turned what had once been a calling for some teachers into a compliance-based career. It forced many worried teachers to abandon their calling to inspire children and instead focus on protecting their careers. The persons held most accountable for the test scores were and still are the teachers, and the methods used to tally the outcomes were and still are not fair.

Sadly, many great educators have decided to leave the profession or take early retirement. They saw the writing on the wall and knew the days of teaching from the heart, teaching the subject they knew how to teach with passion and vigor, would soon be just memories. And the last thing they wanted to spend their remaining years as a teacher doing was following an ineffective curriculum book page by page, day by day, only to be given another curriculum book a few years later once test scores had failed to rise yet again.

No Child Left Behind most definitely forced teachers in the tested subjects of math, reading, English, science, and history to *teach to the test*, as it's called. Even those educators who fought the pressure to teach to the test were still required to spend entirely too much time (if not all the time) at least *preparing* for the test. To put it simply, the policy made school even *more* boring, if that were possible. And when kids get bored, we all know what type of ADHD-like behaviors follow.

The policy prevented many inspired educators from finding the time to even get to know their students and help them progress as individuals. Teachers who have taught for many years understand that this personal relationship is what makes teaching refreshing and rewarding year after year. To put it simply, NCLB gave educators a one-size-fits-all curriculum, a pacing guide that ordained how far instruction should have progressed in the curriculum by any given week, and as a result took away the time that had been used to build relationships, rules, and routines so important to student academic success and personal growth. The policy took a learning process that has the potential to be fun, interesting, and effective, and feel like a day at the beach, and turn it into an experience akin to being forced to spend the entire day inside a nature center with no windows, listening to an automated slide show that lectures about the beach. And why did they do this?

CHANGING ENOUGH TO SAY WE'VE CHANGED AND SETTING COMMON STANDARDS

National education policy was radically changed so that we could annually give our children a multiple-choice test to see if they were learning the facts and how to think critically. But how can you measure critical thinking with a test that asks you to guess between four options and fill in a bubble? Well, the powers that be, our all-knowing government and their politically oriented think tanks, were scared that the United States was falling behind in education and that as a result we would fall behind as the economic juggernaut of the world.

Given that our new Common Core State Standards Initiative policy has really only changed enough to say that we've changed, much of what I have written on education in my previous books pertaining to improving education under NCLB still holds true. The big difference between NCLB and Common Core is that instead of each state creating and using their own standards-based achievement tests based on their own critera, we now have one national test and a Common Core of standards.

This is a good thing when it comes to statistically comparing how states are doing. But given that more than a dozen states at this time have either pulled out of or threatened to pull out of Common Core, one can only assume that the baggage that comes along with this new federal policy doesn't seem worth the effort (to some states, at least) to repeat a slightly different (possibly even slightly improved) version of NCLB or reap the reward of minimal federal funding. You might note again that only approximately 2.6 percent of our federal budget goes to education—this despite the widely held conviction that our global industrial and economic power rests on a first-rate education system.

Furthermore, even though Common Core claims to also be more focused on producing kids who can think critically, it still is fundamentally based on the same belief system that if we increase test scores nationally we will increase our test scores on international tests so that we can show once again that the United States is number one in education. U.S.A.! U.S.A.! But hold on a second, my fellow U.S.A.–chanting patriots; unfortunately this policy has also been built on flawed logic. Why?

Ask any teacher you know, and there is a good chance you will hear that while NCLB kept them occupied with busywork, the new demands of Common Core are burying them alive. When we try to accomplish more with the few hours of instruction we have in a day that were already filled to capacity, teachers only have less time to teach all they are expected to teach. Furthermore, focus continues to shift away from important predicators for academic success (or our achievement scores)—parent involvement, how we deliver the curriculum, the development of the students, educational attitudes, the educator-student relationships, and the school climate. More than fifty years of research has shown that these educational complements create high levels of school effectiveness.

It's a Sad, Sad Situation

But there are still other indications that the current U.S. education system is failing. According to the National Center for Education Statistics, more than a quarter of our students on average are choosing to drop out of school. Depending on what research you believe, that rate could be as high as 33 percent nationally. The high rates of school failure and student dropout plaguing many American cities and rural areas have a variety of repercussions. For example, a study of incarcerated black men born between 1965 and 1969 estimates that 60 percent of high school dropouts go to prison by the time they are thirty-five years old. As Stanford University's Dr. Linda Darling-Hammond points out, failure in school feeds the school-to-prison pipeline.

Teachers also are affected by the current schooling environment. The United States is not retaining its best and brightest teachers, where more than a third of new teachers leave the profession within three years of starting. And half of them must be replaced every five years. Additionally, a great number of our best and most experienced teachers are taking early retirement or leaving to pursue work in another field. Many of these once-inspired educators are leaving because they feel undersupported, unappreciated, and underpaid. They also report concern with student behavior problems and a dislike of the current focus on standardized tests affecting their curriculum choices, instruction, and classroom climate.

Academic success is a worthy goal, but first understanding and doing what we need to do to improve academic success is critical. Yet despite the fact that more than one out of four kids drops out of school and that out of those who stay in school one out of three can't even read proficiently, instead of truly changing how we approach education we have merely changed the test and act like we have changed for the better. For our schools and educators to truly be given a chance to help all kids find academic success, we must do more than this. Instead of discussing the fact that we have not made any adequate progress over several decades, all we seem to hear is that NAEP is not fair, that state tests need to focus on a common core of standards and use a common test, and that we need to continue our unattainable pursuit of 100 percent proficiency.

The Common Horror

This is basically what the Common Core State Standards Initiative is trying to accomplish. If states do not agree to adopt the Common Core state standards, they will not be allowed to apply for certain federal monies. Through this political strong-arming, decision makers at the federal level have managed to push this new policy through. This bullying only decreases the popularity of federal efforts to influence education. But when we look at who funded this program, we find the organizations and corporations that provide the testing services and subsequent texts developed to teach the new standards.

Now, this is truly scary. Even a student reading below proficiency can read the writing on the wall: a conflict of interest exists when a large publishing company funds—or commits resources to—a federal movement to rewrite standards so that the publishing company conveniently *might* have a role in writing the new test, printing the new test, grading the new test, and/or publishing the new books and software to teach to the test. But welcome to Washington, D.C., where common sense is not that common anymore and lobbying and corruption are rampant.

Furthermore, though some of the new Common Core standards have been provided for educators to begin teaching the curricula and different content subject knowledge, the tests are not quite ready. As a result, during these first few years using the Common Core, many have been teaching new, possibly more demanding, standards with inadequate resources and have been using old tests that measure different standards while the powers that be create, pilot, and set new proficiency levels for the new test. With many school districts warning their teachers behind closed doors that scores will not be good for several years to come, we can safely assume the worst.

Please note that in California, Massachusetts, and a handful of other states there was debate over whether the Common Core standards were actually lower than the previous state standards had been under NCLB. Regardless, we know what is needed to move from a cross-sectional comparison of test scores to a more meaningful assessment that allows us to track whether educators are actually helping individuals develop and get better academically.

But rumors are leaking out from behind the closed doors where these tests are being created that they are developing yet another battery of content subject-based knowledge tests with a pinch of critical thinking incompatible between grade levels. In other words, it sounds like for all of their trouble, the new tests still will not allow a child's progress to be tracked. Even though they say the new test will not use multiple-choice-type questions to measure the critical-thinking components, anyone who has thought it through knows they will be unable to efficiently grade essay answers from millions of students, because doing so is not affordable, accurate, or efficient. To steal President Obama's controversial wisdom from the 2008 presidential election, "You can put lipstick on a pig, but it's still a pig."

Using assessments of academic success as a means to hold teachers and administrators accountable has certainly caused an uproar in the past. Even so, it's still likely that Common Core tests will be used as some sort of "value-added" indicator of teacher effectiveness. Never mind that the test typically only starts in third or fourth grade and then often skips grades up to the junior or senior year. How is this fair to the teachers who teach the grade levels tested when so many of their colleagues teach grade levels with no testing? And how, then, will we assess the job performance of teachers of pre-K through third grade or the primary or secondary grades not tested?

And given that the tests typically only assess math, reading, history, and science, how will the tests be used to assess teachers who teach the few existing nontested subjects? And let's address the eight-hundred-pound gorilla in the classroom: why aren't we taking this opportunity to incorporate age-appropriate developmental measures into the new tests to assess the developmental level of our students and possibly the impact of all the other prosocial education efforts put forth by a teacher or principal to help students develop? As you can see, the policy and the way we measure compliance to said policy is not making it easy for educators to truly focus on our kids as individuals.

WHAT DOES THIS ULTIMATELY
MEAN FOR CHILDREN?

So, now that we know what this policy is doing to school systems and educators, what does this strange, alien-like testing policy mean for you and your child? It means that with such unrealistic expectations and unfair assessments dictating whether a school can stay open and teachers can keep their jobs, teachers are challenged and sometimes unable to focus adequately on what really matters to each individual child in their school. The legalities of the policy dictate that all children exhibiting challenging behaviors—such as those associated with ADHD—must be diagnosed, even though our education program had considered those same behaviors to fall within a normal spectrum of behavior for over a century. It means that your school and the teachers in the school are being asked to focus heavily on accomplishing the impossible, to increase academic achievement beyond the normal distribution of intelligence and motivation to want to do well on tests or in school.

During a curriculum night held for parents last year in my kid's district, when Common Core was initially being implemented, a teacher explained to parents that the difference between NCLB and Common Core was that NCLB had teachers cover curriculum a mile wide and an inch deep while Common Core has them cover material an inch wide and a mile deep. On the surface, this looks like a good thing. Under Common Core teachers supposedly were going to cover less material but delve deeper in hopes of helping students think more critically. But as some teachers have expressed after their first year using Common Core, going an inch wide and a mile deep takes more time and work than did trekking a mile wide and an inch deep. Why?

Under the new paradigm a teacher actually still has to cover all of the topics on the test but now they have to make sure that all students truly understand everything much more deeply and can problem solve to figure it out on their own. This is not necessarily a bad thing. But with classrooms growing in size and the school day not getting any longer, it is nearly impossible for one teacher in a classroom to accomplish the task.

Put yourself in the shoes of a teacher: Basically, your boss can't give you a raise this year, and in order for you to keep your job and just maybe get a raise next year, you need to double your production and all of your clients must show they have learned everything you shared at a much higher level than did your clients the year before. Suddenly you find yourself in a frenzy. You know you have a few clients who need much more special attention, but you can't afford devoting precious resources to the few, as it would hurt your efforts with the greater part of the group. As a result of the untenable position in which we've placed our teachers, children have been left behind.

Luckily, there are a few loopholes that allow you to designate these challenging customers as "special-needs" cases. In fact, going back to our metaphor, let's say there's a financial incentive to categorize clients this way. Out of desperation and in hopes of keeping your job, you send word up the chain of command that these clients (students) need to be labeled and possibly assigned elsewhere. Although you like the clients and want to help them, your stress-induced tunnel vision doesn't allow you to see that there are probably more clients than the ones you have noticed that need more help. You only noticed these clients because they were screaming and behaving differently from the rest. They seemed slightly more annoying. They were, however, quite possibly only communicating their unhappiness or dissatisfaction with what was being taught and how it was being taught. Regardless of the what ifs, you do what you need to do to keep your job.

And this is what is going on in schools today: teachers are being stretched too thin and asked to accomplish far too much. And students who cannot keep up, or behave according to expectations, are being unfairly labeled.

Luckily, plenty of excellent teachers tell their administrators they will use the new curriculum, only to shelve the new curriculum book as the first few weeks pass, returning to what they know works best. These are normally the more experienced teachers. The Mr. Finnegans of teachers take the time to turn the kids on to how cool science—or whatever subject—is first and foremost. They develop within each child a motivation to learn the subject. They also build a personal relationship with the child. And then as they get to know each child they start to share the subject matter in different ways that align with the different learning styles in the class.

Some kids are put into small groups. Some are left to learn by themselves because they prefer it. Some tutor others one-on-one because the tutor learns as he or she teaches and the other student gets the help they need from a partner. The teacher also calls certain parents and meets with them to create a plan where they can work together to ensure the students' success. And lo and behold, at the end of the year these kids do just as well if not better than the kids in the other science classes where teachers were consumed with following every page of the new curriculum book and keeping up with the pacing guide.

What these special teachers realize, and what generations of teachers have practiced in the past, is that sometimes we must start slowly. Sometimes we must even backtrack. But in the end, *if* we can get all on board and make it a team effort where every child in the class matters, we gradually catch up and with great momentum surge pass expectations. And guess what? More kids perform better academically and leave with a good feeling about the subject matter.

We must understand what our teachers are up against and appreciate that not all teachers feel confident enough to buck strict policy expectations. But if the situation arises where, for example, a child is being forced into an ADHD diagnosis, we must also ask them to consider whether it's the child or the policy expectations that is causing the real problem. And, most of all, we must be willing to step up and share the responsibility. I've said it before, and I'll say it again: parents who have successfully raised children who did well in school know firsthand that their role in helping the child succeed in the classroom is just as important if not more important than the teacher's role.

SUMMARY

So how does this discourse on national education policy relate back to ADHD? The short answer is that parents always can benefit from being more informed about their child's education. We must learn how the game is being played in order to have a chance at competing. We must realize that our international standing in education is not improving with this focus on testing and, equally important, that a third of our kids have been dropping out of school and we've been unable to stop it. We must see that our education system is not improving, according to tests scores, and that the system is holding back inspiring educators. And in the wake of the senseless murders of so many children in Newtown and in other communities, we must remember that our children's lives mean far more than a proficient test score.

For over a decade I have researched schools, but before that I taught in a juvenile detention center and ran a community-outreach program that tried to help at-risk youth better connect with their communities and schools. I must admit that my desire to help young kids get through some of the most challenging years of life was energized by the years I spent coaching middle and high school students and working with troubled youth, as well as a not-so-wonderful personal childhood filled with far too many family challenges and bad decisions on my part.

The last two books I wrote discussed the challenges and flaws of our education policy, meant not to merely critique its shortcomings but, rather, help educators—as well as lawmakers—better understand how to fix our education system's shortcomings. My coauthors and I wrote these books with the intention of helping our education system to better approach developing the whole child, not just their inner test taker, and supporting the social development of children.

The education policy we have is flawed and misdirected. It values international rankings over our children's personal educations and development. The policy is unfair to parents, and it is unfair to the millions of teachers who have answered a call to inspire and love children. In broad strokes, I write this book to convince you that ADHD is a farce and must be reckoned with, and that medication holds no role in the nurturing of any healthy child's life. This chapter in specific was written to help you understand how it is that our education system is unfortunately drawing too many families into this growing trend to medicate our children for acting like children.

Because our nation's institutions of higher education have been successful in producing top scientists and engineers for many years, it's tempting to believe that current public-education policy must, then, be working. The U.S. education system, however, is intended to be a free compulsory education for all children, not just the well-behaved children or the children who are good test takers or have promise to become scientists or engineers. Therefore, policy must guide education to prepare all students, regardless of potential career or trade, for a fruitful and productive adulthood. Policy changes over the last decade that have emphasized the importance of standardized student assessments as the primary measure of educational achievement have led to an imbalance in the system that may threaten the core of public education.

To make standardized tests useful instructional tools rather than mere instruments of accountability, we need to start using them to diagnose individual student needs and progress, not to indicate whether the class (i.e., teacher) or school has made adequate yearly progress. If we are going to lavish on testing an even greater portion of the meager 2.6 percent of our federal budget earmarked for education and for states with underfunded education systems, we need to start developing tests that actually allow us to track an individual student's developmental growth and academic ability. We need to create tests that inform what we are doing rather than merely serve as an indicator of our children's academic being.

**REFLECTION EXERCISE:
DREAM A LITTLE DREAM FOR ME**

From my experience working with kids who struggle to succeed academically or in education environments, I often find that many do not yet have a dream. By this I mean that they have not yet figured out what they want to become or accomplish in life. Some cannot imagine that maybe they're capable of even achieving a dream like that. But we can help them realize that they can rise above their life challenges and become or achieve whatever they dream, no matter how poor they are or no matter how bad they are performing. I suggest that you sit down with the kids you are concerned about and talk about what their dream might be. Sit down and help them visualize, step by step, how with your help they can achieve whatever their heart and unmedicated mind imagines.

6

Epidemic Distortions

REASON #6: ADHD's cause has never been definitively proven, and no definitive evidence establishes ADHD as a real disorder, disease, or chronic condition.

We are about to close part I of this book, where we've focused on the factors contributing to the ADHD trend, and move on to part II, where we'll look at some common-sense recommendations for better approaching and addressing behaviors and issues associated with ADHD. But first let's discuss in a bit more detail the research often cited by those who support the ADHD diagnosis. This will probably come as no surprise to you at this point, but in the following I'm going to teach you about a few more limitations, shortcomings, and flaws associated with the research that is supposed to be supporting ADHD.

One of the courses I teach at the university level is research methods. In this class students learn the basics of statistical analysis as it relates to behavioral- and social-science research and how to design and write formal scientific studies. While luckily most of my students find this course to be a great asset to their careers, I have heard through the grapevine that some of them believe that my class is too demanding. It's probably an accurate diagnosis.

I think part of the problem is actually that some of these not-so-happy students come to my class with the belief that they are not good at math—or, as my gifted and more-than-occasionally opinionated sixth-grade daughter refers to it, Mental Abuse To Humans (M.A.T.H.). Like many folks out there, some of my students suffer from a slight case of "Numerophobia"—fear of numbers. As a result, when faced with trying

FOCUS ON THE FACTS

- The abundance of ADHD fact lists out there were created to scare you.
- These lists claim that ADHD is a real disease, growing at epidemic proportions, and tied to genetic, biological, and environmental factors.
- These epidemic claims are inconclusive and not or even partially supported by science.
- Pharmaceutical companies are creating pseudo-nonprofit websites and paying for the publication of ghost-written studies to spread these misleading claims.
- Though the pharmaceutical industry has produced its own biased studies linking their conclusions to scientific evidence, other studies contradict their findings.
- The increase in ADHD cases is not a sign of an epidemic but, rather, is representative of effective propaganda that relies on scare tactics and suspect research to legitimize ADHD.
- The increased prevalence of ADHD in the United States is also connected to the rise of increased accountability demands and various education-policy requirements that more kids be diagnosed more often, and at ever-earlier ages, for learning disabilities and disorders.
- Our fascination with standardized testing is turning students into scapegoats.
- The rise in ADHD also mirrors the rise in child poverty.
- This chapter further teaches you how to separate fact from fiction when it comes to ADHD research claims, because the only real evidence supporting ADHD is that there is a lack of real evidence.

to understand what the numbers in front of them mean, their distaste predisposes them to tune out and not absorb the lessons, which means they're missing out on just how important it is to understand what statistics are, how they are used, and how people manipulate them.

I always share with my students on the first day of class, you don't have to be good at math to understand research methods or do research. I explain that my goal is to help turn *sadistics* into *statistics* (bad math humor, I know, but that's what you get from a guy who focuses on using numbers to measure what is taking place in schools and with children). I further explain to them that I realize that not all of them will leave my class experts in research methods or statistical analysis. But every student who finishes my class will at least leave as a better consumer and a savvier critic of research.

This is my goal with you as well. This chapter is intended to help you identify a few more of the bright red warning flags connected to research that insists ADHD is (1) real, (2) an epidemic, and (3) caused by genetic, biological, and environmental factors. By sharing with you just a few more of the many red flags out there, my goal is to help you become a more knowledgeable consumer and savvier critic of ADHD research.

DEBUNKING THE ADHD-EPIDEMIC MYTH

An easy Internet search can call up long lists of famous and historical people who are said to have ADHD. Myriad other Internet searches bring up long ADHD fact lists, maybe on websites with domain names ending in dot-com, dot-org, dot-edu, or dot-gov, most of which fly some serious red flags up their flagpoles. These lists are full of claims that research does not support. This should come as no surprise. If you haven't learned by now, not everything on the Internet is trustworthy, accurate, unbiased, or honest.

Many of the websites focused on ADHD are created by—or work in conjunction with—the pharmaceutical companies that sell ADHD drugs for kids. Others, maybe a little less biased and in some instances much more informative, are provided by government and nonprofit organizations, researchers, and groups that wish to point out just how serious this so-called "ADHD epidemic" is becoming. The point is that there are an abundance of "fact" lists and supposed myth-busting lists created by those who want you to believe ADHD is a real disorder and not a collection of symptoms that define how *normal* or slightly developmentally delayed (or possibly gifted) children act.

These fact lists, however, are full of differing claims suggesting that ADHD is the result of a genetic, biological, brain, or environmentally induced abnormality. Very few ever venture across the line into honesty (and reality) and actually explain that the most obvious contributing factors to the display of ADHD symptoms are tied to challenges with school-learning environments and family life and to developmental or other social challenges.

Every now and then, however, if you go deep enough into your search engine's findings and plow past all of the links to websites supported by the more affluent organizations, which are able to pay computer gurus big money to make sure their numerous websites come up first in every concerned adult's Web search into ADHD, you will find a few sites that tell the truth and expose the myths about ADHD. You will find websites created by clergy, doctors, and educators warning you of the dangers of the ADHD diagnosis and drugs. You even will find websites created by individuals who themselves took ADHD drugs as kids and want to help others steer clear of that mess.

Unfortunately, beyond a few recent informative articles and studies published by the *New York Times, Forbes, Time, Psychology Today*, the *Wall Street Journal*, and the Centers for Disease Control and Prevention, readily available, less-biased research-based information is harder to track down online than are the plethora of propaganda sites funded through the not-so-family-friendly arm of the pharmaceutical industry.

The abundance of research supporting ADHD as a valid diagnosis can be overwhelming to the uninitiated. If we were to dismiss for a moment the fact that nearly all of this research uses an unreliable and invalid measurement to actually measure ADHD, it might even seem like they have evidence to support their claims. But even beyond the fact that they have no way to actually distinguish between kids who do and do not have ADHD, other legit studies contradict the very evidence they claim to be fact.

One of the biggest myths touted as fact is that *ADHD is an epidemic.* Debunking this will highlight a few of the smaller myths propagated about ADHD and the methodological limitations that plague research on ADHD. But first, so as to better understand the research debunking the myths and exposing misleading facts, let's separate fact from fiction.

BECOMING A GOOD CONSUMER OF ADHD RESEARCH

Any good research always first proposes a hypothesis or research question. So let's start by asking, Is there an ADHD epidemic? An *epidemic*, by definition, occurs when the incidence rate of a certain disease substantially exceeds what is "expected." Contrary to what those in the ADHD business would have you believe, although the incidence rate is exceeding what is expected (especially in the United States), ADHD is not an epidemic unless you believe it is actually a disease. Science, however, really hasn't produced evidence supporting that ADHD is a disease. By examining the increase in ADHD cases in context, and exposing the bad science for what it really is, we will see that ADHD is not a disease spreading at epidemic proportions but, rather, is more representative of effective propaganda reliant on scare tactics and suspect research to legitimize and publicize ADHD.

As the following will document, the rise in cases of ADHD—or, more specifically, the increased prevalence of ADHD in the United States—is also due to

- the rise of increased accountability demands from a standardized-testing fascination
- current U.S. education policy that requires early diagnosis for impairment
- more readily available and lax screening by pediatricians and other primary-care givers
- an unfortunate link to children living in poverty and
- the destigmatization of ADHD accomplished through the powerful promotion of propaganda by a few pharmaceutical companies that have masterfully discovered how to push pills for kids and sell ADHD as a legitimate research-supported mental disorder, neuro-biological disorder, and/or chronic neurologically based disease.

With so many factors contributing to this trend or supposed epidemic, where to begin? I might be showing my bias for numbers, but I think the best place to start is by addressing the statistical research so many want you to believe *proves* ADHD's existence (there's that P word again). The numbers, when used strategically, are the main power behind helping ADHD appear to be an epidemic.

Go West, Young Man

Given that many people suffer from "Numerophobia," it is easy to create supportive evidence that scares many into believing ADHD is real, and therefore an epidemic, by throwing an abundance of confusing data at them showing the increase in ADHD cases. Unfortunately, as Andrew Lang (famous poet, novelist, literary critic, and anthropology enthusiast) once so wisely suggested, we "use statistics as a drunken man uses lampposts—for support rather than for illumination." This is often the case when statistics are used in education (e.g., test scores). And we observe the same practice using research on ADHD. In each of these cases, numbers are used to show that something exists—that a problem subsists.

Take a look at figure 6.1, for example, which shows you how the percentage of children *with* ADHD in 2007 increases as we move west to east in the United States. Using only those numbers, some might say, "This clearly proves that ADHD is quite prevalent in the United States and it is worse on the East Coast." What we should be doing, however, is looking at the underlying factors responsible for the numbers. We should be asking why the numbers increase as we move eastward.

But for some it's hard to engage in an honest discussion that could provide more comprehensive research-supported answers and intelligent insights about why so many are being diagnosed with ADHD, especially

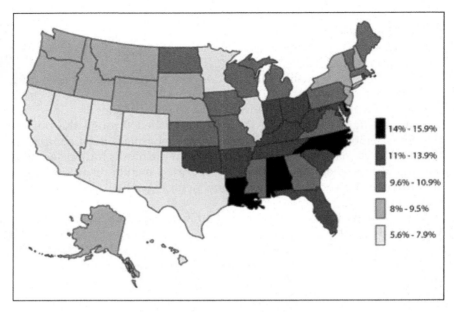

FIGURE 6.1 State-based Prevalence Data of ADHD Diagnoses as of 2007

on the East Coast. Consider the good folks running the "nonprofit" web-site ADHD Awareness Week. They're conveniently *sponsored* by . . . drum roll, please . . . the profitable pharmaceutical company Shire—makers of Adderall and Vyvanse. Instead of addressing the East Coast epidemics they just give you more data (figure 6.2), and then suggest the best way to answer the question, "Are ADHD rates increasing?" is to examine prevalence rates over time.

Following their example, if you were to compare figure 6.1 to figure 6.2, you might easily come to the conclusion that the prevalence of ADHD did indeed increase unexpectedly between 2003 and 2007. By looking at only these two maps you might conclude that ADHD is truly a growing epidemic. And by considering only these two graphics, those seeking to legitimize the ADHD epidemic can popularize their assertion that rates of ADHD are increasing. These two maps show clearly how the highest percentage category of ADHD prevalence in 2003 (6.5 percent) fell into the lowest percentage category in 2007. And with the latest numbers provided by Centers for Disease Control and Prevention, which we looked at in chapter 1, we can only assume that these numbers have increased again.

As world-renowned expert in creativity and education reform Sir Ken Robinson points out quite humorously in his video "Changing Education Paradigms" (which went viral online—check it out if you get a chance),

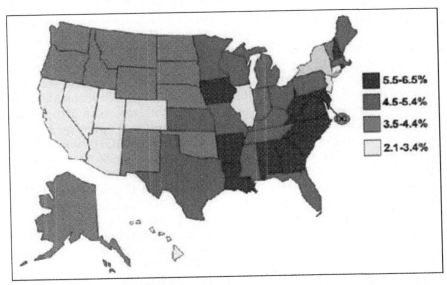

FIGURE 6.2 State-based Prevalence Data of ADHD Medication Treatment as of 2003

"This attention deficit disorder increases as you travel east across the country. People start losing interest in Oklahoma. They can hardly think straight in Arkansas. And by the time they get to Washington[, D.C.,] they've lost it completely." But all kidding aside, why is the prevalence of ADHD increasing, and why is it so different from coast to coast?

More importantly, why does the United States have an 11 percent average prevalence rate that seems to annually increase while the rest of the world is holding steadier at a 5.29 percent prevalence rate? Great Britain, it should be noted, is holding steady at a mere 3 percent. But before providing more evidence that begins to answer these questions and debunk the epidemic theory, let's first look at some of the other scary research the powers that be want you to believe provides evidence of this supposed epidemic. But rest assured, these two maps do not provide enough illumination to explain why the increase is taking place. Rest assured, these two maps do not explain why ADHD is more prevalent on the East Coast. And, most assuredly, these two maps do not *prove* it is an epidemic or explain why the United States' ADHD prevalence rate in some states is two to nearly five times higher than in other parts of the world.

Be Afraid; Be Very Afraid

Some claim that ADHD is a *neurobiological disorder*, which is defined as an illness of the nervous system caused by genetic, metabolic, or other biological factors. Such claims suggest ADHD is something a child is born with or catches from the environment. A few other well-known neurobiological disorders are autism and Tourette's syndrome. This sounds scary, right?

If this is true, ADHD is as serious a condition as autism and Tourette's. Others, like the pharmaceutical company Shire (which, coincidentally, has been marketing ADHD medications to children since 2001), claim it is a chronic neurologically based disease similar to epilepsy, multiple sclerosis, or Parkinson's disease. Such claims suggest ADHD is something a child is born with or inherits. Meanwhile, the new DSM-5 wants you to believe it is a neurodevelopmental disorder. Hearing all this, you might in turn believe that a child who is said to have ADHD truly does have a disease or serious disorder and will never be able to outgrow the related behavioral challenges, enjoy a *normal* childhood, or function as a *normal* adult in society. But before we let megacompanies and organizations that profit from our fear make us too afraid, let's think about this rationally for a moment.

If ADHD is a chronic, neurologically based disease, where is the abundance of evidence supporting these claims? If definitive evidence is hiding somewhere in some academic publication, medical journal, or pharmaceutical research lab, why are we still diagnosing it at a pediatrician's office using a pen and paper to basically complete a checklist of eighteen symptoms that all *normal* children exhibit *often* to some degree?

If it is a chronic, neurologically based disease, why are doctors not performing some sort of medical, genetic, or biological test to identify it as they do with other chronic, neurologically based diseases, like MS and Parkinson's? Or, on the other hand, if it is really a neurobiological disease, why aren't we testing the drinking water and air-quality levels to discover which or what kinds of biological or environmental contaminants are causing the epidemic?

The fact that proponents of ADHD want you to believe ADHD is all of these things provides further evidence they don't know what they are talking about.

Why don't the powers that be—those who make the drugs to *treat* ADHD—put less funding toward sponsoring propaganda advertisements and websites promoting the legitimacy of the diagnosis and instead put more funding toward actively doing research capable of producing evidence supporting a direct link? Might not those findings help identify the specific biological or environmental contaminants (which, by the way, we could safely assume would be much more present on the East Coast) causing the neurological or neurobiological abnormalities that hypothetically contribute to the neurodevelopmental disorder? If this were the case, that the evidence was actually provided that conclusively showed that environmental contaminants are the main cause of ADHD, then we could all work together to get the EPA to help reduce the use of those dangerous contaminants.

For that matter, having that evidence might provide direction to pharmaceutical companies, who could theoretically develop preventative drugs (or drugs designed to remedy the neurobiological or neurological condition) to fight the effects of the contaminants and protect against genetic malfunctions. With this, we might actually have created a preventative approach rather than a reactive approach to medicating our children. So why aren't the pharmaceutical companies focused on selling ADHD drugs to children doing this research? Because there is no need to invest any more of their valuable profit into the research exploring fictional claims that decades of trying to produce pseudoevidence has failed to accomplish. In other words, the pharmaceutical companies don't believe they'll find a link, so they don't want to spend their money looking for a link.

Now, Let's Be Fair

I should be fair and mention that some "research" out there suggests that neurobiological links do possibly exist. For example, one study published in *Pediatrics* in 2010 found that children with higher than normal levels of organophosphate in their urine had higher ADHD rates. Organophosphate is one of forty-some pesticides used on produce in the United States. Other studies have discovered similar findings—that women with higher levels of organophosphate in their urine, for example, were more likely to have a child with ADHD. I have reviewed these studies, and I can tell you that the findings—that is, the numbers, the strength of the statistical significance or effect sizes—are not that strong.

Furthermore, the data set for the 2010 *Pediatrics* study has been massaged more than a Thanksgiving turkey at the White House. And, more importantly, the methods and assessment tools they used to perform the study were questionable. In the world of research methods, we call these shortcomings *major limitations* to the study. Since this study suffers from the same limitations that weaken many other studies, let's take a minute to break down the details.

To begin, the study in *Pediatrics* relied on a phone interview to diagnose children with ADHD. The interview, however, was performed with parents of the children who had taken part in a previous study that had been specifically focused on testing organophosphate levels in the childrens' urine. The phone interview was intended to diagnose the previous study's participating children for ADHD by using a "slightly modified" version of the DSM-IV criteria called the Diagnostic Interview Schedule for Children IV (DISC IV). The authors of the study claim the DISC IV "has evidence of substantial validity, reliability for both its English and Spanish versions, and successful use via telephone in DSM-IV field trials." In other words, it has been used before to consistently misdiagnose normal children with ADHD and was now being used to justify publishing weak studies based on a phone interview.

This supposedly reliable and valid diagnostic interview can identify thirty different psychiatric disorders in children. And such evidence of the DISC IV is based on using it with a whopping eighty-two children. Don't forget (as we learned in chapter 2) the currently flawed DSM-5 diagnosis requires much more than a short interview with only parents at a doctor's office, let alone a short interview on the phone with parents conducted by a "trained interviewer." Don't forget that the DSM is very clear that no such test for ADHD exists.

So to measure the variables of their *groundbreaking* study, they took real scientific findings from a previous study documenting organophosphate levels in urine (through actual lab testing) and combined that data with an abbreviated version of an unreliable and invalid assessment tool (psychometric test) to measure ADHD. Additionally, given the short interview performed by an unqualified mental-health practitioner, they admit to not having followed the details of diagnostic criteria requiring feedback from multiple observers in multiple settings. They didn't take the time to even talk to the children or rule out the sixteen differential diagnoses (which seems strange, given that they used such an amazing interview tool, the DISC IV, supposedly capable of identifying thirty different disorders).

In other words, the authors of this study had underqualified interviewers diagnosing ADHD through the use of an assessment tool that science has not shown to be capable of measuring the same thing over and over again (reliability) or capable of measuring what it says it measures (validity).

Another interesting if not suspect outcome of this study is that of the 1,139 children who participated in the original organophosphate study (that Moe and his non-clinically trained telemarketing colleagues Larry and Curly diagnosed via an annoying dinnertime telemarketing phone call), they identified 119 cases (nearly 10.5 percent of the participating children) displaying the common behaviors associated with ADHD.

As a side note, there were thirty additional children who did not meet the modified ADHD diagnostic criteria via the phone interview, but according to the parents these kids had previously been diagnosed with ADHD and had been taking doctor-prescribed ADHD medication during the previous year. In other words, their modified diagnosis actually missed a few kids previously diagnosed with ADHD but was still capable of diagnosing nearly the same exact percentage of children identified in the United States, which is nearly two to three times higher than in other countries in the world.

Even beyond the many methodological flaws of this study (like letting Moe, Larry, and Curly play mental-health practitioner, creating less-than-stellar diagnoses using an unreliable and invalid assessment tool), it basically only found that kids with *higher than normal levels* of organophosphate compared to kids with *no traces* of organophosphate were *less* than two times more likely to be diagnosed with ADHD via a phone interview with parents.

Without boring you with the statistical details, this study's outcomes are based on a data set that went through more facelifts than Joan Rivers and still only found minimal results using a low-level analysis barely supported by simple descriptive statistics. Given that they did not report any statistically significant differences between those with *normal levels* of organophosphate compared to those with *high levels* of organophosphate, nor did they provide additional results using more discriminating analysis (such as inferential statistics—that is, analysis we can actually draw inferences from), we could assume these findings came from a fishing trip or *data-mining expedition*. This is when researchers dig deeper into analyzing the data set in hopes of finding something, anything, worth claiming because the first analysis attempt did not find anything.

WHAT DOES IT ALL MEAN?

We can look at these findings in a few different ways. We can believe the rhetoric and think that this study shows that pesticides are possibly contributing to ADHD and that ADHD is a neurobiological disease. Or we can look at this and similar studies and believe that pesticides are moderately linked to the behaviors associated with an ADHD diagnosis. In other words, pesticides are bad for kids (duh!), and they possibly make children not think or behave as well as they should. Please note, numerous other studies have documented that there is zero to little effect (no relationship) when it comes to environmental effects and ADHD.

Moe, Larry, and Curly's organophosphate study does suggest a possible link, but we in the research field understand that correlation research (studies that only compare two variables—pesticide urine samples and phone-based ADHD diagnoses) can't *prove* that pesticides *cause* ADHD. Yet this is the study that is cited hundreds if not thousands of times by individuals and websites pleading with you to believe that ADHD is real and pesticides might be the cause.

There are other, similar studies (just as flawed in methodology, weak in measurement, and overzealous in their claims) that have looked for and tried to claim possible links between ADHD and lead exposure, smoking and alcohol use during pregnancy, and food dyes and other food additives. But given that the DSM, every pharmaceutical company's medication guide, and so many other sources claim that evidence of the cause of ADHD does not exist, please just understand that these studies are inconclusive and can't even combine to represent some sort of consensus-based evidence.

Regardless of the pseudoscientific debate taking place, let's just apply a little common sense to this whole dispute. It doesn't take a rocket scientist to understand that these things (e.g., pesticides, lead, and dyes) are bad for kids' brain development and behavior; but do you really think they cause ADHD? As my coauthors and I explained in our book *Multidimensional Education: A Common-Sense Approach to Data-Driven Thinking,* correlation research if used incorrectly can be what we call "corn-fusing":

It was a couple of years ago that one of the twenty-four-hour cable-news networks ran a story on how research had discovered a significant correlation between corn and the increase in autistic children. The way the story was presented suggested that corn might be responsible for the increase in autism. Think about this for a minute before you stop eating corn or feeding it to your children. How many children do you know who don't eat corn? Not just corn but also the endless amount of processed foods that are part of the majority of our children's diets. Whole corn, corn flour, cornstarch, corn gluten, corn syrup, corn meal, corn oil, and popcorn are just a few common forms of corn consumed or part of an endless number of recipes.

Then you have baking powder, caramel, confectionary sugar, glucose, dextrose, fructose, vanilla extract, monosodium glutamate (MSG) . . . The list goes on of other common ingredients that contain corn or corn syrup. Would you think that a large percentage of kids with autism might consume some form of corn? A correlation study identifying a significant relationship between the evils of corn and autism basically tells us that kids with autism eat corn. But so do a large percentage of kids without autism.

We are not big gamblers, but we bet if you replaced the variable of autism with low achievement you will probably once again find a significant relationship ("Corn Causes Low Achievement"). And if you replaced low achievement with high achievement you would probably find a significant relationship to corn again ("Corn Causes High Achievement"). So corn might be significantly related to high and low achievement. It is true that high levels of mercury have been found in corn syrup, and it is also possible that a diet with less corn (and definitely fewer processed foods) *may* help in the battle against autism. But to say corn causes autism is an overstatement.

This is one example demonstrating how we must be careful to act or react to data that is not complete or comprehensive enough to serve as our foundation for change using data-driven thinking. (pp. 56–57)

Another factor to keep in mind with correlation studies that only look at two variables (pesticides and ADHD) is that in the analysis they are not including the many other variables that might explain what else might be playing a larger role in the relationship between pesticides and ADHD. We call this statistically controlling for other possibly related variables (known as *covariates*). For example, if this study might have included statistics in the analysis measuring other variables, such as the family socio-economic status, sex, family structure, age, grade level, and the quality of the education received, the relationship with or impact of pesticides on ADHD might have been weakened if not completely erased. If they were truly interested in finding the truth about a pesticide link to ADHD they could have performed what is called a *regression analysis*, which would have allowed them to discover the role of pesticides in comparison to many other possible reasons or predictors.

It's Not Rocket Science

If you were the billion-dollar pharmaceutical industry making these claims, or more importantly needing real evidence supporting these claims, it would seem like an easy task to find the resources to fund and allow truly unbiased research groups to perform the experiments or even quasi-experimental studies needed to truly study a representative sample of unmedicated kids diagnosed with ADHD. Furthermore, if you were the National Institute of Mental Health, it would seem important to consider how future longitudinal research on ADHD might avoid funding solely researchers on the pharmaceutical companies' payroll. Such studies could even be designed to examine the long-term effects of stimulant use as well as investigate (statistically control for) the biological, environmental, and genetic variables possibly contributing to the cause.

But instead, the majority of research often touted by the pharmaceutical companies selling ADHD drugs is typically focused on showing how the drugs reduce the symptoms (e.g., the MTA studies discussed in chapter 3) or how the drugs improve focus in school. And then you have a smattering of research massaging or even manipulating old data sets (sometimes reeking of urine) to make claims as weak as those in Moe, Larry, and Curly's study or defending the short-term safety and effectiveness of their medications to treat so-called *abnormal* behavior symptoms. The possibility exists, given the track record of ADHD drug dealers, that someone else will have to perform the research if it is to ever be completed.

Please note, Congress has asked the FDA on several occasions (as early as the 1970s) to investigate the possible dangers of stimulant use. But for whatever reasons, and despite a 41 percent increase in ADHD diagnoses in the last decade, no such federal oversight or investigations are being discussed publicly. It is as if the FDA thinks the research is of little importance or not actually able to be produced. It is as if the FDA is not able to read and understand real research and figure out a feasible plan to do sound studies. Since the United States is the worst offender in the world of prescribing ADHD drugs to kids, one would think that if the FDA were actually concerned about this supposed epidemic they could put a little effort into identifying sound research methods and get other government agencies as well as our education system to be a part of the research.

For example, an interesting study from 1973 completed by Safer and colleagues simply asked school nurses to track weight gain, height, and medication use of students taking stimulants. This simple study documented that indeed kids on ADHD stimulants were experiencing serious challenges in maintaining healthy weights. Imagine if Congress actually ordered our government agencies (the FDA and U.S. Department of Education, for example) to do a similar study and we were able for the next ten years to track the development, behavior, and health of kids being medicated for ADHD and compare their results to other children diagnosed with ADHD who had not been taking medication as well as with kids not diagnosed with ADHD. Given the large number of school nurses who are very concerned about the rising trend of ADHD drug use, it's a fair guess that they would love to be a part of the study. We could also safely wager that after just two or four years we would know a whole lot more about the effects and outcomes of this supposed epidemic and the use of ADHD drugs, especially the new extended release medication.

Pharmaceutical companies want you to believe that they are researching the links between ADHD, biological contaminants, brain abnormalities, and mutated genetics. Some in the field might tell you that the research is underway but will take some time, due to technology limitations. But for decades they have been saying the same thing.

They have been saying this because groups like the National Institute of Mental Health, the U.S. Congress, the International Narcotics Control Board, and the World Health Organization have been warning of the evils of youth stimulant use and calling for long-term studies since the early 1970s. Why? Because since the creation of Ritalin and even Dr. Frankenstein's experiments with Benzedrine, we have been told that using stimulants will most likely result in addiction and have adverse effects on children and that before we start prescribing these pills to kids we need to know what the long-term outcomes truly are. This is why Sweden outlawed Ritalin decades ago.

We must not forget that pharmaceutical companies have had since the 1950s to research the long-term effects stimulants have on kids, and it is widely publicized that little research supporting long-term use of stimulants exists today. The billion-dollar pharmaceutical companies that have been selling drugs to kids for more than a decade based on claims that ADHD is linked to chronic neurologically and neurobiological disease have not produced any impressive significant findings related to biological contaminants and genetic links.

With only a few inconclusive studies barely suggesting the links, no medical test for ADHD to legitimize the few existing claims, and the fact that pharmaceutical companies have suppressed or covered up data concerning negative outcomes resulting from the use of their drugs (such as when GlaxoSmithKline suppressed findings on the many dangerous side effects of the depression medication Paxil, including an increased risk of suicide), it would be advisable to not believe their hype. Nearly every other thing you read on ADHD states that "the causes remain unknown." After nearly a century of acting like this is a real thing, maybe it is time to just accept the fact that the causes are unknown because you can't find causes for something that does not exist.

We probably should feel sorry for the researchers out there who have dedicated their efforts to working toward validating ADHD. They have either been duped into pursuing a wild goose chase or are being forced by finances to waste their careers. Either way, they could gain great insight by taking a year off and serving as a substitute teacher. Then they would realize the symptoms they are futilely trying to link to genetics, environmental influences, and brain abnormalities are something that all kids exhibit to some extent.

This Is Your Brain on Drugs

There are a few other things you need to be fully aware of regarding the so-called genetic studies linked to the claim that ADHD is a chronic, neurologically based disease, as well as the brain-scan research still being touted as evidence.

In nearly all ADHD-focused genetic studies published, DNA tests were not used, nor did the researchers discover a chromosome related to ADHD. Instead, they often only looked at similar behaviors reported by family members. Basically all they have been able to say is that the kids studied show similar behaviors to their parents'. Once again, common sense tells us that these studies are incapable of distinguishing nature from nurture. Is it not possible that in living with parents, kids will begin to adopt and exhibit similar behavior patterns as their parents that coincidentally are related to the commonly encountered ADHD symptoms?

In psychology this is called *conditioning*; kids are often conditioned (or programmed) to behave and believe to some extent as their parents do. We also call such things *learned behavior*. It is equally possible that these kids learned the behaviors rather than inherited them. This is what we call the *nurture* side of the nurture-versus-nature debate.

Think about it for a moment. How many of your idiosyncrasies remind you of your parents' behavior? Similar to most adults, you probably have a few that maybe a spouse, partner, or sibling has pointed out before. They exist because when we live with someone long enough we learn from them and often mimic or subconsciously adopt similar behaviors. The research out there on ADHD's connection to genetic, biological, or environmental variables is incapable of supporting any definitive conclusions.

In other words, the duped, bribed, or coerced researchers can say what they want, but at the end of the day the only real evidence is their lack of real evidence (after sixty years of need and opportunity to capture the evidence). As the DSM and medication guides clearly admit, the causes of ADHD and the true impact of ADHD drugs remain unknown.

Ghost Writers in the Storm

But the problems with ADHD research get worse from here. If you decide to read the body of ADHD research yourself out of sheer curiosity, the will to learn more, or to make sure the case for not drugging children presented in this book is not overstepping its bounds, you might also look into the problems with the research related to ghostwriting. What is ghostwriting? In the case of pharmaceutical companies, one form of ghostwriting is when the employees at a pharmaceutical company (or a firm hired by the pharmaceutical company) draft or create a research publication, write up a somewhat misleading and biased analysis, and then, in hopes of making their in-house research look more credible and unbiased, proceed to tempt, dupe, bribe, and sometimes coerce individuals (professors or physicians) or groups of individuals into putting their names on the paper and publishing it.

According to articles investigating ghostwriting in the pharmaceutical industry published by the *New York Times* in 2009 and *Forbes* in 2011, this practice is not uncommon in the pharmaceutical world. For example, according to the *Times*, between 1998 and 2005 a total of twenty-six "scientific" papers were produced and published via a medical-communications firm hired by the pharmaceutical company Wyeth. Wyeth produces hormone drugs for menopausal women, and the studies produced were supportive of hormone-drug use.

While these twenty-six studies were being published, however, a federal study on women using hormones was abruptly stopped because it was documented that these very drugs increased the risk of invasive breast cancer, heart disease, and stroke. When lawyers uncovered the paper trail documenting this pay-for-publication scheme during a lawsuit against Wyeth for selling their dangerous drugs to women, two respected medical journals—*Elsevier* and the *Public Library of Science Medicine* (PLoS)—were rather disturbed by the allegations.

The same thing is taking place with ADHD drugs. According to *Forbes*, and also published in *PLoS*, Dr. Linda Logdberg, an unemployed assistant professor and mother of two children with ADHD, had answered an advertisement in the *New York Times* for a ghostwriting position. At first she enjoyed the work and felt fulfilled publishing again with top researchers and practitioners, as well as being wined and dined in fancy restaurants.

But after a while she began to suspect something was not right with what she was doing. And when she questioned the account executive at the large agency where she worked regarding the benefits of the ADHD drug she was writing about, she was met with "the curt admonition to 'just write it.'" She was told to just write what she was supposed to write and ignore both her common sense, which was telling her it wasn't accurate, and what she was seeing at home with her own kids taking the ADHD drugs.

Now, it should be noted that not all research on pharmaceuticals completed by a ghostwriter is necessarily bad, biased, or inaccurate. Oftentimes it is quite possible that busy physicians or scientists not necessarily adept at writing might need help to publish their findings. Dr. Logdberg's story in *PLoS*, however, paints a vivid picture of how some (even fully employed experts) get pulled into unethical practices and how quite likely much of what is being published via ghostwriting is not on the up-and-up. Why would others with steady employment want to put their names—staking their professional reputations—on these bogus pharmaceutical-industry embellished studies? There are several reasons.

One is that in the world of higher education, we are often held to a high standard of publication. Some call this the "publish or perish" culture. In other words, desperate professors in need of journal publications (essential to their eventual promotion), not to mention a little cash (most professors are sadly underpaid, believe it or not), agree to this kind of ghostwriting due to a moral defect of the brain. Yes, they might have an early form of ADHD. But others in higher ed are also now being pressured to find monies for the university. If we can't land one of the highly competitive grants that universities often take 26 to 46 percent of for use across campus to pay the bills, we must sometimes turn to the corporate world for our funding.

Another reason ghostwriting happens is because pharmaceutical companies fund or sponsor a large number of medical centers, research centers, and academic or medical journals. "If you want to keep your [grants, donations, or advertising dollars] that our wonderfully altruistic corporation is providing you, you will agree to publish this study, Dr. Lackabackbone." It is quid quo pro—this for that.

This same quid pro quo reasoning or coercion extends even beyond ghostwriting. Because institutions of higher education are suffering losses in funding for numerous economic reasons, professors and medical faculty are often pushed by their superiors to use desperate measures to find funding for programs, departments, hospitals, and medical centers. For some this means going to the dark side to ask for help. What starts off as "Sure—we would love to help your community improve its education and medical support" later turns into a similar story: "You need to create research that supports our cause, or we will have to direct our monies elsewhere." Sad but true.

This section on ghostwriting further clarifies how the pharmaceutical powers that be will go to desperate measures to produce research supporting their cause. This shows to what lengths they will go in order to produce more of the same research claims in hopes of drowning out the more credible and damning research that exposes their agenda and lack of evidence. The fact that the pharmaceutical companies continue to hire the savviest of marketing firms on Madison Avenue is just further evidence that they have no real evidence.

Then What Is the Cause?

Definitive evidence (studies with limited methodological research limitations that have been replicated numerous times and consistently identified similar statistically significant findings) doesn't exist to support biological, brain, genetic, or environmental claims (or theories, if you will), and so maybe we should consider looking at the facts we *do* have on hand. We can learn more when we consider the whole body of evidence rather than one little study performed here or there on this or that.

It is more than just coincidence that the United States went from diagnosing an average of 5 percent of the youth population with ADHD to over 20 percent in some districts during the course of the failed policies of No Child Left Behind (2001 to present). There are also other factors, more logical common-sense explanations, unrelated to the spread of disease or evolution of genetic or brain abnormalities, that have led to the increase in children being diagnosed with ADHD.

As Sir Ken Robinson clearly explains, "Our children are living in the most intensely stimulating period in the history of the earth. They are being besieged with information and calls for their attention from every platform—computers, from iPhones, from advertising hoardings, from hundreds of television channels and we are penalizing them for getting distracted. From what? Boring stuff at school, for the most part. It seems to me it's not a coincidence totally that the incidence of ADHD has risen in parallel with the growth of standardized testing."

At the end of the day, medicating the disruptive kids (who have little tolerance for insufficient intellectual stimulation) into better behavior (compliance), greater focus on the one task at hand (e.g., worksheets created to teach Mental Abuse To Humans, or math), and not further disrupting the delivery of standards-based curriculum instruction is directly tied to the standardized-testing movement.

According to the ADHD Educational Institution (www.adhd-institute. com, another advocacy group conveniently funded by Shire), other reasons for the variation of prevalence rates of ADHD between countries is due to geographic location, the diagnostic criteria used, and the requirement of impairment for diagnosis. In other words, the "epidemic" is also reliant on where you live, how easy it is to be diagnosed ADHD, and whether the school system requires diagnoses for everyone suspected of having some sort of impairment.

You are probably also aware of the fact that school systems are focusing more heavily on early-childhood interventions. As a result, we are seeing more and more kids being screened for supposed learning disorders like ADHD at a much higher rate and earlier age. In fact, in my children's school district (which, I have to say, is a great school district) all preschoolers must complete a screening. But there is also the tie between increased diagnosis and socioeconomic factors, which sadly in this country are still closely tied to higher minority populations of children.

In behavioral and social sciences we often refer to this variable as *socioeconomic status* (SES). Although there are a number of specific formulas used to configure SES, it generally represents the economic and educational status of a child's family. In other words, students who come from poorer families with less-educated parents are considered low SES. Many of these low-SES students are considered to be living in poverty, and child poverty is tied to the increase in children being labeled with ADHD. Figure 6.3 illustrates how child poverty has increased between 2000 to 2010. And if you compare figures 6.1, 6.2, and 6.3, you can begin to see how the increase in the prevalence rate of ADHD is related to—or mirrors—the increase in child poverty during the same time frame of the failed policies of No Child Left Behind.

Compare figures 6.1, 6.2, and 6.3. Do you notice anything interesting? Do you notice how the eastern states experienced a greater increase in child poverty between 2000 and 2010? Despite the fact that figure 6.1

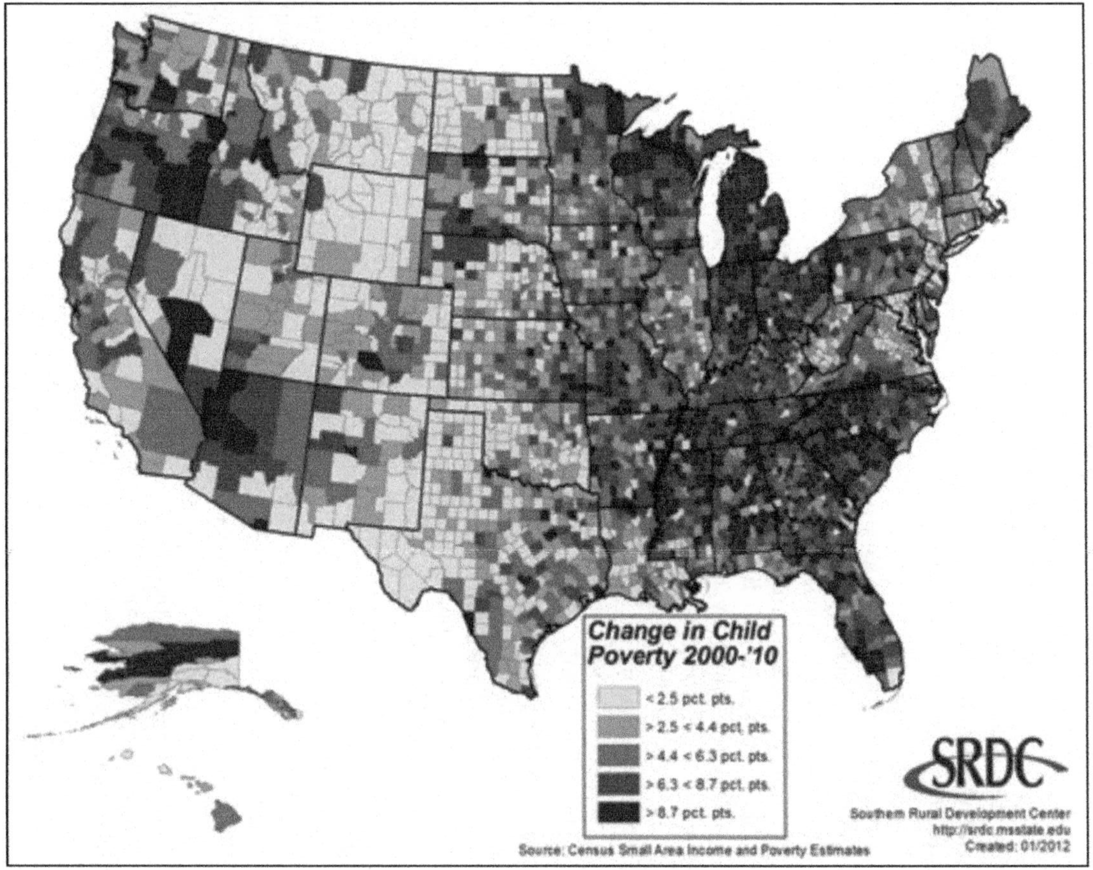

Change in Child
Poverty 2000-'10

< 2.5 pct. pts.
> 2.5 < 4.4 pct. pts.
> 4.4 < 6.3 pct. pts.
> 6.3 < 8.7 pct. pts.
> 8.7 pct. pts.

Source: Census Small Area Income and Poverty Estimates

SRDC
Southern Rural Development Center
http://srdc.msstate.edu
Created: 01/2012

FIGURE 6.3
Change in Child
Povety 2000–2010

and 6.2 are based on state averages and figure 6.3 is based on county averages, do you notice how the dark parts of each figure are similar especially when it comes to the East Coast? Without going into a deep review of the literature on socioeconomic status, the facts are that children of lower-income families tend to have more academic and behavior challenges in school and typically score lower on standardized tests. The fact is that SES has historically been one of the biggest predictors of academic success.

The majority of schools that struggled to meet the grade under No Child Left Behind were schools with larger populations of low-SES students. Title Programs (federally funded efforts to financially support schools with lower-income student bodies) under the current education policy provide loopholes for schools looking to skirt academic-accountability challenges tied to low SES if they can show that the student has a learning disability or disorder. Quite often, ADHD has become the new popular category for managing Title I requirements.

The facts are, however, that even within certain school districts that sit within states with high ADHD prevalence levels, there are schools (in the same city and county) that differ greatly when it comes to the number or percentage of students diagnosed with ADHD. It is as if there are protective bubbles around some schools in a district. While as many as 15 to 20 percent of kids in some schools are labeled with ADHD, the percentage drops dramatically in other schools just a few miles away.

From my experience it would appear that these bubbles are normally the result of more-affluent neighborhoods and suburbs or of schools that have more caring educators and educational leaders who refuse to play the ADHD-diagnosis game. But as I always like to clarify when I present my research findings, I could be wrong. Maybe these communities have truly discovered a way to create a bubble or some sort of ecodome to protect the kids in their communities from the contaminants causing genetic mutations.

SUMMARY

As I began my systematic research into ADHD it quickly became obvious to me why so many parents and educators have decided to become part of the ADHD movement. The pharmaceutical companies pushing their ADHD drugs for kids have flooded the market with an abundance of magnificent marketing and pseudo-evidence highly suggestive that ADHD is real and rampant. It is easy to see why so many adults faced with the dilemma to buy in or opt out often give in to the powers that be. With so much propaganda telling you it is the right thing to do, how could the ADHD experts be wrong?

The task for any parent, guardian, or educator looking for a reason to "say no to drugs" has become an overwhelming undertaking. The proponents of the wing of the pharmaceutical companies selling ADHD drugs for youth have flooded the market and buried the competition's evidence. I would like to believe that this book will begin to change the game. My goal is to help you dismantle the evidence that so many are using to fuel the myth of the ADHD epidemic. My goal is to help you understand the evidence needed to build the case to support what your conscience is screaming in your ear: "Drugging kids because they are acting like kids is wrong and dangerous!"

Researchers in Australia have taken such steps recently. Their study in the *British Medical Journal* documents that the less-restrictive ADHD diagnostic criteria are contributing to a massive increase in the diagnosis of children worldwide. The study suggests that beyond adverse drug reactions, the negative stigma of ADHD and overdiagnosis also leads to kids being perceived as lazier and less clever by their peers and parents having lower academic expectations of them. These findings only further confirm something intuitive. But why so many want to continue the search for evidence supporting the legitimacy of the diagnosis, I cannot understand.

So what has this first part of the book provided as far as evidence? In chapter 1 we learned that allowing children to be drugged for ADHD will, for one thing, stop them from ever knowing what their life would have become had they not been given drugs that most likely cause permanent brain damage. We learned that many of the same behaviors used to diagnose ADHD are the same that identify giftedness and that it all depends on whether the powers that be like the child before deciding if they are to be diagnosed with a questionable mental disorder or placed in advanced programs. In chapter 2 we learned just how easy it is to be diagnosed with ADHD and just how little underpins the research.

In chapter 3 we learned that the drug manufacturers supposedly haven't learned how ADHD drugs actually work or impact a child's brain. But we also learned what research on animals has found to be the case. In chapter 4 we learned about all of the horrible warnings, disclaimers, and outcomes about their products that drug manufacturers had seen before and were forced by the FDA to disclose. In chapter 5 we learned just how crazy our education system has become and how much pressure educators are under to demand conformity.

And in this chapter we have learned more about how the research behind ADHD is flawed and how the pharmaceutical companies are doing a darn good job keeping us distracted elsewhere with trivial findings. Most of all, we learned that you cannot claim to measure whether a child has ADHD or how a drug treats ADHD if you don't first have a measurement for it or any idea or evidence of its cause.

I urge you to read and research more on this topic; but please approach with caution. As I share with my students every semester, you don't have to become an expert in research and statistics to be a good consumer of research. You just have to stop believing everything you read. You have to be a critic who questions a great deal. You need to put on your lab coat and think like a scientist. You need to approach research in hopes of disproving what others claim.

In the end, statistics don't lie. But what you will find is that people often use statistics to tell lies.

REFLECTION EXERCISE: WHERE'S THE BEEF?

You might remember the classic Wendy's commercial that had the cute older lady saying, "Where's the beef?" Not only is this still a good question today for some fast-food chains to answer, it is also a good question for those behind the ADHD movement to answer. The limited amount of research I have shared in this chapter, as well as in other chapters in the first part of this book, should make you ask the same question.

Where is the beef, the substance, to justify these claims that ADHD is a neurobiological disorder or chronic, neurologically based disease? How can pro-ADHD experts claim that kids displaying the same behaviors their parents display is evidence of a genetic link to behave a certain way and not merely nurtured, learned behaviors? How can they claim that environmental contaminants are causing ADHD and not just contributing to bad behavior or lack of attention?

With what I have shared with you so far in relation to thinking about being critical of ADHD research, for this reflection exercise I want you to return to a search engine online. I want you to put on your lab coats and imagine being a scientist. Similar to the way scientists approach research, I want you to be critical of claims and question what you find.

I suggest you remember that since there is no real reliable or valid measurement of ADHD, you should not waste your time looking for claims that a medication treated or successfully reduced the symptoms of ADHD. Instead, look for research that actually provides evidence that ADHD exists. Look for research that connects ADHD with a certain cause, if you will (you know I hate using the C word)—such

---

as brain deformity, environmental contaminant, and so on. Look for real evidence, not just simple claims that medication is the answer.

Once you find the evidence, look for other studies that replicate the research and report the same results. Remember that it takes more than one study to support anything; all findings need to be confirmed. Be critical of the sample they selected to do the study on. Think about what other possible answers might explain the findings.

In other words, go out and do more research on ADHD. But this time, instead of doing the research with the worry that your child might have a mental disorder, do the research looking to see if the evidence even comes close to justifying the claims or putting your child at risk of all of the side effects that come with ADHD drugs and the implications from accepting the label of ADHD.

II

MULTIPLE REALITIES

With part I intended to educate the reader on the main factors contributing to the rise of diagnosing and drugging youth for ADHD, part II is directed at providing the reader with more information to help them avoid becoming a part of this practice—or, for too many readers, to help them navigate their way out of this unfortunate place.

- Chapter 7 provides a crash course in child development (a subject I teach at the university level). For many educators and parents this chapter sheds some light on many other reasons behind behaviors associated with ADHD. This chapter provides an essential piece to fully understanding how a diagnosis using certain generic symptoms can often be explained by what psychologists call a developmental delay or lack of maturation (maturity).
- Chapter 8 provides information on determining and identifying the best education for your child. It takes an inside look at how some schools and classrooms have changed for the better so they can focus more on individual children's behavior and attention issues. This is the prosocial side of education, which is essential to achieving academic success and helping kids reduce issues related to the behaviors associated with ADHD.
- Chapter 9 takes into account how many individuals already recommend therapy for children instead of or in conjunction with drugs to treat the symptoms of ADHD. We expand on the notion of therapy and provide examples of systems-based therapy, which is the basis that many mental health practitioners (marriage and family therapists, among others) already practice. Although the child might be the patient, the symptoms often are the result of family and social dynamics, and we must look at changing the culture a child is

nurtured and educated in if we are to make real progress. This chapter also provides more research, solutions, and suggestions for best practices to shift the focus toward productive, proactive, and holistic approaches to helping kids become better kids and students. To help the reader see that there are multiple alternatives that can become a reality if they can escape from this parallel universe, chapter 9 also explores approaches from decades past, before we started turning to drugs for the answers.

- Chapter 10 closes the book by taking a light-hearted look at what kids want out of life. Readers will be reminded what it is like to be a kid and will hopefully walk away with a new perspective (a little more reason and logic) on the behaviors so many children exhibit. This chapter summarizes the book and also challenges parents and educators to look in the mirror and honestly answer why these kids are on drugs for ADHD. As Dr. Peter Breggin once said, "Every time we drug a child, we are choosing convenience . . . over the child's real needs." I have heard on many occasions what kids really want when it comes to school or their home lives, but not once in all of my interviews and research have I ever met a young child who requested to be put on ADHD medication.

7

DIAGNOSIS VERSUS
DEVELOPMENTAL DELAYS

REASON #7: All of the behaviors associated with an ADHD diagnosis are just common symptoms of childhood development that can often be explained by what psychologists call a developmental delay or lack of maturation (maturity).

When it comes to knowing (learning) how children develop, nothing can replace or compare to the quick and sometimes unforgiving learning curve that comes from actually being a parent or guardian and raising a child. You can read all the books in the world and still not learn the valuable, irreplaceable lessons parenthood provides. With that said, every parent and guardian should read and learn more about the research and theory on child development.

The literature on the subject offers a great deal of information we sometimes miss or overlook as we tackle every new lesson or issue that arises as we scramble to raise our children. Before the chaos of parenthood begins, a lot of expectant parents read books on what they should expect. Many of these are great books that are very helpful to new parents. When it comes to reading about how a child will develop, however, far too many stop reading shortly after the baby's arrival.

Unfortunately, many parents do not read further to learn how a young baby will develop gradually and sequentially (slowly, one stage or level at a time) into a young adult. As a result, they are not given the broader picture that paints how all parents to some degree will observe many of the same development issues in their children. Just like the well-known terrible twos, every age promises certain developmental challenges, and

FOCUS ON THE FACTS

- The literature on child development offers adults a great deal of information we sometimes overlook as we scramble to raise our children.
- Developmental research and theory show that what some want you to believe are signs supporting an ADHD diagnosis quite possibly are just signs of a developmental delay.
- Studies show one of the major reasons a child does not behave to expected standards is often that the ADHD-diagnosed child is not as old as the other kids he or she is being compared to (e.g., not as developed as older third-grade peers).
- The youngest children in a grade are twice as likely as older classmates to regularly use stimulants prescribed to treat ADHD.
- Such diagnoses related to age differences could account for or explain why up to 2.5 million children have been misdiagnosed with ADHD.
- For the youngest kids, it might not even be a delay but instead evidence they might be smart enough to be in the grade yet not mature enough to act like others in their grade; for when their behavior is compared to that of kids the same age in the grade below, they seem perfectly normal.
- Learning- and developmental-theory research provide different theoretical lenses to study how these developmental challenges further explain behaviors associated with ADHD.
- Nearly all child-development theory agrees that children develop gradually and sequentially on a similar but unique time line dictated by an array of issues, with some of them being to some extent out of our control.
- *Stage theory* tells us that children progress through developmental stages.
- Kids labeled with ADHD are probably just one stage away from being considered *normal* once again.
- Much of the developmental process cannot be rushed, but it can be nurtured at home and at school.

knowing about them helps parents recognize that much of what some doctors will want to tell you is abnormal behavior is actually quite normal.

This is why I have often given extra copies of child-development textbooks to many of my friends and family at baby showers. I often have these books lying around my office, sent to me unrequested and free of charge, from publishers trying to get me to use them in my courses. Yes, I will admit, I am a regifter. And, to be sure, a regifted textbook on the science of child development is not as exciting as opening up a beautifully gift wrapped multiprimary-colored Mozart whistling teddy bear covered with geometric shapes that detach and turn into a mobile of flashcards so your baby can read, but these course books are loaded with a great amount of useful information every parent should know.

CHILD DEVELOPMENT 101

Several of the courses I teach are focused on child development. But there is far too much on that subject for us to cover in much detail in this short chapter. So I am basically giving you a crash course in Child Development 101. My goal is to cover about five main points I hope will help you understand a bit more about child development, make you feel a little better about your child, and maybe even inspire you to find out more.

In Child Development 101, among other things we are

1. exploring the basics of what developmental and learning theories tell us about how all children develop
2. further detailing how development impacts a child's emotional and behavioral responses
3. looking at how many of these emotional and behavioral responses are related to brain development
4. looking at how parents and educators should work together to nurture this development and
5. looking at how practicing patience, when raising children, is much more than a virtue—it is a necessity.

But our main goal here is to look at diagnoses versus developmental delays—that is, what some want you to believe are signs supporting a diagnosis for ADHD are quite possibly merely signs of a developmental delay. All of the eighteen symptoms used to diagnose ADHD, if looked at negatively, are only signs that your child has not yet learned to think and behave in a way that some expect of children. No matter if the behavior is due to a developmental delay, unique characteristics of children, or just plain unrealistic expectations of children, it is not guaranteed that the child will never learn how to improve these behaviors.

In other words, while some are a little delayed in learning how to behave like the other kids in their grade, in time most will catch up. And if they don't behave exactly like the other kids, it's typically not a sign the sky is falling. As you are about to read, there are many reasons beyond an ADHD diagnosis that can explain why some children's behavior seems different or more unacceptable than others'.

LISTEN UP, YOUNGIN!

In 2010, an interesting ADHD study done by researchers at Michigan State University was discussed on a twenty-four-hour cable-news service. According to the news reporter, the study had documented that if a child was the youngest in their classroom, they were two times more likely to be diagnosed and drugged for ADHD. The study suggested that quite possibly the diagnosis for ADHD in classrooms across the country was linked to how old the child was in comparison to other classmates.

This news story was intriguing because unlike a great amount of the pseudoresearch publicized on ADHD it made sense—good, common sense. The reason some kids weren't behaving to grade expectation was possibly due to the fact that they weren't as old as the other kids they were being compared to in their grades. They were not as developed or mature.

The study found that a significantly higher percentage of kids labeled with ADHD were born in the month prior to their state's cutoff date for kindergarten eligibility, while the ADHD-diagnosis rates dropped noticeably in the kids born in the month immediately afterward. Quite often kids, who start early, especially young boys, are typically not only the youngest but also the most developmentally immature children within the grade. As the study discovered, the youngest children in fifth through eighth grades are nearly twice as likely as their older classmates to regularly use stimulants prescribed to treat ADHD. The study also found that diagnoses (or, more accurately, misdiagnoses) related to these age differences could explain why up to 2.5 million children have been diagnosed with ADHD.

The study also found that this age difference strongly influenced a teacher's assessment of whether a child exhibited ADHD symptoms. But this was not the case for parents. The findings suggested that many of the ADHD diagnoses might have been driven by teachers' perceptions of poor behavior among the youngest children in the class. If you are a parent who has picked up this book because you are concerned about your own child and ADHD, think about how old your child is compared to the other children in the class. Might this research shed some light on why your child has been singled out for ADHD diagnosis?

Unfortunately, this study shows us that instead of using the behavior of kids the same age (a more similar developmental level) to decide whether the behavior of a child is much different (abnormal) from their peers', researchers are instead using kids in the same grade with differing ages (older kids) as the comparison group. As you probably already know, and as the next chapter will discuss in greater detail, when it comes to comparing kids in preschool or specific elementary grades, we often see a large difference (significant variance) in behavior.

Due to the many different developmental levels through which pre-school- and elementary-age children progress, we observe a wide spectrum of student behaviors in elementary and middle-school children that show us that some have matured more quickly than others. This is due to a child's individual progression along a gradual and sequential path to becoming a young adult. This study and others similar to it show us that for at least 2.5 million children, they have quite possibly been misdiagnosed with ADHD because of their developmental delays. And for the youngest kids in a grade, those who started early, technically it might not even be a delay, but just evidence that though they might be smart enough to be in the grade, they might not yet be mature enough to behave like others in their grade; though they would seem perfectly normal when compared to kids in the grade below them—kids their own age.

I Have A Theory

Although some have said that the work my colleagues and I have done to investigate the multidimensionality of education and the concept of prosocial education may someday provide the basis for theories for improving learning and development, at this point we really don't have a theory. While the comments are quite flattering, you shouldn't take my quip that "I have a theory" literally. My views, as one of my memorable professors labeled them back in the 1980s—when I was younger and dumber and sporting a semimullet—are *Corriganisms*, not necessarily theory. I share this because for theories to truly be considered theories, they must be supported by years of research, where the findings have been replicated by many others so that one can document certain axioms (premises or ideas supported by evidence) related to the theory.

As you might know, a theory is defined as an integrated set of concepts and principles developed to explain a particular phenomenon, like child development, for example. Unlike a hypothesis, known as an educated guess, theories are supported by facts based on sound research. It is important to understand these definitions and expectations of theory, because the learning and developmental theories to be shared in this chapter have decades of research to support them.

And it is not just one theory. There are many theories related to child development. But by having many theories that in many ways complement each other, if not overlap, we are able to look through similar yet slightly different theoretical lenses to study the ways a child's development is guided.

The two things that nearly all theories in child development agree on are that children develop gradually and they develop sequentially. Since these two terms have been mentioned a few times now—gradual and sequential—we should explain them. So, what *does* gradual and sequential development mean to a child?

TAKING BABY STEPS

Unlike Siddhartha Gautama, the Buddha, children are not typically born under sal trees as prince prophets-to-be, able to talk and walk. Nor when they take their first steps do lotus flowers blossom under their feet. It is typically the opposite. And if they are like most children in their early days, destruction often follows in their paths.

As we all know from watching them over many months and years following birth, they slowly develop the ability to lift their heads, roll over, scoot on their butts, crawl on all fours, and eventually walk and then run. During that time they also learn how to grasp things—cabinet doors, pets' tails, and many other objects we thought or hoped were out of reach. They learn how to climb excessively, and they develop ways to climb higher than we ever expected.

These are just some of the milestones that one of the great learning and developmental theorists, Jean Piaget, describes in the first of his four-stage theories (models) of cognitive development. By *cognitive development* Piaget refers, basically, to the ability to gradually and sequentially move toward thinking more deeply and clearly. As table 7.1 illustrates, the four stages of cognitive development that Piaget uses to document a child's gradual and sequential development are, in order, sensorimotor, preoperational, concrete operations, and formal operations.

In the sensorimotor stage, children are learning how to create what Piaget called *schemes*. In this stage they are learning how to use their brains. While in the early days of their lives they could only focus on what was directly in front of their faces for a nanosecond or ten, slowly they begin to develop the brain power to create schemes that allow them to focus on many objects and connect several objects in the room. But slowly they figure out how to use all of them.

For example, I remember one day coming down to the kitchen and finding that my son (about nine months old at the time and unable to

TABLE 7.1 Jean Piaget's 4-Stage Theory of Cognitive Development

STAGE	PROPOSED AGE RANGE*	GENERAL DESCRIPTION	DEVELOPMENTAL EXAMPLES ACQUIRED
Sensorimotor	Birth to age 2	In this stage children develop schemes based mainly on behaviors and perceptions. In the early parts of this stage, due to the inability to focus on anything beyond what is in front of them, they focus on what they are doing and seeing in the moment.	• Object permanence: realizing objects continue to exist even after they are removed or covered from view. • Symbolic thought: develops ability to see physical objects and events as mental entities (symbols). • Trial and error experimentation with physical objects: exploration and manipulation of objects to determine their properties.
Preoperational	Age 2 through age 6 or 7	Due in part to a fast-developing language and the symbolic thought it feeds, children can now talk and think about things beyond their immediate experience. They do not, however, reason or behave like adults yet.	• Language acquisition and development: vocabulary is increasing rapidly as well as the ability to create grammatical structures. • Intuitive thought: some logical thinking based on hunches and intuition rather than on conscious awareness of logical principles.
Concrete Operations	Age 6 or 7 through age 11 or 12	Adult-like logic appears but is limited to reasoning about concrete, real-life situations.	• Class inclusion: ability to classify objects as belonging to two or more categories simultaneously. • Conservation: ability to realize the amount stays the same if nothing is added or taken away, regardless of alterations to shape or arrangement.
Formal Operations	Age 11 or 12 through adulthood	Logical reasoning processes are applied to abstract ideas as well as to concrete objects and situations. Many capabilities essential for advanced reasoning in science and mathematics appear.	• Proportional reasoning: conceptual understanding of fractions, percentages, decimals, and ratios. • Reasoning about hypothetical ideas: ability to draw logical deductions about situations that have no basis in physical reality.

walk at this point) had removed the safety gates blocking his path and pushed the cat's scratching castle from the family room into the kitchen. By *scratching castle* I am referring to a carpet-covered stack of plywood boxes my wife and I had paid entirely too much money for to give our rather moody half-Siamese cat a safe spot to rest, above and away from our two one hundred-plus-pound dogs. My son had discovered that if he put the carpeted castle in front of the counter that led to the cabinet containing the cookie stash, he, with all of his newfound superchild brain power, strength, and agility, could get cookies before we discovered his master plot.

In this sensorimotor stage, children use trial-and-error experimentation to figure out how things work. In this stage, they learn that the guy play-ing peek-a-boo in the seat behind them hasn't really disappeared behind his hands. They learn that physical objects and events have symbolic meaning (e.g., *cabinet door open* means *cookies*, *Christmas* means *Santa comes with presents*).

All kids go through this first stage. But don't let the figure's specified age range of birth to two years confuse you. As the asterisk next to *Proposed Age Range* is meant to clarify, some children reach more advanced stages earlier and others a bit later. So even though they will all go through these four stages sequentially, not all will go through the stages at the same rate of speed. Actually, what we often find is that some will go through one stage really quickly but the next very slowly. Others will go through first one or two stages quite slowly and then excel in later stages. It truly just depends on the kid. But some will go through the first two or three stages quickly and then have troubles reaching the third or fourth. This is where the diagnosis of ADHD comes into play, unfortunately.

All the World's a Stage

Look closely again at table 7.1, giving a bit more attention to the second, third, and fourth stages. Look at the age ranges, and read the general descriptions. Think about how these age ranges relate to different grade levels and behaviors we might expect of young children. If your child's school is similar to most, you will probably find two if not three different ages within each grade level. This is because some start school early, some start on time, and others push the barrier, starting late—or maybe had been held back a year due to an earlier diagnosed developmental issue or learning disability.

Think about how millions of kids being diagnosed today with ADHD are in these younger age ranges that overlap several of Piaget's devel-opmental stages and often exist within several different grade levels. When it comes to ADHD, what we are most likely seeing when kids are diagnosed before the ages of six or even eight (or possibly in some rare cases as late as nine) is that the child is moving more slowly through the preoperational stage than what the parents and educators want.

For these many children moving slowly through the preoperational stage, the adult-like logic we begin to see at the third stage of concrete operations is not happening quickly enough. For example, as the majority of kids in first grade have progressed into Piaget's third stage, some kids are still trying to catch up. For kids diagnosed with ADHD between the ages of ten and thirteen, the case might be that they are not yet displaying the logical reasoning skills associated with the fourth stage of formal operations.

But instead of reviewing the research on Piaget's theory of cognitive development that all educators and therapists are aware of, and remembering or realizing that the research shows us that all kids will gradually reach stages three and four (unless severely mentally challenged with extreme autism or possible intellectual disabilities), our schools and doctors' offices are rushing to judgment. Instead of giving a child the extra support and time to develop on their own predestined or preprogrammed time line, we drug them into at least not misbehaving or disrupting the class with their child-like behavior—that is, their delayed or slower development.

What many are failing to realize is that although a child's development might be slow going in stages one or two, if they are not given ADHD drugs to manipulate their brains they might move with lightning speed through stage three and possibly four. A perfect example of a child who experienced delayed development in the earlier stages is Albert Einstein.

Little Albert Is Not That Different

Historical research suggests that Einstein did not say his first word until the age of four. His parents even worried that he had a learning disability because he was so slow in learning to talk. As a child he also avoided other children and was known for his extraordinary temper tantrums. When he started school, however, he was a good student, creative and a persistent problem-solver. But he hated the rote learning and disciplined teaching styles of the educators at his Munich school. As a result, he had his issues and eventually dropped out when he was fifteen. Luckily for him he was able after several attempts to pass the entrance examination for a polytechnic school in Zurich, and the rest, as they say, is history.

What many are failing to accept or admit is that nearly all children in our country will reach stage three and most stage four. But they will do it on their own time line. ADHD does not have the research to suggest that kids who behave a certain deficient way between the ages of four to fourteen will never change or improve. Although some of them might still have some of those annoying behaviors or ADHD-like traits as adults, to some degree, the great majority if not all of them will at some point grow up. Even if they still display these behaviors, chances are that they are rarely as annoying as they were when they were clueless children. But, for that matter, who would ever want to stop being creative in thought and energetic in life? Child-development theory, however, does have the research to show you that your child will develop and learn how to better manage their behavior.

To some degree, it is a "wait and see" process. But there is much we can do to help them find their path as we wait. What many are failing to do is realize that slow, gradual development is normal. Think about it: If 6.5 million kids are being labeled with ADHD and millions of other kids are being given other labels related to behavioral challenges and learning disabilities, isn't it quite possible a large percentage of these kids are just kids performing at a developmentally delayed level or behaving in a younger, less mature manner? You don't have to look in the back of the book for this answer. The answer is yes.

The Promise of Piaget and Stage Theory

One of the greatest contributions of Piaget's theory of cognitive development is that he studied (tested) his model in many parts of the world and found for the most part that the stages describe well how all children progress into adulthood. Sure, the theory has some weaknesses. For starters, the age groups are just too limited to capture the diverse differences with only four stages. To compare two- and three-year-olds to four-, five-, or six-year-olds seems delusional to those who have raised kids or worked with others in these age groups. These two age groups seem as different as night and day. Maybe it is that ability to actually get off the couch and use the bathroom that amplifies the differences.

Plus, society has changed considerably since Piaget first developed his theory. With advancements in technology, media, transportation, and so much more, kids are exposed to many more and diverse stimuli than were the children he studied. This means that many kids today are possibly performing years ahead of what he had predicted they should, due to advances in technology that help them better and more quickly understand things like *proportional reasoning* related to fractions, percentages, and decimals.

But at the same time some kids—especially kids from lower SES settings—aren't always privileged to have such high levels of stimuli provided. As a result, many kids are behind on development according to Piaget's model. But this means that in any given classroom the range and number of kids displaying signs of advanced development to delayed development has widened and increased, a situation that makes it very difficult to teach. In education they call efforts to teach to this range of learning capabilities and developmental stages *differentiated instruction*. Recent research has shown even more clearly that some cultures aren't even trying to have kids reach stage four because they feel it is irrelevant.

But what Piaget's theory does is show us how there *are* developmental stages that every child must progress through; that's why we call it *stage theory*. It shows us how kids, for a number of reasons, move at different speeds sequentially through these stages. This is why the ages in stages two through four provide such a wide range and no specific beginning or ending age. They say it could start at age six or maybe seven, possibly going through age eleven or twelve. Regardless of the actual age at which it actually happens, Piaget's theory shows us why we see a wide array of different behavioral and emotional capacities within certain grade levels and classrooms.

THE BUILDING BLOCKS OF
HOW CHILDREN LEARN

One of the more popular and accepted theories of learning is referred to as *constructivism*. This idea or theory is basically built on the belief that children build and create their own knowledge. In other words, knowledge is not necessarily shared, but it is learned. Think about how we really learn—and by *learn* I mean figuring out something that forever changes how we behave or do something.

Typically, we do not learn major lessons in life through hearing them from a peer or adult role model. Being told something just doesn't root the lesson in our brain cells for future use. We have to experience it (process it) and figure it out (do it) ourselves. If this were not true, children would learn much more quickly at a much earlier age that we adults are right about how it makes good sense to take a bath, not play around in the parking lot, or not misbehave in school.

Another theorist developed a theory rich in constructivism at the same time Piaget was developing his theory of cognitive development. Lev Vygotsky's theory, similar to Piaget's, posited that there is a sequence or model to how children build knowledge or the ability to think.

Vygotsky believed that children must first build and secure one level of learning (development) in order to move up to the next level of learning. He called this *scaffolding*. In simple terms, you can't build the first floor and third floor of a house (with bricks or cardboard building blocks) without first securing a foundation and also including a second floor.

Children's knowledge (or ability to think and act) must be built one level at a time. To understand how to add numbers, we must first learn to recognize numbers and count. In order to multiply numbers, we must first learn to add and subtract. There are stages, levels of scaffolding, that must be learned before moving upward to harder concepts.

Despite the best intentions of parents, we sometimes miss an important part in helping our children build foundations essential to general learning when they are young. For those parents who have to rely on others or formal day care settings where chaos might seem to be the daily theme, this challenge can be magnified. Unfortunately, these settings often also open the door to kids learning unwanted behaviors or thought processes from observing other less well-behaved or well-nurtured children.

Or maybe the parents and day care settings provided the foundation and first levels of learning essential for preparing a child for school, but upon starting school the kids experienced challenges in building the second levels of scaffolding pertaining to different subject matters or behavior issues. And as they struggle to even get close to reaching the third floor without having established the second floor properly, they now appear to be behind as others finish building their houses of thoughts' third levels. A delay in development, or the ability to develop the cognitive abilities to learn and behave as expected, can happen many different ways.

Let Me Count the Ways

As Vygotsky and other sociocultural theorists have proposed, the role of social interaction and a child's cultural heritage (the culture or setting in which they grow up) is quite important to how that child develops. Sociocultural theory believes that parents, teachers, and peers play an instrumental role in helping a child learn culturally prescribed ways of thinking and behaving. This simple idea that one's culture strongly impacts learning and development, which makes good common sense, is a sign of a good theory. Good theories should be simple.

As you can imagine, given that a child must often try to figure out and connect everything (good and bad) that they have learned from their home, family, friends, school, after-school or day care settings, playgrounds, and neighborhoods, it takes them a while to test and try out these behaviors and cognitive practices. Through trial and error they gradually adapt and adopt behaviors. The question or unknown variable, which will determine whether life is good or going to be tougher when it comes to helping your child develop according to sociocultural theory, is what behaviors they observe and adopt and how they adapt them. As we will see shortly, this adoption and adaptation process is highly reliant on how the behaviors they try out are reinforced or punished.

Vygotsky is also famous for theorizing the *zone of proximal development* (or ZPD), which basically represents a teaching strategy to help children learn. The belief is that there are a range of tasks children cannot yet perform independently but can perform and learn with the right amount of help and guidance from others. ZPD instructs us first to consider the difficulty of each concept or lesson the child is learning. Like the story of Goldilocks, where one bowl is too hot and one is too cold but the third is just right, ZPD reminds us that there are three possible situations that exist for learning life's lessons.

The first is that a concept or lesson is so simple (so easy) that the child does not need any help solving the problem. The second is that the concept or lesson is so hard that there is no way the child will learn it without help. And the third, ideal, situation is that the concept or lesson is hard enough that the child needs our help (our guidance) but with our help can learn the right answers the right way. Think about this for a moment.

Anything that is too simple to do does not create a real learning outcome. Simplicity does not require our brains to think deeply, and, therefore, we do not always register the importance of building the connection between the brain cells to be stored in our memory. A truly hard situation where the child is basically guaranteed failure to learn often creates unwarranted stress, which often leads to the child giving up and not wanting to learn at all. In fact, such stressful learning experiences often result in developing a "mind block" in our brain cells to remind us to shut down when being told to try and repeat this difficult learning experience. But when we can create a situation that challenges the child to think deeply, and we are able to help them (guide them) in solving the problem and learning the lesson on their own, well, this is the zone we want to be in.

Good teachers and smart parents understand the importance of ZPD when helping their children learn anything from common-sense lessons to academic subject matter. They understand that it is normally better to be the *guide on the side* rather than the *sage on the stage*. By not just telling children what to think or know because we are experts and know everything, but instead guiding them to discover the answers themselves, we are practicing constructivism. We are letting children build meaningful knowledge. We are letting children develop the tools they need to learn on their own. Sometimes this is also called *discovery learning*.

Unfortunately, today's hectic family schedules and the inability of our current education structure to allow a teacher (in kindergarten through twelfth grade or even sometimes in preschool) the luxury to truly focus on helping each child find that ZPD mean that attention to controlling the learning environment and offering the support and guidance needed is often left by the wayside. And if this guidance is abandoned too often early in life, the child is left to his or her own devices to learn (without sufficient guidance or support) and falls behind developmentally when it comes to cognition—that is, when it comes to the ability to think and act properly. But even when we do all of the right things and take every precaution to raise the mystical "perfect" child, we still sometimes fail. This is why teaching and being a parent seem at times to be as difficult as rocket science.

Easy as Cake

Raising children is kind of like baking. It requires strict attention to detail and takes a little experimentation to figure out the best way to do it. With children, we have to be fully aware of all of the ingredients needed to help them develop properly and turn out wonderfully. We can't rush the process, and we definitely can't forget about them. But unlike a cake, children are extremely resilient. And even if we fail at some point as a parent or an educator, there is always time to help them learn and catch up.

Many couples have adopted children with very troubled childhoods, and, after a few years of hard work and lots of love and patience, these kids developed into wonderfully adjusted people. Many parents who do a great job raising children during the early years run into problems when the school years start but despite the challenges still manage to overcome behavior or performance issues with just a little more (okay a lot more) effort. Many times a teacher is part of these success stories and is often credited with helping these children catch up with their peers within a year. But there are just some things that will arise along the way that are to some extent out of our control. Even the best and most successful parents and teachers at some point run into challenges. Why is this so?

REPROGRAMMING THE PREPROGRAMMED

To some degree, our kids are wired. By *wired* I don't mean hyper and full of energy but that they are programmed (or preprogrammed) to behave in a certain way and develop by following along a certain path. Some of these things that our children are preprogrammed to do at some point can begin to become a problem. As a result, we often need to reprogram the preprogrammed. Other times the preprogrammed wiring takes a while to connect.

One of these preprogrammed things that unfortunately takes time for kids to develop—but with a little help *will* develop—is *delayed gratification*, which is defined exactly as it sounds: having the ability to delay the need for gratification (fulfillment or delight). Kids of parents who do not try to help their children develop the ability to delay gratification are often quite challenged in elementary school, and let's just say that in the high school and college years they can become a nightmare.

"Are we there yet?" "Are the brownies ready?" Parents, you've probably heard this a thousand times from your kids. These questions are perfect examples of kids' inability to delay gratification. It starts to show when they are babies and toddlers. You take away a toy for just one second, and they start to scream.

My five-year-old reminded me of this slowly developing ability this past spring when we made the unfortunate mistake of telling him four weeks before school was out that we were going on a family vacation to DisneyWorld when school ended. For four weeks we heard the same question: "When are we going to Disney World?" As the weeks went by, the question ended with statements of desperation and disgust: "It's taking forever. We're never going to go!"

Although in grades three through five we start to see progress in a child's ability to delay gratification, it doesn't get much better, or better quickly enough, as they move through elementary and middle school. Technically, delayed gratification is when kids are able to live with small, immediate reinforcers (e.g., rewards) in order to score big if they wait patiently. The fact that kids are often not preprogrammed well enough to exhibit delayed gratification earlier than we want begins to explain how this developmental challenge relates to academic challenges. Not being able to understand that if they pay attention, behave well, and work hard on math for the next forty minutes they will then get to do recess evidences a lack of delayed gratification.

This is why many parents and educators understanding the challenges often provide mini-lessons to help kids practice delayed gratification: "If you work hard this week, we will get ice cream on Friday." Sports or music lessons help them with this challenge as well. Mastering a sport or instrument takes time and requires patience. Such mini-lessons teach children that most good things in life come from waiting and working for it.

Additional Preprogrammed Challenges Related to Social Life

On numerous visits to elementary schools I have seen a few young kids playing by themselves on the playground. They're often talking to themselves. It's quite possible they are trying to convince themselves to wait for the gratification. But at the same time they might be discussing an important issue of global significance with their imaginary friend. Vygotsky called this *self-talk*.

Self-talk plays an important role in cognition development. By talking to themselves, these kids are able to learn and guide their behaviors through difficult tasks or situations. This typically is a sign of their emerging and developing ability to think and grasp language. But let's admit it: we adults have done the same thing on occasion as we drive home after a long day of work.

Unfortunately, if this self-talk goes on into the elementary grades for too long, little Tommy gradually becomes the kid the other kids talk about or pick on. Because, unfortunately, despite how well self-talk helps us to figure things out and vent our frustrations, it makes us look a little crazy. This is why over time kids learn to turn their self-talk into what Vygotsky called *inner speech.*

Inner speech is when we talk to ourselves mentally rather than aloud, and it's something we do all the time. It is an automatic function most of us cannot get our brains to stop doing. But it helps us think. In fact, the smartest people you have met, kids or adults, probably either talk aloud or mentally to themselves quite often.

We do it on tests. We do it to get through long lectures for school, training sessions at work, or sermons at church. We do it as we read a book. We do it as we listen to our significant others explain that we never listen. But kids do it quite often to complete schoolwork or deal with the challenges involved with socialization (fitting in with other kids).

One of the biggest things we all need to feel good about in life is the acceptance of others; none of us set out to not be accepted by others. We want to be a part of *the* group or at least *a* group. This is even more important when you are young and wanting to make friends. And if you haven't noticed lately, kids are still at the most unfortunate times some of the most judgmental and cruel people in the world when it comes to making another child feel like dirt.

Consider the bullying that has become a major issue in our schools. Cyberbullying (bullying via social media) has made conventional bullying (e.g., "Meet me at the water tower after school") seem like a walk in the park. It's quite possible that today's kids experience more frequent bullying and other students' attempts to alienate them from the class. So, on top of all of a child's inner workings and wirings as they develop and try to work things out, they also have the outer workings (the social life) making it even harder for them to think and just focus on becoming better kids and better students.

Other preprogrammed issues kids face relate to temperament and moral development. Temperament, or a child's temper, is believed to be genetic; we get it from our bloodlines. You have probably heard someone say, "I have my father's temper." To some degree, this person is correct. Many children are burdened with not-so friendly temperaments that challenge them daily to not become upset or angry.

Combine a challenged temper with a developing ability to delay gratification, impacted by their cultural upbringings (what they see at home or in their neighborhoods) and some not-so-nice kids teasing them about silly things, like talking to themselves or taking ADHD medication, and it makes progressing through the hard parts of child development even more difficult. Then add to this combination the developing reasoning skills to make the right decision, and suddenly once again you discover why parenthood and educating kids is difficult work and childhood can at times seem downright miserable.

The Morals of the Story

Lawrence Kohlberg offered another stage theory, the model of moral reasoning. Table 7.2 shows how the theory posits that kids gradually and sequentially move through the development process of gaining better moral reasoning skills. According to Kohlberg's theory, in the beginning kids do the right thing basically to avoid punishment or exchange favors. Around middle school or high school age, some start to do the right thing based on what they think will please others or because they are starting to understand that rules and laws must be followed.

Reasons for making the morally correct choice, at the first two levels, are not very altruistic or unselfish. We are not doing it because we know it is the right thing to do. We do it to get something, or we do it because we must do it to stay out of trouble or be seen the way we want to be seen. For the most part, the second level of conventional morality is where most of us set up shop for quite some time. As research into the theory shows, very few ever reach postconventional morality.

As I jokingly explain to my students, the postconventional stage seems to be typically reserved for the Ghandis of the world. But I am not sure I agree with the model in its entirety. I have watched young children do the right thing just because they saw someone crying and wanted to help. I have watched adults rush to help another in need with no thought about how it will affect them and then, as the next days go by, do something completely immoral. At times I have wondered whether the model would be improved if we were to look at it as a spectrum going from the left, preconventional, to the right, postconventional.

This way it might better reflect how some days we are postconventional, wonderful, caring people while on other days . . . Well, not so much. But I do think the stages illustrate how many kids, when they are learning what is expected of them, actually debate internally (inner talk) what the morally right thing to do is. The stages of the theory also help explain how some kids develop the morals needed to avoid displaying the behaviors associated with ADHD while others are delayed. This theory also shows us once again how kids gradually and sequentially develop stage by stage, one level at a time.

TABLE 7.2 Lawrence Kohlberg's Model of Moral Reasoning

LEVEL	STAGE	DEFINITION
1. Preconventional	1. Obedience and punishment	Based on avoiding punishment, a focus on the consequences of actions, rather than intentions; intrinsic deference to authority
	2. Individualism and exchange	The "right" behaviors are those that are in one's own best interest; tit-for-tat mentality
2. Conventional	3. Interpersonal relationships	"Good boy/good girl" attitude, sees individuals as filling social roles
	4. Authority and social order	Law and order as highest ideals, social obedience is a must to maintaining a functional society
3. Postconventional	5. Social contract	Beginning to learn others have different values; realization that law is contingent on culture
	6. Universal principles	Developing internal moral principles; individual begins to obey those above the law

Excuse My Brain Part

Before we put all of these developmental challenges together to consider the whole picture and how so many things cause or contribute to developmental delays that might provide a better explanation for the behaviors associated with the ADHD label, I want to share a bit more about the role a child's developing brain plays. In some instances, the interplay between what children inherit (their preprogrammed wiring) and the environment in which they're nurtured takes the form of what is called a *sensitive period*. Unlike some psychologists who want to be more precise about the exact ages in which these sensitive periods take place, I believe that childhood in general (from infancy to young adulthood) is to some degree one very long sensitive period. But there are times in a child's development when specific remedies are needed for the child to get what they really need in order to continue developing gradually.

For example, the quality of nutrition plays a more critical role in early childhood on cognitive development than in later years during middle childhood or adolescence, the reason being that in early childhood the brain is developing more rapidly and must be nourished properly. During these early years it also is important, no matter what culture you live in, to immerse a child in intensive language development. These first five to ten years of life are very sensitive periods for proper language development.

If a young child is not properly nourished to fuel brain development and the brain is not introduced to a large vocabulary as well as other culturally important subjects, the brain begins to self-prune the tree of brain cells (neurons) just sitting there waiting to be stimulated, nurtured, and programmed. It's kind of similar to deciding whether you are going to nurture a tree to grow as big as an oak reaching high into the sky or as small as a bonsai sitting on a shelf. Unfortunately, research suggests that this self-pruning might take place more often with kids deprived of readily available resources, no matter how hard the parent tries to provide them.

Stay Positive

For quite some time now, research has established that there is a strong relationship between socioeconomic status and academic achievement. Research shows that if a child grows up in a home where the parent or parents have lower education levels and, unfortunately, due to reasons such as economics possess fewer resources and skills to provide good nutrition and academic support, the child is often developmentally delayed (or at least challenged). For example, in 1995 a study by Hart and Risley found that vocabulary growth differed sharply by SES class and that the gap between the SES classes was apparent at a very early age.

In the study, Hart and Risley showed that by age three children from professional parents had vocabularies of about 1,100 words, while children of parents on welfare had vocabularies of about 525 words. The children's IQs correlated closely with their vocabularies. The average IQ among the professional children was 117, while the welfare children had an average IQ of 79. Now, since an IQ test is heavily reliant on vocabulary (even at very young ages), it is quite likely that the IQ tests reflect more that the lower-scoring kids were not necessarily less intelligent but instead less advanced in vocabulary, contributing to a lack of ability to explain or answer questions.

By age three, however, the average child of a professional heard about five hundred thousand encouragements and eighty thousand discouragements. For the welfare children, the situation was reversed: they heard, on average, about seventy-five thousand encouragements and two hundred thousand discouragements. You do not have to be a developmental psychologist to understand how these early-developmental challenges and interplay within a child's culture translate into academic challenges or advantages that persist into adolescence. Just starting school with such a smaller vocabulary and not having the self-esteem needed to believe in one's ability to succeed are two pretty tough challenges to conquer right up front. But there is more to be aware of when it comes to the role the brain plays in development.

Stick with Me

One thing we ought to be aware of that is very closely related to the diagnosis of ADHD is a child's ability to pay attention. And this ability to pay attention is completely connected to the development of the brain. From gestation to adolescence and onward, the brain is experiencing what is called *synaptogenesis*, a process in which one hundred billion neurons (brain cells) are being connected by synapses. *Synapses*, as we discussed in chapter 3, are tiny spaces between the neurons where a variety of chemical substances send chemical messages (that is, where dopamine and other neurotransmitters hang out). These neurochemicals help the neurons' synapses communicate and connect with other neurons' dendrites, and this connecting of neurons is how brains are able to store, connect, and recall knowledge—how brains think, in other words. (Take a quick moment to flip back to figure 3.1.)

Take, for example, when we try to remember an actor's name. First, we usually say something like, "You remember her . . . She was in that movie with Kevin Bacon."

Someone mentions *Flashdance*, and suddenly your brain is flying through the connections of neurons to find *Flashdance* stored deeply in your memory. Your brain first sends you down the path of connected neurons that store memories of bad movies you will never watch again, but it hits a dead end.

You think to yourself that the actor wasn't in *Flashdance*, so your brain backtracks and flies off down another line of neurons holding memories of more recent movies. You think to yourself that this task is like going up a creek with no paddle. And then, Bang. Creek, paddle, river—*Mystic River*, Meryl Streep!

Of course, these memories normally only come to us hours later, long after the chance to look knowledgeable to our friends has passed us by. But this neurological delay is often due to the fact that our brain is constantly cleaning up (pruning off) neurons on the branches of our brain that are not being used. Sometimes the neurons we needed to help us remember have been wiped away since they're never being used or haven't been used for a long time. This is why it's so important to exercise our neurons regularly so that our inner janitor doesn't put them in the dumpster of nonessential knowledge or brain cells to never again be recycled at a later date.

This is why stimulating a child's mind early and often, with as much experience and information (i.e., stimuli) as we can give them, is important to early brain development. We are trying to program neurons early so that they don't feel unused and as a result end up getting pruned. We are trying to help the brain program and connect neurons so kids have better knowledge and quicker recall. By the way, much of this cleanup (pruning) is done by *glial cells*; and one type of glial cell is the *astrocyte*. Astrocytes are intimately involved in developing our learning and memory processes. And one area of the brain critical to managing attention and behavior essential to our learning and memory processes is the prefrontal cortex.

Using Their Noodles

A child's prefrontal cortex is a work in progress. In fact, it is under development until our late twenties. Some research suggests that it's noodle-like when we are young. When we are young our prefrontal cortex is so underdeveloped that we can't often handle emotions very well. This is why infants scream at that octave that numbs the adult brain. This is why teenagers cry and sob so miserably after their first lost love and swear to never love again. This is why kids, especially kids in preschool and elementary grades, have trouble sustaining attention as well as reasoning, planning, decision making, coordinating complex activities, and controlling unproductive thoughts and behaviors.

When it comes to attention, a good rule of thumb is to take a child's age and multiply it times two to five minutes (e.g., four-year-olds can focus maybe eight to twenty minutes). Science has documented this to be true time and again. Attention, however, is contextual, and in order to gain attention the subject needs to be interesting.

From personal experience, a more accurate rule of thumb for gauging attention span when kids don't find a subject interesting is to multiply the child's age times one minute. Regardless of whatever thumb you choose to use, after this attention span has been maximized, science documents that the child needs to be thoroughly refreshed in order to regain even this low level of attention again. And yet, knowing what science has documented many times, we still think that children can pay close, sustained attention for twenty to forty minutes per class period for seven consecutive periods a day in schools where recess and playtime or exercise rarely constitute more than thirty minutes over the course of the whole day—in other words, where little mental refreshment is provided.

Believing this, despite the well-documented science to the contrary, is truly a sign that folks behind today's educational structure suffer from a delusional-based mental disorder. The brain is the organ responsible for a child's behavior- and academic-related development. And no matter how much we want to speed up the learning process to prepare our kids to be better test takers at a much earlier age, the brain will not get to that level for the large majority of kids in elementary school and for a considerable percentage for those in middle and high school. Their prefrontal cortexes are not physically capable of helping them program the rest of the brain needed (or using their already preprogrammed brain) to sustain deep attention and create more complex neural connections. And don't forget that the older they get (the closer they get to puberty), the more hormones start to flood their bodies to combine with the neurochemicals in their brain. And we all remember how hard it was to think while our hormones raged.

One other thing to keep in mind is that research has shown that kids diagnosed with ADHD are quite capable of sustaining attention if given the chance to focus on something they are interested in. What this means is that their behaviors are not necessarily all related to an *inability* to pay attention but, possibly, to what they *want* to pay attention to. And as some educators and adults have learned, the first task in getting kids to focus is to get them interested in the topic at hand.

So, Let's Add Them All Together

If kids, regardless of what type of home life they come from, are

1. working with a slowly developing brain to achieve the ability to truly think (cognitive development)
2. trying to capture more strength to have the patience to wait on being gratified (delayed gratification)
3. dealing with a temperament that is telling them to scream or hit
4. wrestling with determining the morally right thing to do in a crazy social environment and
5. being prevented from paying attention or acting appropriately by much, much more that is going on developmentally in their brains, what do you think the end result will look like on a daily basis for most kids who are behind the curve on development?

You guessed it: children behaving like children. Not because they have ADHD but because they are still developing, still learning.

It is a safe bet that normal developmental issues explain close to six million of the 6.5 million kids with ADHD diagnoses—and explain why the diagnosed kids are being medicated. For a small fraction of kids we might truly be seeing an issue that needs the help of mental-health practitioners. But millions of others who habitually, if not uncontrollably, make the wrong decisions to behave or academically perform on a daily basis have been wrongly labeled by those with a license to pill. But the point of this chapter is to show you that all of these things that all kids are dealing with developmentally (and we've only covered a very few of the challenges children have been documented to confront during normal development) can be quite hard to manage.

Throw into the mix a few home challenges and seven hours spent daily in that social incubator known as school today, and what you get is something not yummy like cake. Add to this the overcrowded classrooms where teachers can barely find the time to call each child's name daily let alone actually work one-on-one with each child to find their ZPD. Add, then, the stress created by more homework and testing than has ever been assigned to elementary children in the history of our education system, and the challenge gets worse. As a side note, research suggests that homework for elementary-age children only helps prepare them for homework when they are older; it does not improve academic outcomes later in school.

There are some things that just take time and a great amount of hard work to nurture in a child. Maturity is more than going through puberty. There are some things that no amount of nurturing will speed up. Even when we think we have accomplished our goal and our children are starting to show signs of progress, it takes them much longer to master.

For example, the ability to delay gratification takes time for all children to develop, as we discussed previously. To be honest, *I* still struggle with it. And after a week at Disney World, I couldn't wait to get back home. Like so many other things in life, child development is gradual and sequential. It's just something preprogrammed in our children's brains that we must learn to accept, and we must understand that time, love, and hard work will overcome, not a label or drugs.

SUMMARY

As the saying goes, patience is a virtue. But with raising and educating children, it is a necessity. It is a necessity for our children as well as for our own sanity. But what I will cover in a bit more detail in the next chapter, and what is known to all parents who have raised successful children, is that parents must make just as much effort as educators, if not more, to overcome the challenges their kids face in growing up. Despite the fact that educators play a crucial role in a child's development process, we cannot continue to blame them for our kids' behavior and school performance. We must take equal or greater ownership of the problem.

We have to make our children just as important as any other task we put on our daily to-do lists. We have to make time for them. We have to make time for supporting them with school work. We have to ask our teachers how we can help. And if we don't know how to do what they suggest, we need to ask them to show us how, help us more. This teamwork will benefit everyone involved.

So, the previous was meant to give you some examples of how all kids develop slowly and go through stages or levels of development. They go through this development process on their own time line—not the school's and not necessarily the parents'. Much of the developmental process cannot be rushed, but it can be nurtured at home and school.

Most of all, I hope I've shown you that while so many people will tell you that these developmental challenges are unique to your child, they are not but, rather, are experienced by billions of children worldwide. For centuries, prior to the modern-day pharmaceutical practice of medicating children for acting like children, kids have been quite capable of getting through these developmental challenges. But as we've seen, they do it according to their own schedule.

Many of the behaviors associated with ADHD are just signs of developmental delays and nothing else. Kids being diagnosed with ADHD at five years of age have only been on this planet for sixty months. Why would we expect anyone to perfect social nuances in such a short time?

But if we are complicit with their diagnoses, we are also most likely agreeing to use ADHD drugs and flood the synapses that are essential to connecting neurons with unnatural levels of neurochemicals. As if a child's brain doesn't have enough to deal with already! If your child has been labeled with ADHD or is being recommended for a diagnosis, I hope you realize that there are so many other things we should be focusing on doing rather than labeling and medicating when it comes to helping our children more efficiently develop.

At the least, I hope this discussion has prompted you to ask those pushing the ADHD diagnosis to help you over the next year to first work on addressing the developmental challenges relating to your child's behaviors that they are concerned about. You will be surprised what a year of hard work void of ADHD drugs can do for a child who is behind the developmental curve.

REFLECTION EXERCISE:
DEVELOPMENTAL DIAGNOSIS

Using the Piaget's and Kohlberg's stage theories as outlined in this chapter, take a moment to diagnose, if you will, where the child you are concerned about falls in relation to cognitive and moral development. Consider their age and grade level. Maybe go online and get more detail to help you identify what stage they are at in the models. Take a week or so to try and gauge the symptoms of the child to help you determine where they fall. And once you have come to a conclusion, list what you might start doing regularly to expedite your child's development to the next level.

8

IN SEARCH OF INSTRUCTIONAL INTELLIGENCE

REASON #8: In many circumstances, the behaviors associated with ADHD can be effectively managed through teamwork between parents and educators and finding the education that works best for your child.

Educators and parents know that it takes more than adopting a new curriculum and relying on standardized-test scores to best help students learn to read and write, add and subtract, multiply and divide, or excel in science and history. Of course, learning all of these subjects is very important, but the best educators know that there are other important ingredients to learning. The best educators want to accomplish more, and they know what it takes to do it. They are fully aware that some kids need more time and attention, which is not always achievable with the current one-size-fits-all curricula. Inspired educators and concerned adults, however, also know it takes more to motivate and teach kids so they can do well in life as well as on tests.

Caring educators and concerned parents also know that schools serve as the social incubators kids need to develop into responsible adults. Most educators and adults recognize that school means more to kids than learning how to read and write or understand math. They know that, unfortunately, some kids are often more concerned with their social status and network of friends than their grades. The best teachers and school administrators, however, also know they are the key people with whom kids need to have a healthy relationship in order to flourish socially and

FOCUS ON THE FACTS

- Since our education system was first established, educators and education researchers have admirably been exploring the best ways to help our children better learn while simultaneously developing into not only good students but good people—productive citizens.
- This two-pronged approach is called *prosocial education*.
- As the research shows, when we complement supporting the academic side of the educational coin with prosocial education (a focus on developing the whole child), academics improve.
- Learning all core subjects is very important, but the best educators know that there are other important ingredients to learning.
- Caring educators and concerned parents also know that schools serve as the social incubators kids need to develop into responsible adults.
- When classrooms and schools provide healthy, supporting learning environments, the social-incubation process is quite beneficial to academic goals as well as to personal growth and our communities.
- For many challenged students, all it takes is one teacher, one year, to turn around problems faced in school.
- Often kids labeled with ADHD just need a more meaningful, inspiring education, delivered by a special teacher who loves every child in that class equally, regardless of slightly annoying behaviors, age, race, weight, IQ, or who their parents voted for in the last presidential election.
- This is what all kids labeled with ADHD need and deserve.
- In the following, we'll review more research and theory to help you find the type of education your child needs to improve and flourish.
- This discussion is intended to help you find the instructional intelligence that, believe it or not, is quite abundant even in that parallel universe, Planet ADHD.

ethically. And when classrooms and schools provide healthy, supporting learning environments, the social-incubation process is quite beneficial to our academic goals as well as our communities.

This chapter is intended to share with you what *good* education looks like and to assure you that it does exist and is available to all who wish to provide their kids the best education that meets their needs. Although I have been critical of what current U.S. education policy has done to educators who have a strong desire to inspire kids to greatness, there are plenty of educators out there not letting policy turn their calling into a compliance-based-testing career.

There also are many admirable individuals at the state- and federal-administrative levels who want education to focus on making education more meaningful to every child's life but whose hands are also tied by policy and politics. This chapter is intended to help you identify and better connect with educators to help your kids get through certain challenging developmental phases and identify better types of education to fit their learning styles as well as developmental and individual needs. This chapter is intended to help you find instructional intelligence in the parallel universe of Planet ADHD.

PONDERING THE PYGMALION EFFECT

There is a classic study that I and many other professors still share with students of education every semester. This study's findings provide a lesson that every educator and parent should understand. This study highlights the type of education every child should receive.

In 1968, researchers Rosenthal and Jacobson did an experiment that is known as the Pygmalion-effect study (or sometimes referred to as the Pygmalion-in-the-classroom study). They named it after the legendary Greek figure Pygmalion, who was a sculptor who fell in love with the statue he carved. Why they named the study after Pygmalion will make more sense in a moment.

In this study, the researchers told a group of elementary teachers at the beginning of the school year that they were going to do an intelligence test on the students. They explained to these teachers that this test was special and designed to identify students who were "late bloomers." The researchers told the teachers that once this test was administered and graded, the tests would identify which students in their classrooms would blossom academically in the coming year.

In truth, the test was just a regular, run-of-the-mill intelligence test. The test had no magical capabilities of identifying who would blossom academically. For this experiment, the test basically served as a pretest to set a beginning measurement of how smart the kids were at the beginning of the school year and post-test to see if the students showed significant increases in intelligence by the end of the year. Once they collected the first round of intelligence scores for the pretest, however, they did not use the scores to select who were the smartest or who were the late bloomers. Instead, they chose at random a percentage of students' names in each classroom.

These children chosen randomly (basically, the same as pulling names blindly out of a hat) were the students the experimenters *labeled* late bloomers, and as part of the experiment the researchers shared the names of these random students with the classroom teachers. It did not matter one bit what the childrens' test scores had been on the pretest. At the end of the year, the test was administered again, and the students randomly identified as late bloomers showed significantly higher increases in test scores than the control group (those students not chosen randomly and labeled late bloomers).

For the whole study (before the first test was taken to after the second test scores came back) teachers had thought the experiment was focused on studying student intelligence and using the test to identify late bloomers. The educators did not know that this study was actually focused on studying the impact of teachers' attitudes and perceptions of students on academic success. As Rosenthal stated in 1997, "the only difference between the experimental- and the control-group children, then, was in the mind of the teacher."

When the teachers were informed of the real reason for the study, they reported that they were unaware of having treated the experimental and control subjects differently. Yet as the classic study suggests, teachers did treat them differently, verbally and nonverbally. The kids identified as late bloomers, who supposedly had incredibly more potential, received more positive compliments from the teachers than did their control-group peers, the students not identified as late bloomers. The teachers were proud of the beautiful academic late bloomers they had sculptured.

So what can we learn from this study? We can learn the secret to helping kids succeed in school. The "late bloomers" received the kind of attention and support that every child wants—to be looked at as a child (a person) who can conquer the world and has the brains and ability to accomplish anything. The "late bloomers" received the kind of attention and support that the best teachers strive to give every child in their class every day. The "late bloomers" received the education that every child needs and deserves. From the Pygmalion-in-the-classroom study we have learned, once again, that students don't care how much you know until they know how much you care.

One Good Teacher, One Good Year

For the late bloomers in the Pygmalion study, it was most definitely the luck of the draw. Given the fact that so many people have a personal story about how one teacher in one year changed their life, taking part in the experiment that year probably changed the lives of the kids chosen to be late bloomers. When you take the time to listen to different people tell their stories about how one teacher changed their life and inspired them to succeed, you find that the stories are all so similar.

The stories normally start with how that person struggled in school for many years and never felt as smart as the other kids or how they didn't fit in. Then, one year, a certain teacher actually showed interest in them and expressed how impressed they were with their ability. The teacher in one way or another made them feel they had a future where they could become something wonderful. The teacher made them feel appreciated and wanted. The teacher gave them the dream that every child needs to succeed. That year, as the stories go, was the year they discovered they could be successful. They decided they were smart enough to go to college or achieve whatever it was that could make their life meaningful.

Personally, I am a firm believer that all it takes is one teacher, one year, to turn around a child having problems in school. Beyond the fact that as chapter 7 shared one year can make a huge difference when it comes to developmental challenges, one teacher, one year, can give meaning to a child's life and give them a glimpse at what they can achieve with a good education.

This belief is what inspired me to share with students I taught in the juvenile detention center that being in jail was not the end to their future but instead could be looked upon as a wake-up call. I explained to them that there was only one direction to go in their life, and that was up. I tried every day to share how they could start over and direct their brains (their actions) into doing good and being productive. Some took my advice and rose above the challenges. Some did not. But at least my efforts helped a few; we teachers cannot often expect perfection with so many variables that are out of our control.

For students in middle and high school, who have many teachers, like my students in the jail, things can be harder to turn around. For older kids, however, I still think one teacher, one year, can be the difference; but it might also require a good school that offers a caring and supportive environment.

Maybe for your child this means you need to sit down with your child's teacher and explain your dream. Maybe for your child this means you need to ask the principal to put them with another teacher. Maybe for your child this means you need a new school with a principal who has a different perspective. Maybe for your child you need a school with smaller classrooms. Maybe for your child you don't need a legal designation (e.g., IEP, 504, or RTI) but, rather, a personal promise and commitment from the educators to help you achieve what your child needs. Regardless, when all is said and done, you and your child need a teacher surrounded by a team that wants to help your child succeed as much as you do. As we talked about in chapter 5, you want educators who are just as concerned with preparing your child for the test of life as they are for your child's life of tests.

WHAT KIDS LABELED WITH ADHD NEED

I mentioned previously that some colleagues and I recently finished a handbook on the promise of prosocial education. *Prosocial education* is a term we coined to show that there is a vast amount of research and successful practices documenting that truly effective education, just like a coin, has two sides. One side is to teach kids academics, and the other is to help them grow as people.

I share this with you because I want you to understand that I'm not just a whiner, complaining how bad education has become. I want you to understand that beyond writing this book, my colleagues and I are actively trying to provide our country's lawmakers with research and best practices that could let our educators truly do what is needed to improve our education system. Our intentions are to help educators get back to what they do best—inspiring young minds. And as many educators would attest, Amen! But most of all, I share news of the *Handbook of Prosocial Education* because this is the type of schooling your child needs if he or she is being labeled with ADHD.

For more than a century now in the United States and abroad, educators, psychologists, philosophers, and researchers from many other disciplines have produced a body of evidence that quantitatively and qualitatively informs us about what has worked and not worked in education. As the *Prosocial Education* handbook shares, a respectable portion of this body of evidence on what works in education is supportive of the present-day benefits of practicing prosocial education and its historical roots in the American education system.

As the chapters and case studies in the handbook explain, since the inception of our education system, educators and education researchers have admirably been exploring the best ways to help our youth learn better while simultaneously developing into not only good students but good people—productive citizens. This is the dualistic goal or two-pronged approach of prosocial education. As the research shows, when we complement supporting the academic side of the educational coin with an equal dose of prosocial education (a focus on developing the whole child), academics get better.

With so much evidence documenting what has historically worked in education, it is difficult to understand why some schools are allowing the testing focus to consume nearly every moment of the day and take so many away from also focusing on the prosocial side of education. Schools that focus equally on developing kids into outstanding citizens are seeing higher test scores. Schools that have supported or are helping parents support kids' prosocial development are seeing higher test scores. Schools that focus on prosocial education have happier teachers. So if schools, or, more importantly our government, want higher test scores, then they should start focusing on the kids as much as the test scores. Easy enough, right?

What Is Prosocial Education?

Once again, as with most supposedly "new" discoveries, prosocial education is nothing new. But since there was no name to describe the philosophy that encompasses so many differing yet quite similar efforts in education that focus on developing better kids, we decided to create a new umbrella term and try to unite the forces beneath it. This focus has been around in various forms since the U.S. education system was first developed. In fact, to some extent, it was our initial goal to educate our youth into informed citizens, capable of developing the best country (democracy or republic) in the world.

There are many organizations, programs, and educators still out there today supporting and doing prosocial education. The Association for Supervision and Curriculum Development (ASCD), a large organization doing good work in education, is supporting educators. ASCD says they are "developing the whole child." And there are many foundations and smaller programs trying to do the same.

Rachel's Challenge, a great organization based in Colorado, is using the tragic yet inspiring story of Rachel Joy Scott (the first student killed in the Columbine shootings) to help kids discover their *why*, their reason for wanting to succeed, and create a chain reaction of compassion in schools to help kids achieve their dreams. We see efforts in schools focused on character education, social-emotional learning, civics, service learning, and so much more. Within every school you will find educators practicing prosocial education in their classrooms and hallways and teaching kids essential life skills.

Unfortunately, current policy has successfully loaded the plates of educators so full that the hours they used to spend focusing on developing good kids have now dwindled down to a few precious minutes a day, if not a week. In many schools, new policy requirements have frightened school administrators into further pressuring teachers to focus mainly on preparing for standardized-achievement tests. As we discussed in chapter 5, unfortunately the teachers and the schools are the only ones truly being held accountable for the test, and their livelihoods and existence are dependent on the test scores. But the good news is that there are plenty of schools and educators that know what it takes to achieve and inspire.

How to Find Instructional Intelligence

Believe it or not, it is quite possible that good, prosocial educational opportunities exist in your child's current school. Therefore, much of what I am about to recommend can be accomplished without changing schools. In fact, I urge you to try the following in your existing school before looking elsewhere.

Although we normally use numbers to evaluate the effectiveness of schools, we can typically tell if the school is a keeper just by spending some time there. To do this, you should meet with the principal and the leadership team (staff, vice principals, counselors, etc.) and try to understand their focus and philosophy. Also, meet with the teachers to see how much they like the school and the kids; try to get a feel for the morale.

When it comes to individual teacher's capabilities, you can typically tell if a teacher is *good* by just spending a little time with him or her and seeing how well he or she interacts with students and how the students respond. In other words, the numbers or ratings of schools you find readily available online (typically based on test scores) are not necessarily the answers to determining or finding the instructional intelligence needed by kids who have been labeled with ADHD. Unfortunately, sometimes you just need to go with your gut feeling.

To more accurately inform your intuition, you might start by getting a better feel for the relationships in the building and a taste of what the school climate feels like. A simple way to begin to measure this is to nicely ask what percentage of teachers have been at the school for a long time. I tell my students wanting to find their first teaching job to do the same thing. I explain to them that it is important to know the turnover of the school's teachers and principals. If the school is experiencing high teacher turnover (teachers leaving the school every year) or if there have been a lot of principals or recent turnover with principals, it could be a sign of an underlying problem. Also, take a look around and see how clean the school is, no matter if it is new or old; that tells you a lot about school pride.

Another warning is to not be fooled by words on the wall or words in the hall. I studied character development's relationship to academic achievement for the U.S. Department of Education, and some schools' idea of developing character consisted of hanging up a few posters throughout the school or on bulletin boards with words like *respect, honesty,* and *perseverance,* or with other positive character traits on them. This is not a bad thing, but building character, civic pride, and social-emotional capabilities doesn't happen just through reading posters. Prosocial-education focuses do not develop through osmosis or subliminal programming. Rather, it takes time and focused, strategic hard work to develop kids' ethical, behavioral, and emotional capabilities.

In your review of the school, also ask what they do to help all students feel welcome and cared for as individuals. Ask about how much recess or down time the kids get. Ask about art, music, and physical education. Basically, get a feel for what your child's school day consists of (or is going to consist of) from the first bell to the last. Make sure they are going to get a well-rounded education and not just an endless daily pelting of the four subjects appearing on the standardized-achievement test.

Once you have a feeling that the school has respectable intentions, now is the time to get more specific. What is the average class size? How many students are in each class, and how many teachers or aids are in the classroom to help? Ask what the expectations of the leadership team and teachers are when it comes to communicating and working with parents. Find out if they expect all teachers to be readily available to help parents and students at any time. They need to do more than just require children to sacrifice their recess or break time to ask any questions about what they did not understand in class, as some elementary and middle schools do. Make sure from a parent-support perspective that their policy or definition of parent involvement doesn't just consist of volunteer opportunities to help raise money for the school, attending sports, music, or drama events, or holding occasional parent-teacher conferences.

Ask how they approach supporting kids with ADHD. For instance, at some schools, as long as the "ADHD kids" are not being disrespectful or causing undo distraction, they are permitted to walk around the back of the room during instruction time. As the educators in these schools have learned, this really helps kids with ADHD-related behaviors not feel so constrained. Discuss some of the behaviors associated with the ADHD label that you want help with pertaining to your child, and listen to how they suggest working together. Most of all, do this with someone from the leadership team as well as the teacher or teachers your child will be assigned to if you transfer. Finding out the little things they do, the unique approaches they take, can mean a world of difference to your child.

In most communities there are options for kids to attend other schools if you think a transfer is needed. Beyond other public schools you might have to do the driving to and picking up from, there are often charter and private schools. If you have no choice but to stay in the same school where your child is encountering issues related to an ADHD label, you can accomplish much of what was just shared with the staff and teacher. Maybe the discussion is centered on having your child switch classrooms to be with another teacher who is more understanding of your situation and wants to help.

Communication Is the Key

In most cases, though not all, improving communication and teamwork has been the answer to helping kids get through a tough developmental period. All too often we parents think we are doing enough to support our child but eventually come to realize that we need to do more or something completely different. What you might find out is that the school is doing everything possible to help your child and the only reason they are recommending a diagnosis of ADHD is because they don't know what else to do. This is where you come into the picture.

A little work early on in retrospect will seem trivial to the work and frustration you will encounter if you don't immediately tackle the challenges at hand. Talk to the counselor, who may be able to offer invaluable help. Explain that your child will not be taking medication, they might not even be given permanent IEP or 504 designation, but that you want to work with the educators to provide the systems needed to modify and change your child's behavior and academic performance for the better.

What this means is that you need to have a talk with your child as well, maybe even in the company of the educators involved in the discussion (after you have all had a chance to work out the plans), discussing both the help offered and also what will be expected of your child. Explain to the teachers that you do not want to be a thorn in their sides but only want to make sure that you are communicating so that you know how and what to help your child with, but also so that you and the teaching team are on the same page.

Too often we believe too much of what our child tells us about the teacher and do not hear or listen enough to the teacher's side of the story. Believe it or not, kids are quite good at playing teachers and parents against one another. As one of my kid's teachers wisely explained to the parents at the beginning of the school year, "If you believe half of what your child tells you about me, I promise I will not believe half of what your child tells me about you." To this day I have yet to hear wiser words that so accurately paint the communication challenges between students, teachers, and parents.

Again, this does not mean you should go in and ask for your child's teaching team to create an individual education plan (IEP) or 504. We should not assume this is the right path to take. In fact, I personally believe that if more parents encountering these normal and quite possibly temporary childhood-behavioral and -developmental challenges avoided legal avenues, educators would have much more valuable time and latitude to help those who truly need those designations. With hard work, it is possible to make all of these problems more manageable within a year. So why label your child for the rest of his or her education years with a disorder, disability, or legal designation?

Instead, sit down with your child's educators, and explain that you understand what their concerns are but want to know what they and you can do together to help your child understand (learn) what it takes to make things better for everyone. A good school, and caring educators, will appreciate your efforts and wishes to not rush to judgment to have your child labeled or medicated. Communicate that you want to make sure that the challenges are not just related to a developmental issue or delay before you take additional steps.

CHALLENGES TO BEHAVIORS
ASSOCIATED WITH ADHD

Take a quick look back in chapter 2 or the appendix at the behaviors (symptoms) associated with the ADHD label. Choose which ones describe your child's ADHD-like behaviors. Is your child fidgety, bored, and not paying attention or unable to sustain attention? These behaviors can provide challenges to learning in classrooms, but they are not something we can't overcome.

One thing for sure, however, is that telling a child to get over it and buckle down (". . . or else, young man!") is not always enough to accomplish any progress. For real progress not only must the child try and change, but the teachers and parents will also have to try and change. This is why my friends Doctors Phil Vincent and Doug Grove wrote a book on the three Rs—relationships, rules, and routines.

We must help our kids who are having trouble organizing their days and achieving in school to develop the relationships essential to getting the support they need, the rules that give them guidelines to abide by, and the routines that provide the familiar structure essential to getting through each day. For autistic children, these three Rs have been found to be quite helpful. And as many have discovered, they are helpful to everyone young and old, challenged or not.

We have learned that kids displaying the eighteen behaviors associated with the ADHD label are either perfectly normal kids who are good at being overly annoying or are in fact gifted or experiencing a developmental issue or delay. And what science has taught us is that kids displaying these behaviors often need more structure or want a different approach to learning.

Divergent Thinking versus Convergent Thinking

One other famous person you don't often find on the lists of famous people with ADHD is a man named Socrates. Most of us have heard of this famous Greek sage and how he is considered to be one of the most intelligent people in our short history here on earth. Some don't know, however, that Socrates was a daydreamer; and this is an understatement. Holy cow, could this guy turn out the lights quickly and for quite some time.

It is said that Socrates was known to spend hours in a nonresponsive state. He would be in the middle of discussions (you know, one of those toga-clad debates on the existence of man) and then suddenly tune out everyone as he gazed into the emptiness before his eyes. He even did this on the battlefield. Can you imagine lying down on the battlefield for hours thinking, daydreaming, while the fight raged on? Socrates did.

The point is that even the smartest of people have trouble paying attention or even being polite enough to act like they are paying attention. Daydreaming, not paying attention and thinking about something else, is a sign of a mind that can think divergently. Unfortunately, much of today's education is focused on thinking convergently. Let's explore what this means to children exhibiting the behaviors associated with ADHD.

Divergent thinking, in simple terms, is when we take an idea and try to think of many other things that are related. Some call this brainstorming. Convergent thinking is just the opposite. This is where we take many ideas and try to simplify them into one thing. As the research suggests, divergent thinking is a highly valuable tool or ability essential to harnessing creativity. Though convergent thinking takes some creativity or ability, whittling many things down to one simple focus (a valuable tool in life), convergent thinking for most of us seems a bit easier. Why?

Well, for some strange reason, some of us have a challenged ability or even inability to think creatively. What do you want to eat tonight? Some of us will list all the options, comprising every possible permutation of everything in the refrigerator and cabinets to everything available for takeout, while others will answer "Food." One interesting classic study looked at how many uses a child can think of for a paper clip. When they are young, the list is endless. But as they continue through formal schooling, the number of creative ideas they can think of dwindles down to a few, and not so very creative at that.

Kids who exhibit the behaviors associated with ADHD are showing many of the same signs associated with highly creative minds. Unfortunately, in classrooms today, when something is explained and the teacher asks for an answer to a simple question, like what is an X-ray, they don't want to hear little Johnny ask, "Why are there so few words that start with the letter X?" But guess what? Johnny does! In fact, even though once Johnny is told to concentrate and answer the question, he continues to count the X words in his head. Little Johnny thinks divergently. And this is a good thing.

But if a child thinks divergently, he or she will have difficulties learning from instruction that is trying to force kids to think convergently. Given that it is not as hard to think convergently (e.g., to solve these addition problems on the math worksheet this one way that will produce only one answer), most creative kids find assignments requiring convergent thinking to be uninteresting and want to direct their minds elsewhere. To some extent, the differences between divergent and convergent thinking relate to nearly all of the symptoms associated with ADHD.

It's not that these kids can't put sustained attention to anything. No, it's just that they aren't interested in paying attention to *one* thing they find uninteresting. It's not that they can't stay still or seated; they're just excited and want to do more or something else. It's not that they can't be quiet or wait their turn to answer; there is a lot going through their minds that is screaming to get out and be shared. That voice inside is telling them, "This is a very good idea! Share it with everyone." If you don't believe me, give one of these kids a smart phone, and they'll sit for hours, not moving, playing quietly, perfectly content and focused on the task in front of them. And when you ask what a certain type of angry bird does, they will tell you exactly what it does—as well as the rest of the flock.

The problem is *what* we are teaching these kids and *how* we are teaching it to them. And this is why we must find schools, teachers, and classrooms that understand the challenges and have figured out how to get these kids to participate in the learning process without first medicating them or labeling them with a disorder or disability. It's not always special needs that kids need.

Instead, what kids often need is a more meaningful, inspiring education, delivered by a special teacher who loves every child in that class equally, regardless of annoying behaviors, age, race, weight, IQ, or who their parents voted for in the last presidential election. There are thousands of these teachers and principals in schools today, and they want to help you accomplish this task you face now as a parent. It is what makes their years in education meaningful and fulfilling. It is what confirms their calling to inspire children to greatness.

I Could Be Wrong

As I often say at the end of my lectures and workshops, I must admit that I could be wrong. I can't end this chapter without pointing out the obvious, something I'm sure a few of the educators and mental-health practitioners reading this book keep thinking. And this is the possibility that some kids might truly have some sort of disorder.

Some kids might exhibit severe behaviors associated with the ADHD label that require a more strict and disciplinary-based treatment—what some call tough love. It is quite possible that a few kids who have been labeled with ADHD are truly exhibiting abnormal, extreme behavior—behavior that is so off the charts that one year, one teacher, isn't enough to change. In these severe cases, the solution may require more than teamwork and simple changes to how we teach this child.

If this describes your situation, you should look more closely at the differential diagnoses associated with ADHD. These diagnoses might provide more accurate answers to why your child is behaving aggressively and irrationally. But, don't forget, ADHD-drug manufacturers warn against giving ADHD drugs to kids with aggression issues.

Out of the 6.5 million kids currently labeled with ADHD in our school system, given the many shortcomings of the ADHD diagnosis, it is quite possible that some of them exhibiting more extreme behaviors have been misdiagnosed. If you suspect this is the case with your child, you might want to consider an IEP or 504. It's quite possible your child is going to need you and a whole host of experts to help them get through an intense behavior-modification program that might take several years.

Ain't Misbehaving

In some cases, however, some of the kids have just been . . . how should we say it politely . . . spoiled or raised in an environment where no consequences have been established for bad behavior. And even though the parents have stepped up to support and work with the teacher and the teacher has agreed to work with the parent, there still is little progress being made. Why?

The simple answer is that some kids know what they can get away with. They have worked under this arrangement for so long that it is all they know and they find it quite hard to give up. A few decades ago, educators used to spank students who were out of order, and unfortunately this happened a lot to me too. Did it work? I can tell you from personal experience that this medicine did keep me from misbehaving for several days or weeks. It also taught me to not get caught the next time, which probably helped reduce classroom disruptions. In the short run, however, it only increased the fidgeting I did in my seat, because my butt was sore.

Spanking, or other corporal punishment, was still legal in close to nineteen states as of 2012, believe it or not. Luckily, we don't see it very often due to the extremely high probability that educators will be sued in court for employing corporal punishment. But we have learned over time that this kind of punishment doesn't work very well and often only results in ratcheting up resentment and the likelihood that these behaviors will reoccur or even escalate. If being beaten helped us to behave better and be grateful for being beaten, then we wouldn't hear about the abusive prison guards being the first people murdered in prison-yard riots.

Dr. B. F. Skinner's work in the area of operant conditioning also showed us that punishment, though occasionally effective, gradually, if not quickly, becomes ineffective. What Skinner and others studying operant conditioning discovered is that a response followed by a reinforcing stimulus (a reinforcer) is more likely to occur again. I mentioned these reinforcers earlier and provided rewards as an example of a reinforcer. But rewards are somewhat misleading, because often what might be reinforcing to a misbehaving child (rewarding) might not seem like a reward to others.

Often when bad kids are noticed and reprimanded for bad behavior, they get a positive reinforcement from the interaction. Seems strange, but a study back in the day found that orphaned rats found being shocked by electricity to actually be rewarding when that shock was received while they were cuddling in their cage with the electrically charged mother rat made of wire. Sad, but, then again, isn't science sometimes sad but strangely interesting?

An online search will show you that operant conditioning directs us to look at four things:

1. negative punishment (also sometimes referred to as *presentation punishment*—spanking, for example)
2. positive punishment (also sometimes referred to as *removal punishment*—taking away something of value, for example)
3. negative reinforcement (removing something undesirable, such as the possibility of being spanked, for example) and
4. positive reinforcement (giving something good that is desired, for example).

Basically, to get the response we want from children, we can punish them by presenting them with or giving them a punishment, or we can take away something they have and like. We can reinforce them by taking away something they don't like or give them something they do like.

None of these work all of the time. Even rewards don't work all of the time. For example, we might give young kids a piece of candy if they do something good, but after a time the piece of candy becomes a bag of candy, and then later they must have a king-size bag of candy. You know how it goes.

What we have learned is that we must use a combination of these tools and reduce predictability. It all depends on the child, however, and what gets them to learn that the response they are giving (the way they behave) will produce some sort of outcome, good or bad. Skinner's theory shows us that all kids are different and that for some we have to more deeply consider the role of punishment and reinforcement in order to reprogram their learned behavior.

WHAT DO WE TAKE AWAY?

You would be surprised how much some kids actually like their school when threatened with being sent to another school. The question is whether we can actually follow through on our threats and promises. But often when we begin to take action, explore transferring schools, the kids get the big picture. They realize that they would be leaving their friends behind.

Out of desperation, my mom did this to me once and took me to visit a hoity-toity private school. She had a wealthy and generous long-time friend who offered to pay for it. Upon visiting, I saw all of the other kids in their uniforms, and I just got the sense that they could tell I was a poor kid stepping into their world. For the next week, I begged my mom to not send me to the private school. I promised I would stay out of trouble. And after much debate I was able to stay with my friends.

Did I behave better? Well, I had a few more missteps along the way, but for the most part I was able to make her proud. For most kids, from pre-school to high school, presentation punishment and removal punishment, when used in moderation, can be quite effective when reinforcement is not working. But if this is not the case, you might need to consider some fairly unconventional education alternatives.

For example, some take their kids to military-based boot camps. Others prefer even more extreme measures and explore short-term wilderness-survival boot camps, or, as I prefer to call them, Outward *Bounded* camps. For these camps, children are often woken out of their beds and flown on a redeye, or driven during the dark of the night, to a remote location. The child realizes the next morning that for the next three weeks or months they will need to learn how to listen and behave in order to survive as they travel across the wilderness with a few other bad kids and a couple of tough hombres who they will call Sir or else. These are the extreme measures that only the tired and desperate should ever consider (with much caution) after at least giving it one year, one teacher, or maybe even two.

But some kids might just need a different type of schooling for a while in order to realize that they actually like or at least miss school. Maybe home schooling or online education will work. Though some of these alternative education approaches might seem extreme and maybe more work and risk than they are worth, there are all kinds of alternatives instead of accepting the diagnosis of ADHD and agreeing to drug your child into submission and compliance.

You Are Their Real Answer

As we will see in chapter 9, whether we want to admit it or not we parents are part of the problem and an even bigger part of the solution. While some of the pharmaceutical-sponsored websites want to tell you that ADHD is genetic and that you had nothing to do with your child's behavior (which is an oxymoron to begin with) and, meanwhile, the blinking icon on the right of the computer screen says "Click here for more details on ADHD medication," the truth is something much different.

We parents have spent the longest time with these kids of anybody. Your teacher this year has worked with your child for a fraction of the time. Most of the behaviors kids have adopted are a result of where they were raised and how they were raised. And if that doesn't put the burden on us parents, what does?

Unfortunately, however, many of the serious behavior cases we see in schools are children of single parents. These types of cases are unfortunate because one parent is shouldering the burden of both parents. Plus, most single parents are already stretched thin and to increase their burden is at times impossible. Regardless, we signed up for Child Development 101 and, gosh darn it, we are going to pass this reality-based course!

But if these last two chapters haven't already made it clear, there is a lot of work for parents to do when it comes to nurturing child development and supporting academic success. If anybody tells you differently, it is because they are trying to sell you something that you shouldn't buy. (And all I have is a book, and you already bought it.)

SUMMARY

Although there are some extreme cases related to child behavior that some want to link to ADHD, most of the behaviors associated with ADHD can be managed without the label, without the drug, and without a legal designation. The bottom line is that we just need to get more involved as parents and work with our kids and their teachers more or, if that is out of the question, find a new school or teacher. But often it just takes one teacher, one year, for you and your child to learn how to move forward and improve.

You might have had a similar experience growing up. I can remember a few teachers from high school and graduate school who helped me rise above the litany of things holding me back. Both of them were men. Mr. Hayes was one of my English teachers. He was a little man who was very hard and demanding when it came to schoolwork. But he was funny and witty, which was about the only thing that helped me to attend class and pay attention. And though I have probably forgotten every Latin root and noun, and a great many other things I learned that year, it doesn't matter.

Mr. Hayes pulled me aside one day about halfway through the year and told me that though I probably wouldn't get a very good grade in his class that grading period due to all of the assignments that I didn't do (or do well), he wanted me to know that he thought my writing was wonderful. He said he had rarely enjoyed reading a student's paper more than mine. And he thought I had a future in writing. For the rest of that year, I paid much closer attention in Mr. Hayes's class.

It actually reminded me and inspired me that I did want to go to college and be the first person in my family to get a four-year degree. I suddenly found myself studying, reading, and writing more. It reminded me that my problem wasn't that I was stupid. My problem was that I was lazy and I didn't care. My problem was that I was more interested in being Mike Corrigan the Social Man and Athlete rather than Mike Corrigan the Student.

I don't think kids are that different today. They just need someone in addition to their parents to show interest in their schoolwork and abilities. They just want someone to say they are impressed and show they care. They just want an education where the school and teachers are sincerely just as concerned about helping them succeed in life as they are in helping them succeed in school.

9

ALL SYSTEMS ARE GO

REASON #9: For children exhibiting the behaviors associated with ADHD, the challenges to behaving appropriately are often due to external factors that labels and medication cannot fix.

As a few friends and colleagues have cautioned me, given what I have written about the DSM's shortcomings in providing reliable or valid diagnoses for ADHD, some might think I am suggesting that many of the disorders in the DSM suffer from the same challenges as ADHD—little to no sound scientific evidence. This is true, and many other individuals have stated this for quite some time. Although the National Institute of Mental Health has vowed to no longer fund studies that only use the DSM's diagnostic criteria as their tool for assessment and sampling, I am not implying that the whole DSM is a joke and shouldn't be trusted. Nor am I suggesting the field of mental health is of no value; quite the contrary.

Many of the disorders in the DSM are real and do exist. Though the science behind many of the disorders' documentation still might be in need of help (i.e., more science, better measurements and medical tests), the collection of disorders in the DSM provides mental-health practitioners ways to identify and provide effective therapy to treat disorders that actually exist. This book was intended to show that the way we approach and treat this mythical diagnosis of ADHD specifically is flawed in so many (too many) ways. In most cases, the majority of other DSM diagnoses serve as a starting point to help children, parents, and individuals better understand the symptoms they face. Furthermore, many of the other disorders identified in the DSM are not being used haphazardly to justify and immediately medicate 4.5 million children daily with dangerous drugs.

For example, autism and other learning disorders typically are first treated with behavioral-based interventions, talk therapy, and other

---

FOCUS ON THE FACTS

- The DSM's collection of disorders provides mental-health practitioners with many excellent ways to identify and provide effective therapy for disorders that actually exist.
- In most cases, the majority of DSM diagnoses being used to label children serve as a starting point to help children and parents better understand the symptoms kids face.
- Most of the disorders in the DSM are not used haphazardly to immediately justify medicating 4.5 million children daily with dangerous drugs.
- Not every problem associated with slightly annoying childhood behaviors equates to a mental-disorder diagnosis and prescription.
- The way the DSM approaches diagnosis and treatment of the mythical ADHD disorder is problematic in so many (too many) ways.
- Most adults understand that the behaviors children exhibit associated with ADHD are not always due to a medical or mental problem resting within the child.
- Most adults understand in many cases that behavioral challenges are due in part to a larger system of variables encompassing the child's family environment, larger social structure, and educational experiences.
- This chapter is intended to help you improve the systems being offered to children.

---

more holistic approaches. The diagnosis, for many disorders in the DSM, only serves as a starting point to figuring out how to help children (the patients) improve. Many understand, however, that it is not always the disorder (the diagnosis) that is the origin of the problem.

Many understand that the origin of the problem(s) for disorders such as ADHD is not always due to a medical problem resting within the child. Most understand the problematic challenges are due in part to a larger system of external variables encompassing the child's family environment, larger social structure, and educational experiences. The diagnosis often is just the byproduct of the child's existing dysfunctional environments, relationships, rules, and routines, a system comprised of many variables that impact a child's life.

This chapter is intended to help you improve the systems being provided to children. The goal is to get you to widen your view and extend your insights far beyond accepting a label of ADHD or some other disorder, and most definitely beyond accepting advice to medicate children. The goal of this chapter is to provide you with a brief summary of what many other books and resources offer to help you get active if not proactive in helping your child rise above the behavioral and academic challenges they face.

This chapter provides research, solutions, and suggestions for best practices to shift the focus away from labels and drugs and more toward productive, proactive, and holistic approaches to helping kids become better kids and students. Through considering various ideas for improving the structure and systems contributing to children's challenges when it comes to the behaviors associated with ADHD, creative outlets can be started.

IT'S A FAMILY AFFAIR

Typically under the current approach, once a child is labeled with ADHD, the parents are then recommended to give medication and sometimes encouraged to get the child counseling or mental-health therapy as well. Many studies suggest that therapy or behavioral-modification interventions combined with medication are the best routes to take. As you know already, I disagree with the medication advice, but I do agree with the therapy and behavior-modification part. In fact, you should consider therapy not just for your child but for you and your child if not the whole family.

For example, systems-based therapy is the foundation from which many mental-health practitioners (e.g., marriage and family therapists, or MFTs) already practice. Instead of a mental health practitioner sitting down and focusing exclusively on the child, systems-based therapists zoom out and address many external variables that surround the child. Although the child might be the *main* patient leading the family to a therapist, the symptoms are typically a result of years of conditioning fed by the dynamics existing within family, social, and educational environments. Therefore, in order to truly help a child change or improve their behavior, one must look at changing the culture a child is nurtured and educated in if one is to make real progress. For therapy to be more effective, we must look equally at what we offer and provide as adults.

One way to better understand this approach is to consider how one is treated for a heart condition, stroke, or heart attack. When such a life-threatening condition arises, doctors immediately focus on diagnosing the health of the heart. If surgery is needed it is performed as soon as possible. But to keep the treated heart from relapsing back to its troubled state, the doctors also recommend changing one's lifestyle.

The patient is awakened to the fact that many other things need to change, and they must often be educated as to what the next steps are to follow. Soon after, for those who heed the warning, their diet changes, and they begin to exercise more regularly. They understand that their routines must change and that more sleep or adequate rest is a good thing. They change in ways so that life becomes less stressful. In other words, they are trained or reminded as to how they need to modify their behavior.

Systems-based therapy, or more specifically systems-based family therapy, is not that much different than treating other medical conditions holistically or systemically. But instead of the child feeling singled out and forced to go sit with a therapist, possibly making them feel even more like they are solely responsible or being blamed for everything, they get to go with their parent or parents (and possibly siblings) and work together as a team. During this type of therapy a family learns together what the healthy and unhealthy practices currently embraced are doing to the child (the main patient) and quite possibly other family members or the whole family. They learn and work together to find consensus as to what must change. They learn how to help each other.

What's the Problem?

For some parents the idea of therapy or counseling for the family might seem ludicrous. Some families might have multiple children and only one is showing the behaviors associated with ADHD. They might think this is a sign the one "problem" child is the only one with the problem. Beyond individual challenges the child might face related to developmental and educational issues, often such outcomes can be related to sibling rivalries or inconsistent parenting styles. Another situation that might contribute to resisting systems-based family therapy is that the parents have been convinced that ADHD is genetic and that all of their children have ADHD.

Given that the research supporting genetic links is very weak and ADHD only supposedly exists worldwide within 5 percent of the population, it is hard to understand why such parents don't see that it is strange that 100 percent of their children supposedly have ADHD. Typically from my experience, such denial is a sign that much needs to change within the family dynamics and parenting styles.

One Mother's Wake-Up Call

I remember being approached at an outdoor function at one of my children's schools by a mom of another student I knew. As she stood there drinking her extra-large cup of soda, she began to disclose many details about her personal life and explain to me that all of her children were on ADHD drugs. Hoping to avoid discussing the specifics about the many other personal and family issues she'd begun sharing, I asked her why she thought this ADHD epidemic happened to her family. She explained that ADHD is genetic and that her pediatrician confirmed it was in their family tree. Out of morbid curiosity I asked her what a typical day was like with her kids.

She began by telling me how they woke up early to get ready frantically for school. I asked her if the children ate breakfast before they got on the bus. She said typically they just had a pastry and a soda pop. I asked her what the rest of the day was like *typically* after school. She explained that the kids came home and normally watched television or played video games until dinner. I asked if they ate a healthy snack after school. She said they normally drank more soda and just ate chips or something.

She then explained that they would eat a lot of take-out or fast food because she just doesn't have time for shopping or cooking. The kids would continue to drink soda and watch television into the night. I asked when they did their homework. She explained they typically waited until the last minute before bed to do their homework. Curious still, I asked what time the kids typically went to bed. She said about eleven or twelve. Her kids at that time were seven, eight, and sixteen years of age. And, by the way, the bus came around seven A.M. to pick the younger kids up.

I learned that the kids rarely went outside to play or exercise. I realized she rarely helped her kids understand how to do their homework or reviewed their homework. Knowing I was a psychologist at the local university who studied kids, and realizing that I was starting to wonder what planet she lived on, she asked me what I thought about ADHD. Without dropping the whole story on her as to my beliefs, I just suggested that it was highly unlikely that all of her kids had ADHD.

I softly suggested that maybe she try cutting soda out of their diets and feeding them more balanced meals and avoid eating out so often. I suggested she try to set aside time several days a week where they could go outside or to a park and exercise and play as a family. I suggested she have them do their homework shortly after they got home from school or better yet after exercising. I asked her to not let video games be a daily routine. I also suggested she make them go to bed earlier so they could get eight to ten hours of sleep every night, something very important for kids. I then shared a little more detail on the side effects and warnings associated with ADHD drugs before my kids requested my attention elsewhere and our conversation ended.

This incident happened when I had first started researching ADHD. Honestly, I never thought that my talk with her was of any value. I figured parents that had bought whole hog into this farce that ADHD is genetic and all of their kids have it were incapable of being persuaded differently. But recently I ran into this mom again, and she stopped me to explain that all of her kids were off ADHD drugs. She told me that the talk we had made her "think twice" about what she had agreed to related to the ADHD diagnosis.

On that day several years ago when we first spoke, I only provided solicited common-sense-based advice to her, similar to what you have read in this book. A licensed systems-based therapist or family counselor would most likely have offered similar advice and a whole lot more (especially if they don't believe in medicating children). They would meet with the family as a whole and if need be meet privately with individual family members. They would investigate family and social dynamics. They would ask more questions about challenges at school. They would equally focus on possible mental disorders or abnormal behavior the parents and other siblings might exhibit, and they would look closely at parenting styles, marital relationships, and sibling relationships.

As the research shared with you in this book documents, behaviors related to ADHD emanate from and are nurtured by forces reaching far beyond the child's brain. As suggested, we adults in the children's lives often are responsible for a large percentage of the problems children face. We are equally if not more responsible for offering the support to fix such problems.

When considering therapy or counseling for behaviors associated with ADHD, you should seriously consider systems-based family therapy. Although many adults might not want to share with a therapist details explaining how they might be responsible for such behaviors related to ADHD, the other option is giving our kids dangerous drugs on a daily basis for a long time to come. By approaching therapy as a family unit, greater potential for success exists when the problem behaviors and extraneous variables contributing to the problems possibly stemming from the home environment are addressed simultaneously.

The possibility exists that many parents need more help in figuring out just what they could do better to help their child develop and mature. Regardless of whether you believe such views, most would agree that it couldn't hurt to be a part of the therapy the child is receiving. You must remember that the intent of any respectable therapist or counselor is not to cause harm or place blame but to help you treat the symptoms. At the least family therapy could provide more opportunities to experience firsthand what a therapist is thinking, doing, and recommending in order to treat a child. Maybe the family counseling will allow issues related to the parent-team dynamics to be addressed in a comfortable, blame-free environment. The possibility exists that adults can learn and develop as much as the child.

BEHAVIORAL MODIFICATION
AND PARENT TRAINING

Not many parents would readily admit or feel comfortable with the fact they might need more *training* when it comes to being a better parent. Just the mere mention of such advice makes a parent feel immediately slightly inadequate, not to mention defensive. But let's face it, as parents we are rarely ever informed or prepared for all that we will encounter raising children. So please in this section let us just consider that parent training (learning what has worked for other parents) is just one way of finding help (answers); and let's not try to take it personally. When push comes to shove, however, most parents will admit they could use a little *help* raising their child.

Parents of children diagnosed with ADHD describe their family environments as less organized and higher in family conflict than do parents of children not diagnosed with ADHD. Children without ADHD in general experience higher levels of family cohesion, organization, and expressiveness, and lower levels of family conflict. Such favorable outcomes are positively associated with better behavior and helping children think more rationally.

Children in lower-SES homes more often experience environments where higher levels of family conflict exist and less positive affirmation is shared. Also, a higher percentage of children living in lower-SES homes are labeled with ADHD. Does this mean that all homes of children labeled with ADHD have higher levels of family conflict and other negative stigmas? Of course it doesn't. Does it mean all lower-SES homes are less pleasant places for children to grow up? Of course it doesn't.

But what the research does show is that many kids diagnosed with ADHD have many problems at home that are contributing to their problem behaviors at school. And though schools might be able to provide various academic-focused behavioral-modification interventions, parents still need to be aware of what they can change and do at home that also can contribute to lowering the severity of behaviors associated with ADHD.

If you are not familiar with *behavioral modification*, in simple terms it just means putting a plan in place that provides adults with the structure and procedures needed to try and reprogram children to change the conditioned behaviors they have embraced or adopted. For example, many parents turn to the tested time-out approach to help young children deal with issues related to bad behavior.

By giving a time-out, adults are able to set up consistent routines with rules and consequences that children learn to expect when an incident occurs. As time passes and if the time-out approach is practiced consistently, children slowly learn to think before doing something bad, because otherwise they will end up in a time-out; thus their behavior has been modified. Believe it or not, this simple time-out approach when used appropriately works with a wide range of kids who display some of the uncooperative behaviors associated with ADHD.

There are many resources that can provide you with additional behavior modifications you can try at home. The previous discussion on B. F. Skinner's operant conditioning (the differing use of rewards and punishment) is a theory that guides numerous behavior modifications. From positive reinforcement to negative reinforcement to punishment, operant conditioning guides parents in placing the structure needed to establish consistent rules and routines. Whether you are actively providing rewards or consequences with consistency, such structure is what many children often need and want. For some kids it might even work to ignore such behaviors; some refer to this form of negative reinforcement as *differential attention*.

Most experts believe that behavior-modification methods are never unsuccessful; they are either used ineffectively or inconsistently. This is why it is important to find one that works for you first and foremost so that you pick an approach you can stick with. The last thing you want to do is not follow through on rewards promised or try to be more strict or organized in reconditioning such learned behaviors and then not follow through. But another thing you do not want to do is adopt rules that are too hard or demanding for you to enforce or are too extreme and unfair to the child.

Although this chapter cannot provide you with details on all of the behavior-modification approaches that exist (a simple search on the Internet can provide you with many options), you need to be aware there are many to choose from that might feel better to you and work better for your child. What you will learn when you adopt a behavior-modification program for your child and implement it with fidelity is that not only does it slowly train your child to behave in a different manner, it will also train you how to parent in a different manner. Also, don't forget, effective counseling that typically involves behavior-modification programs were just as effective as the ADHD drugs in the NIMH MTA study and many others.

Plan Your Work, and Work Your Plan

Beyond implementing behavior-modification efforts to develop structure and adopt consistent rules and routines, such structure, rules, and routines can also be very helpful in better organizing our daily practices. If there is one thing we have learned from research on juvenile delinquents and children challenged with conditions such as autism, having structure, rules, and routines can be very beneficial to making every day seem like an average day, hopefully void of or less filled with bouts of high drama and chaos. Structure is why military schools work so well for many troubled youth. Structure is what kids with autism need to guide them and feel more stable. Structure is what all kids want or at least need when it comes to being successful in school. Structure provides stability amid the ups and downs of life.

If we know structure helps kids behave better in general and learn better at school, then it makes complete sense that it could also help with behavior and learning at home. Adopting structure, rules, and routines at home can help a child to understand what is expected of them and when it is expected. Structure provides more organization to set aside time for studying, planning, and eating well-balanced meals. Such organization and schedules can help to more regularly allot time for exercise. And when all of the chores, essentials for a healthy mind and body, and expectations of school have been accomplished, rewards can be earned.

Adopting stricter structure, rules, and routines can still allow for a reasonable amount of time for personal indulgences, not to mention more quality family time. It is important to consider that if we are expecting educators to be responsible for using such behavior modifications at school, parents should also be mirroring such efforts at home.

If we don't have a plan or a daily schedule, we end up too often consumed by spontaneous chaos, indecision, and inconsistency. Constant lack of structure and behavioral expectations (that is, too much free time and too little supervision) lead to kids reverting to their child-like ways. Dogs are a perfect example of this downfall of structure. When my dogs are at home, they know the rules and most of the time behave well. When they are with me on a leash, they are the best dogs you could ever want. Let them loose at the dog park, free to wreak havoc on the masses, and they are two hundred pounds of unadulterated canine commotion that, let's just say, the rest of the dog-park visitors don't appreciate or find to be as enjoyable. By the way, I refer to this condition as *dog brain*.

Some parents who don't yet have a schedule system in place and probably already feel as if you have too much to fit into any given day might look at my suggestion to be more organized and provide more structure and think it's something you can't accomplish. But it is something you should at least consider. Because when your to-do list is too long, that is when you most need to prioritize what you should actually be doing, step by step.

You could start by creating a rough schedule for homework and study time, dinner, exercise, and quality time together. Get a little chalkboard for the kitchen to write this schedule on, and be flexible to adjusting it slightly day to day if extracurricular activities and events arise. If we can at least focus on five of the core components essential to helping kids develop and be successful in school, it's a great place to start as we remain patient, waiting for a child to reach the next developmental stage.

GETTING TO THE CORE OF THINGS

Although structure holds great promise for helping kids challenged by extreme behaviors associated with ADHD, we must also not forget the specifics to the behaviors linking such challenges to ADHD. We must not forget that such children are highly energetic, creative, imaginative, and full of life. And if we do forget this and create structure that takes all of the fun out of actually coming home, we are probably creating more problems for ourselves. This is why we must not forget to keep the *fun* in the fundamental components we use to shape our new or improved structure.

Several years ago, my research colleagues and I were asked by a state's department of education to do a little research into the effectiveness of their after-school programs. We spent about a year consulting on the project. What we discovered in our research was that for several reasons (economics, staffing, and resources) many of the after-school programs throughout the state were lacking the structure and essentials needed to provide the kids with a well-rounded, productive afternoon following a long day of demanding standards-based education.

After completing the project and the report for that state's department of education, we determined that there were five components all schools and youth-focused organizations should be trying to implement in their after-school programs. Given that we knew a good many experts in the fields of the five components we'd recommended, we decided we should invest our time and resources into creating a resource for after-school directors to use so they would have everything they needed (for free) to help kids become better people and better students.

But as we recruited many great partners to help us develop the free online resource for after-school directors, we decided it should be designed to be just as useful for elementary teachers and parents of kids four to twelve. The online resource we created, beneficial to helping children live, learn, and grow, is just a mouse click away.

From our research we determined that after a long day of school kids need to receive more support related to those five core components. What you will find when you visit our educational clearinghouse, www .Core5AfterSchool.org, are videos, activities, lessons, web links, and many more resources and publications that focus on fitness, nutrition, character, academic enrichment, and parent involvement. Our goal is to provide adults who work with or raise young children free access to resources to make every day a great day for their kids. If you want your child to do better in school, behave better in school, these five core components offer structure. In other words, if you want to proactively address the reasons that most are encouraged to seek medical help related to ADHD—these five components hold great promise to help your child succeed.

Play Attention

As you are probably aware, we have a serious issue with childhood obesity, as levels reach the highest they've ever been in both our country and internationally. According to the Centers for Disease Control and Prevention, as of 2011 childhood obesity has more than tripled in the past thirty years, and the percentage of children age six to eleven years in the United States who were obese increased from 7 percent in 1980 to nearly 20 percent in 2008. Similarly, the percentage of adolescents age twelve to nineteen who were obese increased from 5 percent to 18 percent over the same period. Numbers also suggest that close to 60 percent of adolescents are overweight. As a result, the spread of diabetes is plaguing our kids at ever-earlier ages.

Research supports the need for more exercise in our children's lives. Besides the obvious role physical fitness can play in fighting the obesity epidemic and the benefits exercise holds to the health of the body, one must also recognize the neurological benefits that come from the exercise-induced endorphins that produce happiness and more efficient brain functions. If physical education and recess are being reduced during the school day to make room for more instruction, then after school and evenings offer a great opportunity to address issues related to childrens' lack of exercise.

Unfortunately, kids are not getting enough time for play or exercise to reverse this growing epidemic. Despite the fact that physical education has been cut drastically in many schools nationwide, and recess and other creative outlets are disappearing too, educators and parents can do something to fight back. Whether it is formal exercise or exercise designed around providing children time to play, there are many benefits to making this a fun part of a normal day in the life of children displaying behaviors associated with ADHD.

Believe it or not, fitness can be fun. Furthermore, fitness provides many academic, health, and mental-health benefits. For example, many schools are required to take part in a national fitness test every year. These tests are called *FitnessGrams*, and research documents that there is a positive correlation between passing FitnessGrams and increased academic achievement. In other words, the better shape a child is in, the better they do in school.

Research also indicates that physical exercise has an impact on the total development of the child. The Centers for Disease Control and Prevention note that "regular physical activity can help keep your thinking, learning, and judgment skills sharp . . . [and] also reduce your risk of depression and may help you sleep better." Research shows that doing a mix of aerobic and muscle-strengthening activities three to five times a week for thirty to sixty minutes a day can provide many mental-health benefits.

In their 2011 article "Promoting Mental Health through Physical Activity: Examples from Practice," Martin Jones and Carol O'Beney note that "the physical health benefits of exercise are well established, but there is also growing research evidence of links between physical activity and mental-health benefits, including mood elevation, better cognitive functioning, and improved self-perception, self-esteem, and self-efficacy." There is endless evidence to suggest that physical activity has a positive effect on mental health in adolescents and emerging adults.

In other words, physical activity not only improves the body and the academics of students, it also has a positive effect on the mental well-being of individuals, including children. When we exercise, our brains produce endorphins, and these endorphins help to wake up our minds and our bodies. Plus, when it comes to the behaviors associated with ADHD, kids who have high levels of energy need more exercise to release the energy. In fact, they might need more exercise than the child not labeled with ADHD. Exercise not only helps find an outlet for extra energy, it also helps work off stress and rejuvenate.

You might also consider reading the bestselling book *Last Child in the Woods*. It is an interesting take on how children today are being deprived of the outdoors. As author Richard Louv suggests, our children are suffering from a nature deficit, and he shares research that relates the nature deficits to ADHD. Playing outside in a park, in the woods, wherever, is a great way to get some fitness in a child's day as well as give them a chance to breathe some fresh air and connect with nature. There are so many ways to get kids moving. And there are so many ways to keep it novel and fresh.

We Are What We Eat

As mentioned in chapter 7, children need good nutrition to develop. With their brains developing at a rate faster than at any other time in life, they must be fed well and often when they are young. Unfortunately, many live in a fast-paced society where making time for planning and preparing quality meals is a challenge. But as a ton of research on child development emphasizes, a balanced and nutritious diet is not a component we can ignore.

Good nutrition is what a child's mind (brain) and body need. The need increases when children exercise regularly. Even on a stretched budget, you can find a way to give children the nutrition they need. But too many kids are eating not-so-nutritious food on a daily basis.

Some parents allow the child to dictate what they will eat. When given no consequences or monitoring, kids will typically eat a form of fried chicken complemented by a side of sugar, fried starch, and fat-laden carbohydrate. Most of us already know that fried foods, and high amounts of sugar and fat-laden carbohydrates, do not make for good nutrition, but recently researchers at Columbia University have been finding that soda consumption is contributing to ADHD-related behaviors. In fact, children who downed four or more servings per day were more than twice as likely to destroy others' belongings, get into fights, and physically attack people.

Strangely enough, many of the pharmaceutical industry-sponsored ADHD websites want to say that nutrition plays no role in ADHD. When organizations marketing medications that suppress the appetite of children suggest that eating food is not related to ADHD, yes, this is a red flag. But when you read studies on child development, there is an endless amount of research as to how diet and nutrition impact cognition and brain development heavily. Think about it for one second. If you don't eat all day, how well do you do at work? If you don't eat all day, how well do you exercise?

Our brains and body need good food, and when we let children eat foods that are not so high in nutrition, they end up depleting their brains and bodies of the nutrients, energy, and fuel they need to think. And if you can't think well, you probably won't perform well academically or think rationally enough to behave well.

There is an endless amount of research and numerous websites available to you to accomplish this important essential component to positive child development. One such website worth checking out that can help with this component of nutrition is www.nourishinteractive.com. It was started by an amazing nurse named Maggie Labarbera and some concerned adults who wanted to stop the diabetes epidemic. And what nourishinteractive .com, Core5AfterSchool.org, and many other websites will help you see is that, similar to fitness, nutrition also can be approached in a way that is spontaneous and fun for kids and families.

Becoming the Person Our Dog Thinks We Are

The third component of our Core5 focus is character. Research into the character development of children is important. Children cannot become the successful students and citizens we want them to be if they do not have the character traits essential to getting them there. They need help developing perseverance, responsibility, and so much more. And we as adults must be that moral compass in their lives. We must become that person our dog (the one who loyally waits at the door every time we come home, wagging its tail in utter joy and excitement) thinks we are.

There are all kinds of folks out there who want to sell you some sort of gimmick, game, or program, promising to transform your children's or students' character. Some are good products, but many are not so good. But in the end, all a child really needs is you. They need you to help them learn right from wrong. They need you to model the right way. They need you to introduce them to the beauty of all of the diversity that exists in the world. And they need you to help them learn patience and forgiveness.

Much of this can be accomplished by being active in their life and showing you care about them and others. All it takes to get started is prompting discussion about school, what's going on in the world, and what's going on in their life. They need you to exemplify what a work ethic demands. They need you to show them reading is important. They need you to believe that they can achieve anything if they put their minds to it. And some days they need you to push them a little outside their comfort zone in order to truly learn life's valuable lessons. They need you to be there for them when life throws a curveball. And they need you to keep them busy with novel new ways to grow as a person.

I am not a clinical psychologist. So when I offer advice, it is just advice, not counseling or therapy. But sometimes friends come to me with their problems because they know I am a psychologist and for some reason think I can help. Sometimes they are depressed and they are wondering what they should do to get better. On many occasions I have listened to their worries, and then I recommend they volunteer at an organization that provides valuable services to those who need so much help. Personally, this worked for me years ago. And though I thought at the time that my life was so horrible, when I saw the faces of those I had helped and heard their stories, I typically drove home thinking life really wasn't that bad. I drove home thinking that I was not really that bad either.

Kids can build character by volunteering. Such novel activities often help them see that they have it pretty good in comparison to others. As a family you can volunteer together and discover what lessons can be learned through helping others. Getting them to serve as mentors or tutors can be good too. Often times it seems childrens' problems are rooted in their view that they are the ones who need help. And if we can just get them to see things differently, develop more character, and grow as people, this is when we begin to see such annoying behaviors associated with ADHD start to transform into truly super powers. In my opinion,

ADHD is not a moral defect, but the ADHD behaviors are related to the gradual development of morality (or ethical behavior). There is no time like the present to double down on your focus on building your child's or children's character. With so many resources readily available, this is a great way to make structured after-school time fun and meaningful.

Being That Guide on the Side

With spending the time after school focused first on fitness, consuming some good nutrition, and growing as a person (developing character), it is just possible that a child's brain might be refreshed enough and ready for a bit more academic enrichment after a long day of school. Academic enrichment is the fourth Core5 component parents should focus on after school, and it requires more than just having your child studying and doing homework. Once again, structure is important to kids with extreme behaviors associated with ADHD (and kids in general), but keeping one's interest level in mind is very important as well. We must keep things new, fresh, and interesting if we are to keep any child's or young adult's attention for long.

Most of all, we must keep them interested in learning and motivated to learn. Decades of research show time and again that how a child feels about school (what is referred to as *affect*) and how motivated to learn a child is predicts with 20 percent accuracy whether or not a child will do well in school. Throw in three other major predictors of success, such as socioeconomic status, IQ, and how involved the child's parents are in the education process, and suddenly you have painted a picture for what is needed to help a child academically succeed.

If there is one thing I have noticed over my years as a professor, however, it is that more and more kids these days seem to think they should get straight A's in school. Back in my day, this was not the case. Back in my day, an A was for excellence, a B was for good work, C represented average, D meant at least you would get your diploma, and F . . . Well, you forgot to drop the class. But today's view brings along several challenges.

First, it puts a lot of pressure on a child to perform at a specific level of excellence. Second, it sometimes results in kids feeling entitled to top grades. The reason I share this is because not all kids are going to be straight-A students. Some are going to work harder than others. Some are going to possibly even struggle at different grade levels or on different subjects. Some are going to struggle when they switch schools or go to college and realize, "Wow, these teachers expect a whole lot more."

This is why we can't just do our kids' homework. This is why we can't just sit down and make them do their own homework every day at the same time. We must help them in the early years to learn through trial and error, not to mention a good bit of guidance, the best ways to study and prepare. We must mix things up so that we keep learning interesting and keep their young minds wanting to know more. We must help them at the earliest age possible to develop a strong connection to education and an intrinsic motivation to learn. And it is essential to help kids develop early in life the study techniques that can help them be better prepared to succeed in school and also to discover whatever it is they want to learn on their own. We call this *academic enrichment.*

Just like developmental stages, when it comes to what type of academic enrichment a child needs, different kids are often at different stages. Some will need your help in figuring out how to be organized and prepared. Others might have challenges when it comes to different courses they are taking. Others might be smart in all areas and know how to study and do homework well but have reached a point where they are lacking in the motivation to want to learn.

Meanwhile, many parents need help in being the best guide on the side they can be. For instance, some parents aren't sure how best to tutor their child in a subject area. At other times we sit down to help and realize we have no idea how to assist them with a subject we thought we were good at. Others might not be aware of what the child needs to master before they go on to the next grade. This is why approaching academic enrichment as a team is important.

When we developed our materials for the Core5 website, we decided to help others understand how best to help kids study. We also sought out websites that could help kids with different coursework. And then we looked for other resources and Web links that could allow children to explore the world from their own computer (e.g., tour the most famous art museums and aquariums). There is so much support online to help you accomplish becoming a parent who better guides their child at home in doing better at school. But we have to make time for such efforts every week, day, and, sometimes, weekend.

It sounds like a lot, but the new U.S. education policy, the Common Core Standards, has pushed so many teachers to assign so much and move so fast. And if we don't help a struggling child try to keep up, or better yet get a step ahead, behaviors associated with ADHD will most likely persist if not get worse. Sometimes such challenges might require you to reach out to a teacher, counselor, or principal. Do not be afraid to do so. By meeting with them you can find out where they think your child needs more help. By meeting with them you can discover what the school system expects your child to master at each grade level. By meeting with them you can work together and communicate better so you know exactly what your child is expected to complete and how you can help.

Academic enrichment at home needs to be carefully juggled. You need to set up the structure and routines to help a child finish assigned work from school, but you also need to make sure to take the opportunity to turn them on to learning whatever it is their little heart desires. To do this we cannot become just a repeat of what they get in school. We need to turn them on to learning. And by parents showing concern for the importance of school, most kids will see the same picture eventually.

GET INVOLVED

Parent involvement is the key to any child's success in school. Parent involvement is what has been found to be the secret to students' scoring the highest on tests worldwide. This does not mean we have to be with them every moment of their day or volunteer for the PTO and every other fund-raising effort for which the school asks for volunteers. It means we need to help shape our children's days early in hopes of helping them learn to shape their own days effectively in the years to come.

Parent involvement probably holds the greatest potential for helping all children overcome education-related challenges. Parent involvement is what helps to eliminate the differing scores we often see between the haves and the have-nots. Dr. Joyce Epstein, a respected expert in parent involvement, argues that school, family, and community are important *spheres of influence* on children's development and that a child's educational development is enhanced when these three environments work collaboratively toward the same goals.

Many of the foundational learning and developmental theories and philosophies taught to teachers (and shared in chapter 7) focus on these same spheres of influence. Vygotsky, Piaget, Erikson, Kohlberg, Dewey, and many other educational visionaries stressed the importance of the larger community's and parent's impact on developing the whole child and helping them accomplish higher levels of learning. Numerous literature reviews clearly demonstrate the relationship between parent involvement and a student's success in the test of life as well as the life of tests. We know that no matter the child's economic status, having an involved parent can be the difference between academic success and failure.

To better understand why some students do well on the Programme for International Student Assessment tests (PISA, which, as mentioned earlier, is the international test for fifteen-year-olds used to rank education systems internationally), Andreas Schleicher of the Organisation for Economic Co-operation and Development (OECD, the group in charge of administering the PISA) was encouraged by the countries participating in the PISA to look beyond the classrooms. So, starting with four countries in 2006, and then fourteen more in 2009, his PISA team went to the parents of five thousand students and interviewed them about how the children were raised and then compared that with the test results. The OECD study found that

- fifteen-year-old students whose parents often read books with them during their first year of primary school show markedly higher scores than students whose parents read with them infrequently or not at all
- the performance advantage among students whose parents read to them in their early school years is evident *regardless of the family's socioeconomic background* and
- parents' engagement with their fifteen-year-olds is strongly associated with better performance.

According to the OECD, typically students in socioeconomically advantaged households experience an environment more advantageous to learning in many ways, including having more-involved parents. However, even when comparing students of similar socioeconomic backgrounds, those students whose parents regularly read books to them when they were in their first year of primary school scored fourteen points higher, on average, than did students whose parents did not.

What they found was that when parents read with students at an early age, or discussed with their children what they had done that week in school, or even cared enough to ask how their day was, students did better in school (regardless of SES status). Furthermore, when parents were willing to discuss political or social issues, books, movies, or television programs, the kids did better on the tests. And the more involved the parents were, the smaller the test-score gap was between those of lower socioeconomic status and others.

A lot of parents often think we don't have time to be involved with our kids. For some reason we think it will require more time than we have to give or that work and other things in life should get more priority. But being involved does not necessarily mean hovering over them like a worried hen or alpha wolf. In fact, you don't always have to be the sage on the stage or try to play the role of all-knowing alpha parent (or tiger mom).

It often helps, when it comes to school and helping them try out their social skills, to be in the background. There are all types of resources to help you figure out things to do on those days you really need and want to interact with your child (be with them one on one). But when we can't find the time to be actively involved, we just need to be nearby and available to guide and monitor them.

They just want to know that you care for and love them. They just want to have some fun every now and then with you. They just want to know you can help and are willing to walk beside them as they learn.

SUMMARY

As parents and even educators, putting efforts toward improving structures combined with a bit of creativity focused on making learning fun and interesting can go a long way toward helping behaviorally challenged kids. Although current practice suggests it is the problem child who needs the counseling, therapy, or behavioral modification, it is quite evident that all who play a part in a child's life should contribute to and benefit from the therapeutic process.

What you have just read hopefully has encouraged you to further explore what specific efforts and approaches you might add to your existing efforts or adopt as a new approach. But sometimes we don't need to look for things to do. Sometimes they are right in front of us and we just need to think back to what we did as kids.

So as you have learned by now, I have a few kids. We were blessed first with a beautiful, wonderful daughter, and then our second amazing child was a boy. They are five years and, sometimes it seems, light years apart. So, for the first five years of parenthood we raised a little girl who was pretty easy to please. Put on some music, pull out the plastic *Beauty and the Beast* tea set, and you were good to go for hours. But as you might have learned, little boys sometimes aren't as easy.

Little boys, the ones more likely to be diagnosed with ADHD, can be a little more energetic and physical. While many little girls like to dress things up, a lot of little boys like to tear things up. As a boy I was not that different, and as a father I have a boy much like me.

It was just a month or two ago that I was watching both of the kids for the day but had a ton of yard work to do. My son wanted to help, but the rake was too heavy. And then the shovel was too big. And then the sun was too hot. And then he couldn't understand why the hose couldn't be left on all day long. Finally, I noticed he was fiddling around with the hammer and nails I had out to fix the fence. He was pounding away as I was trying to determine whether I should take the hammer away so he didn't get hurt or show him how better to hold the hammer and maybe give him some new nails and a big board to go to town on.

That day, I remembered how my dad on many occasions would give me a hammer and some nails and let me pound forever. At first I thought this might not be a good idea, because many of my father's ideas related to child development are not readily cited in parenting guides. This was the same guy who occasionally would take me to the bar to be his seven-year-old pool partner. This was the guy who decided it was a good idea for me to walk home three miles at the age of nine because I'd misbehaved on a fishing trip. But with no other good idea floating around in my head, and my window for getting all my chores done closing quickly, I decided, What the heck? Let the kid play.

I went to the barn (it's more like a large outbuilding, but I call it a barn) and got a huge piece of wood for him. I grabbed a smaller hammer and a whole handful of big nails. I showed him how to hold the nail and hammer and how to swing the hammer. And my last words, before I went back to working on the fence and garden, were, "Don't hit your finger."

A few hours later, I realized I had not heard from him or my dogs for a while. I went around the barn to see if he had given up. He had not. In fact, he had found more wood and more nails. He had built what he called a fort and wanted me to put it in a tree. Meanwhile, my dogs had found more wood too and were busy gnawing away. I chuckled and told my son to keep working on it and we would use it as a prototype for next year's tree fort. To make a long story short, he had a fun day and I was actually able to get a lot of work done. We then later walked around the yard discussing what tree we should build a fort in, and his imagination ran wild.

Parent involvement can take many forms, and keeping our children occupied, learning, and imaginatively active just takes a little creativity on our part. In other words, more television, video games, and homework, things most likely contributing to the problem, are not always the answer. As most would agree, adult supervision in determining alternatives to occupying our children's time is a good thing. But too much adult supervision takes the fun out of things. Too little adult supervision leaves too much room for things to go wrong. There are many ways we can help our children escape from this parallel universe of ADHD. And many of the approaches can come from what parents did in decades past, before we started turning to drugs for the answers.

Similar to the efforts parents of infants take to "child-proof" a house in order to make it safe for the new infant, parents of children being labeled with ADHD must put forth a similar effort to child-proof every day. We must take a close look at everything our child might get into or be distracted by. We must put up gates, so to speak, to lead them away from not-so-healthy choices. We must provide them with novel objects and activities to keep them occupied. We must stay involved as parents.

REFLECTION EXERCISE:
THERE IS NEVER NOTHING TO DO

Far too often as parents we are forced to be the bearers of bad news. We are forced to be the ones who must remind our kids to "Do your homework," "Study for the test," "Go to bed," or "Clean your room." Far too often adults are so preoccupied with what must be done that we forget that there are other things to do that might be more fun but still serve a purpose (e.g., build character, increase one's motivation to learn, allow a child to use their imagination). So for this reflection exercise, I urge you to sit down with your child and ask them what they would like to do or learn more about. Make a list of these things and keep them handy to remind you to explore possible alternatives to just turning on the television. Again.

Take the list, and explore some of the resources I have mentioned. Maybe add to the list ideas you have thought of that you think might also be of interest or value to the child. Begin to create a file of activities you can do together or what you might be able to give the child to do on their own as you remain available to help. In other words, if you have a child who needs to be kept busy in order to focus their ball of energy in constructive directions, get better prepared to put their creativity and imaginations to work.

10

REFRAMING REALITY

REASON #10: We should never drug children for acting like children!

I first want to sincerely thank you for reading this book. I hope that you have found it to be of value in your efforts to navigate this place called Planet ADHD. I hope that I have provided you with substantial research and suggestions to consider. I hope the information has helped you to reframe what appears at times to be the all-too-harsh reality we live in. But I hope, most of all, that this book has alerted you to the fact that ADHD should not be considered a real mental disorder for children and that ADHD drugs are most definitely dangerous and wrong.

It was not that long ago that First Lady Nancy Reagan challenged our children and parents to "just say no to drugs." And now, just a few decades later, millions of parents wake up every morning and force their children to take drugs, or, as some like to call it, "medicine." It's a planet where parents somehow go from obsessing and stressing over whether to give two or three drops of Mylicon^R to help their gassy, crying baby fall asleep to drugging a young child with ten to twenty milligrams of ADHD stimulants every day as if it were a new product line of Flintstone's Chewables^R.

Under the advice of doctors, people we have been raised to trust, today many parents force their children to take stimulants. I was not sure how to lightly break the news to you, but as chapter 3 shared, stimulant medications for ADHD are basically causing brain damage one pill at a time, which is quite possibly irreversible. Maybe this is why the makers of the drugs claim to not know exactly how the drugs produce the effects to reduce the symptoms of ADHD or how the drugs impact a child's brain or neurological development.

FOCUS ON THE FACTS

- For a moment, reflect back on childhood and remember that we—the sometimes mature and possibly sporadically responsible adults—were once not that different than our kids are today.
- Our children are living the one childhood they have and we have with them.
- Your kids mean so much to you.
- And no one has the right to experiment with their brains.

We do know, however, that these stimulants produce a neurochemical reaction that overstimulates a child's mind, causing it to basically slow down or, to some extent, shut down. But using an ADHD stimulant-based drug has nearly the same overstimulating effect on a child's brain as cocaine. Can you imagine giving your child cocaine every morning? Of course not! But many of you reading this book either are an adult who has agreed to give children stimulants (or an alternative ADHD medication) as a means of controlling their behavior or are an adult who is considering it. I urge you, however, at your earliest chance to get off this pharmaceutical freight train or if possible to not get on in the first place.

My goal in part II of this book has been to provide you with sound research and suggestions to explain and better guide you in dealing with those of your child's behaviors that some want you to believe are signs of a mental disorder. And I hope the explanations and advice I have provided feel like something you can start to strongly consider, investigate further, and eventually (if not really soon) incorporate into your parenting or teaching efforts. At the end of the day, every day, as the parents and teachers of children being labeled with ADHD, we are their last resort for helping them overcome these challenges of childhood and the normal development process.

But before we part ways, I want to spend just a bit more time together remembering childhood. I want to, for a moment, reflect back on childhood and remember that we (the sometimes mature and possibly sporadically responsible adults) were once not that different than our kids are today. To do this, let us start by remembering the story of Peter Pan—or, more specifically, let's talk about the classic movie *Hook*.

"BANGARANG!"

One of the movies I remember watching often with my nephews, and that my kids own a copy of as well, is *Hook*. It is a movie from 1991 where

Dustin Hoffman played the role of Captain Hook, Julia Roberts played Tinkerbell, and Robin Williams played Peter Pan. I know imagining Robin Williams in a tight Peter Pan outfit might not seem pleasant, but he is brilliant, and it's a great movie that kids still love and adults find amazingly insightful.

In this twist of the classic Peter Pan story, Peter is an adult with a family, but he has forgotten that he was once Peter Pan and that he could fly. He has two kids and a wife, and life at times seems far too chaotic. But on one crazy night he is pulled back into the world of Peter Pan and must once again face his nemesis, Captain Hook, and his own demons as well. Without explaining the whole plot, climax, and ending in too much detail, thus ruining the whole movie if you haven't seen it or watched it in a while, Peter Pan is forced to revisit childhood. And at the moment he discovers what it feels like to be a child again, he screams out, "Bangarang!"

In the process, he is reminded that it feels so good to be a kid and that childhood passes in the blink of an eye. He is reminded of the magic that fills a child's mind and that only through unbridled imagination can one really fly among the stars and dream. And through revisiting his childhood he discovers that much of what is consuming his life as an adult is of little importance compared to the role he must play as a parent.

What many adults, myself included, often need to be reminded of or recognize is that our children are living the one childhood they have and we have with them. And if we spend the whole time constantly being worried and serious about behavior and school, they just might miss out on the opportunity to fully be a kid and we adults might miss out on one of the most amazing times in parenthood. We might also miss out on a wonderful opportunity to revisit our own childhoods.

Now, I'm not saying we need to embrace their childlike ways forever. In no way do I want anyone to experience Peter Pan syndrome, where one refuses to grow up. What I am suggesting is that we just try to remember, on a daily basis, that kids are kids and that they deserve to some extent to enjoy such pleasures as they learn how to become young adults.

Getting Meta-kid-i-cal

One thing I would suggest, to any parent considering accepting the ADHD label as legit and also considering ADHD drugs as a medically sound approach to treating the supposed disorder, is to sit down with your child and dream for a while. Maybe you have done this before, but if not, I suggest you try. If the weather is nice, grab a blanket, and go find a place in a field or under a tree, and, side-by-side, lay down for a bit, and let your child share with you what they see and think. But instead of dismissing them with thoughts like, "That's so childish," for a moment really consider what they're saying.

Try to remember, like Peter Pan in *Hook*, what you were like when you were a child, their age. Try to drift back into the deeply filed memories that haven't been revisited possibly in years and allow your inner child to come out. Think about and possibly share what you liked to do as a kid. Maybe share some old stories of what you did as a kid. Spend the day exploring trees, leaves, flowers, bugs, birds, creeks, crawdads . . . Run, roll, jump, skip. Spend the day being a kid with your kid.

On many occasions, during my research projects I have taken the opportunity to ask kids what they think of random topics. It's a fun exercise, and you can learn a lot about young people this way. You learn that although they might be still learning the value system and behaviors our society expects of adults, they live in a different world where many aspects and expectations are valued differently. I understand we are trying to help kids grow up and get to adulthood as planned, but I suggest we approach our mission with caution and much patience.

Plus, there is often a happy medium that can be reached in most circumstances where kids' and adults' ideas and expectations conflict. If we take the time to better understand where kids are coming from, we might have a better chance of relating what we want to what they might be willing to consider. And by connecting with children in a fashion one might not have tried before, one can begin to win more of their respect.

There is research on numerous parenting styles. The research tells us we cannot act like a kid with them forever, play the role of just a friend, or be a pushover. We unfortunately as parents must play hardball at times. But we parents can neither be inflexible nor too demanding. Although some want to believe that adults are the sergeants and the kids are the privates going through basic training, research shows that authoritarian parenting often does not produce good outcomes. In fact, it may increase problems. We can be authoritative, but we must not cross the line into authoritarianism. It is so much more enjoyable for everyone involved in the "why don't you grow up" debate if both sides can feel they are a part of the planning and decision making.

Basically, what I am suggesting is that if you have hit your wits end when it comes to your child, as hard as it might be, try again to understand and connect with them. Before rushing into or continuing to embrace the ADHD label and ADHD drug use, just take a deep breath and try again. Who knows . . . maybe they have developed and matured more since the last time you tried. Maybe this time your new approach will work to help you and your child better understand the goals and what is needed to accomplish what you wish for them to achieve. No matter what you decide to try, as long as it is a structured, creative, and nurturing approach, it can't be markedly inferior to just accepting a diagnosis that science at this time cannot verify is factually accurate or supported. It can't be worse than the dangers that come with ADHD drugs.

Mirror, Mirror on the Wall

Not to intentionally spend more time in this last chapter reminding you of more wonderful Disney movies, but I can't help but think about the movie *Snow White and the Seven Dwarfs*. The reason it comes to mind is because, beyond resorting to prayer, I think that too many parents are left with the lone option of looking in the mirror daily and asking their reflection what else they can do—or what is the right thing, the fairest thing, to do—when it comes to managing their child's ADHD challenges. Parents do this because they care and are worried and because their consciences keep whispering that drugging children for acting like children is wrong.

Parents do this because the disclaimers and warnings that are shared in the pharmaceutical drugs' medication guides are scary. Parents worry about these things because after months and years of doling out the drugs every morning to their kids, they start to feel more like nurses treating a questionable disease and less like caretakers. Parents worry because they know that only they—the person in the mirror—have the answers and in the end are the ones who make the final decisions about their child's supposed disorder.

Diseases without any known causes are referred to as *idiopathic*. *Idio* is a Latin root meaning "peculiar," and *pathic* basically means "illness"; thus, we have a *peculiar illness* or *disease*. And if any supposed disease or illness should be called peculiar I think ADHD fits the bill. ADHD is idiopathic because the DSM and pharmaceutical companies admit often to the fact that there are no known causes. Though they want us today to think ADHD is a medical condition, the evidence they have does not support these claims. And depending on which website or resource you reference, they all claim something slightly different.

If it is an epidemic fueled by environmental contaminants, why are *their* studies (the studies provided by the ADHD cheerleading squad) not producing hard, irrefutable evidence identifying these contaminants or showing how the genetics of kids labeled ADHD are more susceptible to the biological or environmental contaminants? If it is a chronic neurodevelopmental or neurological condition, where are the confirming series of experiments and brain scans?

The few genetic studies that exist utilizing questionable sampling techniques, psychometric tools, and data sets (e.g., studying old data sets or combining past studies' findings related to studies on twins) are not giving us any real or conclusive scientific findings. The unsubstantiated analytical or statistical modeling techniques that they are using to try and make their minimal findings look really impressive and scientific are not passing the test. And, as I've said before, you can't claim you are measuring how something exists or is being effectively treated if you don't have a reliable or valid test to begin with.

It wouldn't be the first time in history that we have discovered that doctors or clinicians are incapable of identifying who has a mental illness and who doesn't. The Rosenhan Study classically illustrated these challenges. The Rosenhan Study sent a bunch of people out to mental-health hospitals to pose as mentally ill patients. They were faking their symptoms in an attempt to show that the processes we use to identify mental illness are subjective and flawed.

What the study discovered is that, indeed, a significant percentage of the confederates faking mental illness were admitted to hospitals and diagnosed with serious mental disorders. Some were admitted with such serious diagnoses that legal action was needed to actually get them released from the hospital at the study's end. But the real twist was that the only people in the hospital that realized the confederates were faking mental illness were the truly mentally ill patients who'd already been admitted. As the saying goes, it takes one to know one.

From the Mouths of Babes

Over the course of my research, I have spoken with many young adults, from late teens to late twenties, who had at one time been put on ADHD drugs. Their stories were quite similar but, to me, sad in different ways. At first, many of them didn't mind being labeled with ADHD and being put on drugs. But as time passed, some began to wonder why they were still on the drugs, while others made the label of ADHD and the drugs they took daily a defining characteristic of their self-image. Many who remained on the drugs sought out extra accommodations for their diagnosed condition, even into college. Some of them even admitted to not taking their drugs regularly or abusing their medications.

This might explain why it is believed that a large portion of ADHD stimulants prescribed to kids labeled with ADHD are actually sold illegally to people who have not been diagnosed with ADHD. As studies have shown, ADHD drugs are supposedly effective in increasing concentration in all children over the short term. Such "benefits" might explain why so many high school and college students are making Adderall and other stimulants their drugs of choice when looking for something to help them study or stay up all night. Some call it a "study drug."

But as one young man told me when he explained the many reasons he took himself off the medication, "I didn't do steroids to play football, and I figured I didn't need a steroid-like drug to do better in school." In fact, this young man also explained that after six months of being forced by his parents and educators to take the drugs, and feeling like a zombie, he did his own research and found websites explaining many of the same limitations to the diagnosis and dangers to the drugs I have shared with you. He begged his dad to speak to his mom about it, and, luckily for him, he was allowed to at last stop the medication. But, as he admitted to me, although his parents suggested he use his ADHD label to get special accommodations in college, he did not. From the time he left his high school, he never admitted to anyone else that he had been diagnosed with ADHD.

Other younger kids seem to think it is a *medicine* they must take. They have been told they are sick and that this medicine will make them better. I truly find this despicable. It is not like the child is taking antibiotics for a virus. Any pill whose impact on a child's brain we don't understand—and yet for which we have evidence that it is most likely causing a brain malfunction that is irreversible—should not be considered a medicine.

But believe it or not, most kids eventually realize they are being drugged for their behavior. They realize at some point that what they are taking is not medicine. Some might want to get off the drugs, but after years of being on it and the feelings they get when they forget to take it, they are afraid to stop taking the pills.

I have also been told by some young men they are sure their facial tics are from the medication they were forced to take as a child. Some have wondered to me whether the drugs stunted their growth. One person jokingly explained that either it was the ADHD drugs or mom found another man, because his brother and father were two to four inches taller than he is.

IT'S PERFECTLY NORMAL

On several occasions I have been asked by parents (normally friends, friends of friends, or adult students of mine) to help them in discussions with their child's school. Similar to the embellished story on drugging da Vinci in chapter 1, this normally happens because the parents have been told that they need to have their child diagnosed for ADHD and *possibly* medicated. In one such conference, one of my graduate students had asked for my help because her child's second-grade teacher was strongly suggesting her child be medicated for ADHD. I vividly remember the discussion, which basically began that day with the teacher yelling at the parent, school nurse, principal, and me that "There is no other alternative for this student!"

The room grew quiet after her outburst, and the parent looked at me as if to say, "Help me out here!" As calmly as I could, I asked the principal, "Which teacher in this school annually forces you to have this type of discussion with parents the most?" As he looked down the table at the teacher, he then looked away and dropped his head into his hands without saying a word. I then proceeded to share with them the facts as to what else might be the cause of the child's recent behavior.

What those three educators had failed to do prior to the conference was ask the young mother of that child if anything had recently changed in their lives that might have caused her child to behave poorly. They had not bothered to take the time and ask the child's kindergarten or first-grade teachers about their experiences with the child. With the parent's permission, I explained to all gathered that the boy's father had recently abandoned the family—a father whom, despite his demons, was dearly loved by his boy. The boy could not understand why his father would just leave.

The mother was then forced to work two jobs in order to pay rent for their small apartment, and still she could barely put food on the table. Needless to say, the quality time she had once been able to spend with her son was greatly reduced. She had no "reliable" or "safe" family members to help out. She had few resources to seek quality help from mental-health professionals for her son. There were several other family secrets contributing as well. She told me these details one day in my university office as she broke down in tears and explained to me why she was thinking about dropping my class and quite possibly completely out of graduate school.

But what truly blew my mind during the meeting at her son's school was that as the school nurse and principal showed visible signs of being truly sorry and upset for bringing this parent in for the ADHD drug talk without first having found out the whole story, the teacher actually said in response to what this child was experiencing, "I do not care!" I admit that at that point in the conversation I did lose my temper a little and in a not so politically correct manner made a strong suggestion for that teacher to find a new career that had nothing to do with her being near children.

With this said, the school and father were not the only ones sharing the responsibility of the behavior and performance of the child. As I spent more time that academic year advising this mother and trying to help her stay in school, I would occasionally hear updates on her son's situation. It became apparent from the discussion one day that she was having trouble feeding the child a nutritionally correct diet. Once she acknowledged this and read some literature on the connection between behavior, development, cognition, and diet, she discovered a great improvement once she focused more on a well-balanced, less-processed foods-based diet and cut back on the expensive sugar-laden juices, sodas, and cereals she had been feeding him at night and before he went to school.

She discovered improvements when she set a reasonable bedtime for him and set stricter rules for watching television and playing video games. She discovered a better relationship with him when she realized that he needed her more than ever now to fill the void of his missing father. As I watched her dig her way out of the quagmire that semester, I saw that, though observably more tired than ever before, she was also smiling.

I ran into her the next year, and she told me that her son was doing really well in school. He had a wonderful new teacher, and life was getting better. And, by the way, she never agreed to the ADHD diagnosis, and he never did go on drugs. Why? She told me, as she learned in my class, "There is no reason to have a child diagnosed for ADHD just because the child exhibits ADHD symptoms that document he is a perfectly normal, obnoxious young man with unlimited potential to change the world."

Was my student's child gifted? I don't think so, but who knows? He might have been a late bloomer. But his energy level, creativity, imagination, ability to know bad education when he saw it . . . these were all gifts in a way to me and not signs of a disorder or disease or chronic condition. His disruptive behavior due to family circumstances was also something I would diagnose as perfectly normal. And, most certainly, his symptoms did not justify medication.

Obviously I believe that the only people who benefit from ADHD drug use are pharmaceutical companies and the prescribing doctors. But to be honest, I kind of respect them in a weird way because they are so darn good at making it look like they are right. They understand human nature and how we often look for the easiest path to get from point A to point B. They understand the persuasion game, and right now they are winning. But I hope that I have convinced you to join my side in this debate. It was my number one goal. The child you are concerned about deserves nothing less than living a childhood where his or her imagination runs free.

SUMMARY

I wrote this book because I am against drugging children to treat ADHD. I wrote this book to help you consider the possibility that the symptoms associated with ADHD might very well suggest that your child is normal or temporarily developmentally delayed or even has a gift and not a disorder. I wrote this book to show you that the diagnosis for ADHD at best will only serve as confirmation that your child's supposed abnormal behavior is similar to billions of other children's behavior (in other words, that your child is normal) and, yes, that parenthood can at times seem like a not-so-pleasurable experience.

Too many parents, guardians, and educators have been misled into believing that ADHD is a legitimate diagnosis and that the process of modifying a child's behavior through drugs is a healthy practice. To help you better understand why I feel this way, I have shared some of the bizarre experiences I've had as an educator and researcher studying hundreds of schools and thousands of kids and parents. I shared research to help you help your child navigate the confusing Planet ADHD. I hope this book provided you with an abundance of evidence to more clearly determine that drugging an active, creative, and energetic child who cannot sit motionless at an uncomfortable school desk quietly for seven hours is *not* the best path to take.

As Dr. Peter Breggin once wrote, "the drugging of children for behavior control should raise profound spiritual, philosophical, and ethical questions about ourselves as adults and about how we view the children in our care. Society ignores these critical questions at great peril to itself, to its values, and to the well-being of its children." No matter whether we believe in a higher being, multiple higher beings, rebirth, or a view that life ends at death, most would agree that this time we have on earth is precious. No matter what religious belief or worldview you hold, most of you will agree that we are but a speck in the universe. With science today having shown us just how large the universe actually is, we can acknowledge that we play such a miniscule role. Our existence as humans on this planet is no more than a blip on the universe's timeline, spanning billions of years. And when you look at the history of ADHD on this same timeline, it is not even important enough to be picked up on the timeline. It's just a label some want you to believe is real and important. It's just a reason—an invention—created to justify medicating children for acting like children.

Regardless, if our personal role in the circle of life is of minimal importance or great consequence to the existence of humans, it does not change the fact that we define our world—our own existence—by those who surround us. Our children, friends, family, and neighbors, and many others we don't even know, shape our existence and define who we are. Each and every one of them plays an important role in shaping how we view the past, present, and future, but our children . . . Our children are everything.

On some days we might kid ourselves and act as if we will be happy when they move out and get on with their lives. But I have not met many parents I respect who have not shared how hard it was to let them go when the time came. Millions of empty nesters will confirm that childhood is far too short. I am confident the years will fly by and before we know it our little babies will have become men and women. And so this is why I believe that we must not waste valuable and precious time playing stupid games with our children's health and well-being.

I'm hoping that what I have shared has helped you to reevaluate your view of ADHD. I hope that what I have shared is helping you to think more deeply about how important your child is to you. I hope that what I have shared has helped you see how dangerous it is to blindly trust those who benefit or profit from your fear. When it comes to ADHD, they don't really know what their advice will bring.

Your kids mean so much to you. And no one has the right to experiment with their brains. I know you probably picked up this book and read every chapter, every page, because you care about them so very much. I sincerely thank you.

REFLECTION EXERCISE:
SAY KNOW TO ADHD DRUGS

One of my goals in writing this book was to create a vehicle and possible grassroots movement to inform the masses of just how insane the ADHD diagnosis is and how wrong and dangerous ADHD drugs are for kids. The ten reasons highlighted at the beginnings of each chapter should serve as commandments for shutting down the for-profit trade related to ADHD. At the least, I hope this book serves as the evidence you need to say no to the ADHD diagnosis and medication as it relates to your children or students. But if what I have shared has made perfect sense to you, and the evidence you have read has provided the knowledge you need to be convinced ADHD holds no role in the lives of our children, I ask you sincerely to share your knowledge with others. The more who know about the falsehoods of ADHD, the better our kids' childhoods will be.

APPENDIX

ADHD-INATTENTION SYMPTOM CHECKLIST

*Directions: Put a check mark next to the symptoms that
reflect behaviors associated with you or you as a child.*

a. Often fails to give close attention to details or makes careless mistakes in schoolwork, work, or during other activities (e.g., overlooks or misses details, work is inaccurate). ____
b. Often has difficulty sustaining attention in tasks or play activities (e.g., has difficulty remaining focused during lectures, conversations, or lengthy reading). ____
c. Often does not seem to listen when spoken to directly (e.g., mind seems elsewhere, even in the absence of any obvious distraction). ____
d. Often does not follow through on instructions and fails to finish schoolwork, chores, or duties in the workplace (e.g., starts tasks but quickly loses focus and is easily distracted). ____
e. Often has difficulty organizing tasks and activities (e.g., difficulty managing sequential tasks; difficulty keeping materials and belongings in order, messy, disorganized work, has poor time management, fails to meet deadlines). ____
f. Often avoids, dislikes, or is reluctant to engage in tasks that require sustained mental effort (e.g., schoolwork or homework; for older adolescents and adults, preparing reports, completing forms, reviewing lengthy papers). ____
g. Often loses things necessary for task or activities (e.g., school materials, pencils, books, tools, wallets, keys, paperwork, eyeglasses, mobile telephones). ____
h. Is often easily distracted by extraneous stimuli (for older adolescents and adults, may include unrelated thoughts). ____
i. Is often forgetful in daily activities (e.g., doing chores, running errands; for older adolescents and adults, returning calls, paying bills, keeping appointments). ____

ADHD–HYPERACTIVITY AND
IMPULSIVITY SYMPTOM CHECKLIST

Directions: Put a check mark next to the symptoms that reflect behaviors associated with you, your male child, or your young boy alter ego.

a. Often fidgets with or taps hands or feet or squirms in seat. ____

b. Often leaves seat in situations when remaining seated is expected (e.g., leaves his or her place in the classroom, the office, or other workplace or in other situations that require remaining in place). ____

c. Often runs about or climbs in situations where it is inappropriate (Note: In adolescents or adults, may be limited to feeling restless). ____

d. Often unable to play or engage in leisure activities quietly. ____

e. Is often "on the go," acting as if "driven by a motor" (e.g., is unable to be or uncomfortable being still for extended time, as in restaurants, meetings; may be experienced by others as being restless or difficult to keep up with). ____

f. Often talks excessively. ____

g. Often blurts out the answer before a question has been completed (e.g., completes people's sentences; cannot wait turn in conversation). ____

h. Often has difficulty waiting his or her turn (e.g., while waiting in line). ____

i. Often interrupts or intrudes on others (e.g., butts into conversations, games, or activities; may start using other people's things without asking or receiving permission; for adolescents and adults, may intrude into or take over what others are doing). ____

Please note: According to the *Diagnostic and Statistical Manual of Mental Disorders* (DSM-5), using the symptoms of ADHD as a checklist is not the appropriate way to use the DSM diagnostic criteria for diagnosing ADHD. There are many other caveats that many medical or mental health professionals are not following. For example, the DSM also states that "six (or more) of the following symptoms have persisted for at least six months to a degree that is *inconsistent with developmental level* and that *negatively impacts directly on social and academic/occupational activities*" and such extreme behaviors existed before the age of seven. The checklists provided in the appendix are meant to be used as an activity and in no way serve as a test for ADHD.

REFERENCES

PREFACE

American Psychiatric Association. 2013. *Diagnostic and statistical manual of mental disorders*. 5th ed. Arlington, Va.: American Psychiatric Publishing.

Golden, G. S. 1991. Role of attention deficit hyperactivity disorder in learning disabilities. *Seminars in Neurology* 11 (March): 35–41.

Hechtman, L., and B. Greenfield. 2003. Long-term use of stimulants in children with attention deficit hyperactivity disorder. *Pediatric Drugs* 5 (12): 787–94.

Mojtabai, R. 2013. Clinician-identified depression in community settings: Concordance with structured-interview diagnoses. *Psychotherapy and Psychosomatics* 82 (3): 161–69.

MTA Cooperative Group. 1999. A 14-month randomized clinical trial of treatment strategies for attention-deficit/hyperactivity disorder: Multimodal treatment study of children with ADHD. *Archives of General Psychiatry* 56 (12): 1073–86.

———. 2009. The MTA at 8 years: Prospective follow-up of children treated for combined-type ADHD in a multisite study. *Journal of the American Academy of Child & Adolescent Psychiatry* 48 (5): 484–500.

Schwarz, A., and S. Cohen. 2013. ADHD seen in 11% of U.S. children as diagnoses rise. *New York Times*, March 31, 2013. http://www.nytimes.com/2013/04/01/health/more-diagnoses-of-hyperactivity-causing-concern.html?pagewanted=all&_r=0.

INTRODUCTION

Baughman, F. A., Jr. 1993. Treatment of attention-deficit hyperactivity disorder. *Journal of the American Medical Association* 269 (18): 2368–69.

Breggin, P. R. 2002. *The Ritalin fact book: What your doctor won't tell you about ADHD and stimulant drugs*. Cambridge, Mass.: Perseus Publishing.

Breggin, P. R., and G. R. Breggin. 1995. The hazards of treating "attention-deficit/hyperactivity disorder" with methylphenidate (Ritalin). *Journal of College Student Psychotherapy* 10 (2): 55–72.

Corrigan, M. W. 2012. A body of evidence. In *Handbook of prosocial education*, ed. P. M. Brown, M. W. Corrigan, and A. Higgins-D'Alessandro, 731–66. Lanahm, Md.: Rowman & Littlefield.

Elder, T. E. 2010. The importance of relative standards in ADHD diagnoses: Evidence based on exact birth dates. *Journal of Health Economics* 29 (5): 641–56.

Evans, W. N., M. S. Morrill, and S. T. Parente. 2010. Measuring inappropriate medical diagnosis and treatment in survey data: The case of ADHD among school-age children. *Journal of Health Economics* 29 (5): 657–73.

Haiken, M. 2013. ADHD drug emergencies quadrupled in 6 years, says government report. *Forbes*, August 13. http://www.forbes.com/sites/melaniehaiken/2013/08/13er-visits-from-adhd-drugs-quadrupled-in-past-six-years-report-says/.

Hechtman, L., and B. Greenfield. 2003. Long-term use of stimulants in children with attention deficit hyperactivity disorder. *Pediatric Drugs* 5 (12): 787–94.

Institute of Medicine. 2006. Medication errors injure 1.5 million people and cost billions of dollars annually: Report offers comprehensive strategies for reducing drug-related mistakes. July 20. Available online at http://www8.nationalacademies.org/onpinews/newsitem.aspx?RecordID=11623.

McGuinness, D. 1989. Attention deficit disorder: The emperor's new clothes, animal "pharm," and other fiction. In *The limits of biological treatments for psychological distress*, ed. S. Fisher and R. P. Greenberg, 151–88. Hillsdale, N.J.: Lawrence Erlbaum Associates.

MTA Cooperative Group. 1999. A 14-month randomized clinical trial of treatment strategies for attention-deficit/hyperactivity disorder: Multimodal treatment study of children with ADHD. *Archives of General Psychiatry* 56 (12): 1073–86.

MTA Cooperative Group. 2009. The MTA at 8 years: Prospective follow-up of children treated for combined-type ADHD in a multisite study. *Journal of the American Academy of Child & Adolescent Psychiatry* 48 (5): 484–500.

Organization for Economic Co-operation and Development [OECD]. 2011. What can parents do to help their children succeed in school? *PISA in Focus* 10 (November). http://www.pisa.oecd.org/dataoecd/4/1/49012097.pdf.

Robinson, T. E., and B. Kolb. 1997. Persistent structural modifications in the nucleus accumbens and prefrontal cortex neurons produced by previous experience with amphetamine. *Journal of Neuroscience* 17 (21): 8491–97. http://www.jneurosci.org/content/17/21/8491.full.pdf.

SAMHSA [The Substance Abuse and Mental Health Services Administration]. 2013. Emergency department visits involving nonmedical use of central nervous system stimulants among adults aged 18 to 34 increased between 2005 and 2011. *DAWN Report*, August 8. http://www.samhsa.gov/data/spotlight/spot103-CNS-stimulants-adults.pdf.

Schwarz, A., and S. Cohen. 2013. ADHD seen in 11% of U.S. children as diagnoses rise. *New York Times*, March 31, 2013. http://www.nytimes.com/2013/04/01/health/more-diagnoses-of-hyperactivity-causing-concern.html?pagewanted=all&_r=0.

Symonds, W. C., R. Schwartz, and R. F. Ferguson. 2011. *Pathways to prosperity: Meeting the challenge of preparing young Americans for the 21st century*. Cambridge, Mass.: Pathways to Prosperity Project, Harvard University Graduate School of Education.

U.S. Food and Drug Administration. 2007. FDA asks attention-deficit hyperactivity disorder (ADHD) drug manufacturers to develop patient medication guides. February 21. http://www.fda.gov/drugs/drugsafety/postmarket drugsafetyinformationforpatientsandproviders/ucm107918.htm.

Vatz, R. E. 1993. Attention-deficit disorder mythology. *Wall Street Journal*, March 1, A-15.

Wang, S. S. 2013. ADHD drugs don't boost kids' grades: Studies of children with Attention-Deficit Hyperactivity Disorder find little change. *Wall Street Journal*, July 8. http://online.wsj.com/news/articles/SB1000142412788732336870457859 3660384362292.

Wedge, M. 2012. Why French kids don't have ADHD. *Psychology Today*, March 8. http://www.psychologytoday.com/blog/suffer-the-children/201203/why -french-kids-dont-have-adhd.

CHAPTER 1

Andersen, W. 2001. *Freud, Leonardo da Vinci, and the vulture's tail: A refreshing look at Leonardo's sexuality*. New York: Other Press.

Centers for Disease Control and Prevention. 2013a. Suicide and self-inflicted injury. http://www.cdc.gov/nchs/fastats/suicide.htm.

———. 2013b. Youth violence: National statistics. http://www.cdc.gov/violence prevention/youthviolence/stats_at-a_glance/lcd_10-24.html.

Freud, S. 1989. *Leonardo da Vinci and a memory of his childhood*. Repr. ed. Trans. Alan Tyson. Ed. James Strachey. New York: Norton.

Frontline. 2013. Federal laws pertaining to ADHD diagnosed children. http://www.pbs.org/wgbh/pages/frontline/shows/medicating/schools/feds.html.

Guffanti, S. 2011. ADHD diagnosis is worth money to schools. HowToLearn.com, July 25. http://www.howtolearn.com/2011/07/adhd-diagnosis -is-worth-money-to-schools/.

Ormrod, J. E. 2006. *Educational psychology: Developing learners*. 5th ed. Upper Saddle River, N.J.: Merrill.

———. 2011. *Essentials for educational psychology*. 3rd ed. Columbus, Ohio: Pearson.

Schwarz, A., and S. Cohen. 2013. ADHD seen in 11% of U.S. children as diagnoses rise. *New York Times*, March 31, 2013. http://www.nytimes.com/2013/04/01/health/more-diagnoses-of-hyperactivity-causing-concern.html?pagewanted=all&_r=0.

CHAPTER 2

American Psychiatric Association. 1973. Homosexuality and sexuality orientation disturbance: Proposed change in DSM-II, 6th printing, page 44; Position statement (retired). APA Document Reference No. 730008. Available online at http://www.torahdec.org/Downloads/DSM-II_Homosexuality_Revision.pdf.

———. 2013. *Diagnostic and statistical manual of mental disorders*. 5th ed. Arlington, Va.: American Psychiatric Publishing.

Baca-Garcia, E., M. M. Perez-Rodriguez, I. Basurte-Villamor, A. L. F. Del Moral, M. A. Jimenez-Arriero, J. L. G. De Rivera, J. Saiz-Ruiz, and M. A. Oquendo. 2007. Diagnostic stability of psychiatric disorders in clinical practice. *British Journal of Psychiatry* 190 (3): 210–16. Doi:10.1192/bjp.bp.106.024026. PMID 17329740.

Bentall, R., and N. Craddock. 2012. Do we need a diagnostic manual for mental illness? *Guardian*, February 10. http://www.theguardian.com/commentisfree/2012/feb/10/diagnostic-manual-mental-illness.

Bradley, C. 1937. The behavior of children receiving Benzedrine. *American Journal of Psychiatry* 94 (November): 577–85.

Cosgrove, L., and S. Krimsky. 2012. A comparison of *DSM*-IV and *DSM*-5 panel members' financial associations with industry: A pernicious problem persists. *PLoS Med* 9 (3): e1001190. Doi:10.1371/journal.pmed.1001190. http://www.plosmedicine.org/article/info%3Adoi%2F10.1371%2Fjournal.pmed.1001190.

First, M. B. 2010. Paradigm shifts and the development of the *Diagnostic and Statistical Manual of Mental Disorders*: Past experiences and future aspirations. *Canadian Journal of Psychiatry* 55 (11): 692–700. http://publications.cpa-apc.org/media.php?mid=1062.

Frances, A. 2012. DSM 5 is guide not bible: Ignore its ten worst changes. *Psychology Today*, December 2. http://www.psychologytoday.com/blog/dsm5-in-distress/201212/dsm-5-is-guide-not-bible-ignore-its-ten-worst-changes.

———. 2013. The new crisis in confidence in psychiatric diagnosis. *Annals of Internal Medicine*, May 17. http://annals.org/article.aspx?articleid=1688399.

Friedman, R. 2012. *Spiegel* interview with Jerome Kagan: "What about tutoring instead of pills?" *Der Spiegel*, August 2. http://www.spiegel.de/international/world/child-psychologist-jerome-kagan-on-overprescibing-drugs-to-children-a-847500.html.

Furman, L. M. 2008. Attention-deficit hyperactivity disorder (ADHD): Does new research support old concepts? *Journal of Child Neurology* 23 (7): 775–84. Doi:10.1177/0883073808318059.

Golden, G. S. 1991. Role of attention deficit hyperactivity disorder in learning disabilities. *Seminars in Neurology* 11 (March): 35–41.

Grohol, J. M. 2013. DSM-5 changes: Obsessive compulsive and related disorders. Psych Central Professional, May 28. http://pro.psychcentral.com/2013/dsm-5-changes-obsessive-compulsive-and-related-disorders/004404.html.

Harris, G. 2011. Talk doesn't pay, so psychiatry turns instead to drug therapy. *New York Times*, March 5. http://www.nytimes.com/2011/03/06/health/policy/06doctors.html?pagewanted=all&_r=0.

Kendell, R., and A. Jablensky. 2003. Distinguishing between the validity and utility of psychiatric diagnoses. *American Journal of Psychiatry* 160 (1): 4–12. Doi:101176/appi.ajp.160.1.4 PMID 12505793.

Lane, C. 2013. The NIMH withdraws support of DSM-5. *Psychology Today*, May 4. http://www.psychologytoday.com/blog/side-effects/201305/the-nimh-withdraws-support-dsm-5.

Lange, K., S. Reichl, K. M. Lange, L. Tucha, and O. Tucha. 2010. The history of attention deficit hyperactivity disorder. *Attention Deficit and Hyperactivity Disorders* 2 (4): 241–55. Doi:10.1007/s12402-010-0045-8.

Langley, K., J. Martin, S. S. Agha, C. Davies, E. Stergiakouli, P. Holmans, N. M. Williams, M. Owen, M. O'Donovan, and A. Thapar. 2011. Clinical and cognitive characteristics of children with attention-deficit hyperactivity disorder, with and without copy number variants. *British Journal of Psychiatry* 199 (5): 398–403.

McCommon, B. 2006. Antipsychiatry and the gay rights movement. *Psychiatric Services* 57 (12): 863–68.

Parry, W. 2013. *DSM-5:* Saying goodbye to Asperger's Syndrome. *Huffington Post*, June 11. http://www.huffingtonpost.com/2013/06/11/dsm-5-aspergers -syndrome-autism_n_3422677.html.

Rogler, L. H. 1997. Making sense of historical changes in the *Diagnostic and Statistical Manual of Mental Disorders*: Five propositions. *Journal of Health and Social Behavior* 38 (1): 9–20.

Sanders, J. L. 2011. A distinct language and a historic pendulum: The evolution of the *Diagnostic and Statistical Manual of Mental Disorders*. *Archives of Psychiatric Nursing* 25 (6): 394–403.

WGBH. 2013. Misunderstood Minds: Difficulties with attention. *PBS.org*. http:// www.pbs.org/wgbh/misunderstoodminds/attentiondiffs.html.

Williams, N. M., I. Zaharieva, A. Martin, K. Langley, K. Mantipragada, R. Fossdal, H. Stefansson, et al. 2010. Rare chromosomal deletions and duplications in attention-deficit hyperactivity disorder: A genome-wide analysis. *Lancet* 376 (9750): 1401–8. Available online at http://www.ncbi.nlm.nih.gov/pmc/ articles/PMC2965350/.

CHAPTER 3

Ackerman, P. T., R. A. Dykman, and J. E. Peters. 1977. Teenage status and hyperactive and non-hyperactive learning disabled boys. *American Journal of Orthopsychiatry* 47: 577–96.

Battaglia, G., S. Yeh, E. O'Hearn, M. Molliver, M. Kuhar, and E. De Souza. 1987. 3,4-methylenedioxymethamphetamine and 3,4-methylene-dioxyamphetamine destroy serotonin terminals in rat brain. *Journal of Pharmacology and Experimental Therapeutics* 242: 911–16.

Baughman, F. A., Jr. 1993. Treatment of attention-deficit hyperactivity disorder. *Journal of the American Medical Association* 269 (18): 2368–69.

Borcherding, B. V., C. S. Keysor, J. L. Rapoport, J. Elia, and J. Amass. 1990. Motor/ vocal tics and compulsive behaviors on stimulant drugs: Is there a common vulnerability? *Psychiatric Research* 33 (1): 83–94.

Breggin, P. R. 2002. *The Ritalin fact book: What your doctor won't tell you about ADHD and stimulant drugs.* Cambridge, Mass. Perseus Publishing.

Breggin, P. R., and G. R. Breggin. 1995. The hazards of treating "attention-deficit/ hyperactivity disorder" with methylphenidate (Ritalin). *Journal of College Student Psychotherapy* 10 (2): 55–72.

Castner, S., M. Al-Tikriti, R. Baldwin, J. Seibyl, R. Innis, and P. Goldman-Rakic. 2000. Behavioral changes and [[123I]] IBZM equilibrium SPECT measurement of amphetamine-induced dopamine release in rhesus monkeys exposed to subchronic amphetamine. *Neuropsychopharmacology* 22 (1): 4–13.

Dougherty, D., A. Bonab, T. Spencer, S. Rauch, B. Madras, and A. Fischman. 1999. Dopamine transporter density in patients with attention deficit disorder. *Lancet* 354: 2132–33.

Edmonds, M. 2008, August 20. Why are people's brains different sizes? HowStuff-Works.com. http://science.howstuffworks.com/life/inside-the-mind/human -brain/brain-size.htm (accessed November 15, 2013).

Ellinwood, E. H., and H. L. Tong. 1996. Central nervous system stimulants and anorectic agents. In *Meyler's side effects of drugs: An encyclopedia of adverse reactions and interactions*, 13th ed., ed. M. N. G. Dukes, 1–30. New York: Elsevier.

Gilberg, C., H. Melander, A. L. von Knorring, L. O. Janols, G. Thernlund, B. Hägglöf, L. Eidevall-Wallin, P. Gustafsson, and S. Kopp. 1997. Long-term stimulant treatment of children with attention-deficit hyperactivity disorder: A randomized double-blind placebo-controlled trial. *Archives of General Psychiatry* 54 (9): 857–64.

Goode, E. 2002. Brain size tied to attention deficit hyperactivity disorder. *New York Times*, October 9. http://www.nytimes.com/2002/10/09/health/09BRAI .html.

Guffanti, S. 2011. ADHD diagnosis is worth money to schools. HowToLearn .com, July 25. http://www.howtolearn.com/2011/07/adhd-diagnosis-is -worth-money-to-schools/.

Hechtman, L., and B. Greenfield. 2003. Long-term use of stimulants in children with attention deficit hyperactivity disorder. *Pediatric Drugs* 5 (12): 787–94.

Jaffe, J. 1995. Amphetamine (or amphetamine-like)-related disorders. In *Comprehensive textbook of psychiatry*, vol. 6, ed. H. Kaplan and B. Sadock, 791–99. Baltimore: Williams and Wilkins.

Lerner, M., and T. Wigel. 2008. Long-term safety of stimulant medications used to treat children with ADHD. *Psychiatric Annals* 38 (1): 43–50.

Loney, J., J. Kramer, and R. Milich. 1981. The hyperkinetic child grows up: Predictors of symptoms, delinquency and achievement at follow-up. In *Psychological aspects of drug treatment for hyperactivity*, ed. K. D. Gadow and J. Loney, 381–415. Boulder, Colo.: Westview Press.

Melega, W. P., M. J. Raleigh, D. B. Stout, S. C. Huang, and M. E. Phelps. 1997. Ethological and 6-[18F]fluoro-L-DOPA-PET profiles of long-term vulnerability to chronic amphetamine. *Behavioural Brain Research* 84 (1–2): 258–68.

Melega, W. P., M. J. Raleigh, D. B. Stout, G. Lacan, S. C. Huang, and M. E. Phelps. 1997. Recovery of striatal dopamine function after acute amphetamine- and methamphetamine-induced neurotoxicity in vervet monkey. *Brain Research* 766 (1–2): 113–20.

Moisse, K. 2013. Brainwave test for ADHD: For patients or profit? *ABC News*, July 17. http://abcnews.go.com/Health/brainwave-test-adhd-patients-profit/ story?id=19686712.

MTA Cooperative Group. 1999. A 14-month randomized clinical trial of treatment strategies for attention-deficit/hyperactivity disorder: Multimodal treatment study of children with ADHD. *Archives of General Psychiatry* 56 (12): 1073–86.

MTA Cooperative Group. 2009. The MTA at 8 years: Prospective follow-up of children treated for combined-type ADHD in a multisite study. *Journal of the American Academy of Child & Adolescent Psychiatry* 48 (5): 484–500.

NEBA Health. 2013. Summary of NEBA clinical investigation: Key results. July 22. http://www.nebahealth.com/MRK0027_form_for_clinician%20-%20key%20 results%20summary_20130722__%282%29.pdf.

Porrino, L. J., and G. Lucignani. 1987. Different patterns of local brain energy metabolism associated with high and low doses of methylphenidate: Relevance to its action in hyperactive children. *Biological Psychiatry* 22 (2): 126–28.

Rettner, R. 2013. ADD drug may spur brain changes, study suggests. *Livescience*, May 15. http://www.livescience.com/32044-adhd-drug-treatment-brain-changes.html.

Robinson, T. E., and B. Kolb. 1997. Persistent structural modifications in the nucleus accumbens and prefrontal cortex neurons produced by previous experience with amphetamine. *Journal of Neuroscience* 17 (21): 8491–97. http://www.jneurosci.org/content/17/21/8491.full.pdf.

Sachs, B. 2009. Foot on the gas, foot on the brake. *Psychotherapy Networker* 33 (5): 39–43.

Sonsalla, M. V., N. D. Jochnowitz, G. D. Zeevalk, J. A. Oostveen, and E. D. Hall. 1996. Treatment of mice with methamphetamine produces cell loss in substantia nigra. *Brain Research* 738 (1): 172–75.

U.S. Food and Drug Administration. 2007. FDA asks attention-deficit hyperactivity disorder (ADHD) drug manufacturers to develop patient medication guides. February 21. http://www.fda.gov/drugs/drugsafety/postmarket-drugsafetyinformationforpatientsandproviders/ucm107918.htm.

Vastag, B. 2001. Pay attention: Ritalin acts much like cocaine. *Journal of the American Medical Association* 286 (8): 228–33.

Wang, G. J., N. Volknow, J. Fowler, R. Ferrieri, D. Schlyer, D. Alexoff, N. Pappas, J. Lieberman, P. King, D. Warner, C. Wong, R. Hitzemann, and A. Wolf. 1994. Methylphenidate decreases regional cerebral blood flow in normal human subjects. *Life Sciences* 54 (9): 143–46.

Wang, G.-J., N. D. Volkow, T. Wigal, S. H. Kollins, J. H. Newcorn, F. Telang, J. Logan, et al. 2013. Long-term stimulant treatment affects brain dopamine transporter level in patients with attention deficit hyperactive disorder. *PLoS ONE* 8 (5): e63023. Doi:10.1371/journal.pone.0063023. http://www.plosone.org/article/info%3Adoi%2F10.1371%2Fjournal.pone.0063023.

Weiss, M., U. Jain, and J. Garland. 2000. Clinical suggestions for management of stimulant treatment in adolescents. *Canadian Journal of Psychiatry* 45 (8): 717–23.

CHAPTER 4

American Psychiatric Association. 2013. *Diagnostic and statistical manual of mental disorders*. 5th ed. Arlington, Va.: American Psychiatric Publishing.

Breggin, P. R. 2002. *The Ritalin fact book: What your doctor won't tell you about ADHD and stimulant drugs*. Cambridge, Mass.: Perseus Publishing.

U.S. Food and Drug Administration. 2007. FDA asks attention-deficit hyperactivity disorder (ADHD) drug manufacturers to develop patient medication guides. February 21. http://www.fda.gov/drugs/drugsafety/postmarket-drugsafetyinformationforpatientsandproviders/ucm107918.htm.

CHAPTER 5

Brown, P. M., M. W. Corrigan, and A. Higgins-D'Alessandro, eds. 2012. *Handbook of prosocial education.* Lanham, Md.: Rowman & Littlefield.

Corrigan, M. W. 2012. A body of evidence. In *Handbook of prosocial education*, ed. P. M. Brown, M. W. Corrigan, and A. Higgins-D'Alessandro, 731–66. Lanham, Md.: Rowman & Littlefield.

Corrigan, M. W., D. Grove, and P. F. Vincent. 2011. *Multi-dimensional education: A common sense approach to data-driven thinking.* Thousand Oaks, Calif.: Corwin Press.

Darling-Hammond, L. 2010. *What we can learn from Finland's successful school reform.* National Education Association, January 10. http://www.nea.org/home/40991.htm.

———. 2011. *The flat world and education: How America's commitment to equity will determine our future.* New York: Teachers College Press.

FairTest: National Center for Fair and Open Testing. 2007. Would foreign students score proficient on NAEP? *Fairtest Examiner* (July). Available online at http://fairtest.org/would-foreign-students-score-proficient-naep (accessed December 28, 2011).

Fan, X., and M. Chen. 2001. Parental involvement and students' academic achievement: A meta-analysis. *Educational Psychology Review* 13 (1): 1–22.

Flynn, J. R. 1999. Searching for justice: The discovery of IQ gains over time. *American Psychologist* 54 (1): 5–20.

Fusarelli, L. 2004. The potential impact of the No Child Left Behind Act on equity and diversity in American education. *Educational Policy* 18 (1): 71–94.

Lynn, R., G. Meisenberg, J. Mikk, and A. Williams. 2007. National IQs predict differences in scholastic achievement in 67 countries. *Journal of Biosocial Science* 39 (6): 861–74.

McCabe, C. 2010. The economics behind international education rankings. *NEA Today*, December 9. http://neatoday.org/2010/12/09/a-look-at-the-economic-numbers-on-international-education-rankings/ (accessed January 3, 2011).

McNeal, M. 2011. Proportion of schools falling short on AYP rises, report says. *Education Week* 30 (29): 22. [http://www.edweek.org/ew/articles/2011/04/28/30ayp.h30.html

National Center for Education Statistics. 2011. *National Assessment of Educational Progress.* Washington, D.C.: Author. Retrieved January 24, 2012, from http://nces.ed.gov/nationsreportcard/.

National Commission on Teaching and America's Future. 2008. *Learning teams: Creating what's next.* Washington, D.C.: National Commission on Teaching and America's Future. Available online at http://nctaf.org/wp-content/uploads/2012/01/NCTAFLearningTeams408REG2.pdf.

Obama, B. 2011. Remarks by the president in the State of the Union address. Speech given to joint session of Congress, January 25, Washington, D.C. Available online at http://www.whitehouse.gov/the-press-office/2011/01/25/remarks-president-state-union-address (accessed December 29, 2011).

Organization for Economic Co-operation and Development [OECD]. 2011a. What can parents do to help their children succeed in school? *PISA in Focus* 10 (November). http://www.pisa.oecd.org/dataoecd/4/1/49012097.pdf.

———. 2011b. What is PISA? http://www.pisa.oecd.org/pages/0,3417,en _32252351_32235907_1_1_1_1_1,00.html (accessed December 27, 2011).

———. 2012. Programme for international student assessment (PISA). http:// www.oecd.org/department/0,3355,en_2649_35845621_1_1_1_1_1,00.html (accessed January 31, 2012).

Ormrod, J. E. 2006. *Educational psychology: Developing learners.* 5th ed. Upper Saddle River, N.J.: Merrill.

———. 2011. *Essentials for educational psychology.* 3rd ed. Columbus, Ohio: Pearson.

Paulson, A. 2010. US students halt academic 'free-fall,' but still lag in global testing. *Christian Science Monitor,* December 7. http://www.csmonitor.com/ USA/Education/2010/1207/US-students-halt-academic-free-fall-but-still-lag -in-global-testing/%28page%29/2 (accessed December 23, 2011).

Peterson, P. E., and F. M. Hess. 2008. Few states set world class standards. *Education Next* 8 (3): 70–73.

Popham, J. 2001. *The truth about testing: An educator's call to action.* Alexandria, Va.: Association for Supervision and Curriculum Development.

Rosenberger, B. 2008. Study: State must improve test scores. *Herald-Dispatch* (Huntington, W.Va.), March 21. http://www.herald-dispatch.com/news/ x2087241981 (accessed January 18, 2012).

Simonton, D. K. 2001. Talent development as a multidimensional, multiplicative, and dynamic process. *Current Directions in Psychological Science* 10 (2): 39–42.

Stotsky, S., and Z. Wurman. 2010. Common core standards still don't make the grade: Why Massachusetts and California must regain control over their academic destinies. Pioneer Institute white paper, no. 65 (July). Available online at http://truthinamericaneducation.com/wp-content/uploads/2012/03/ common_core_standards.pdf.

Strauss, V. 2011. What the new NAEP test results tell us. *Washington Post,* November 1. http://www.washingtonpost.com/blogs/answer-sheet/post/what-the- new-naep-test-results-really-tell-us/2011/11/01/gIQADSOtcM_blog.html (accessed December 28, 2011).

Swearer, S. M., D. L. Espelage, T. Vaillancourt, and S. Hymel. 2010. What can be done about school bullying? Linking research to educational practice. *Educational Researcher* 39 (1): 38–47.

Symonds, W. C., R. Schwartz, and R. F. Ferguson. 2011. *Pathways to prosperity: Meeting the challenge of preparing young Americans for the 21st century.* Cambridge, Mass.: Pathways to Prosperity Project, Harvard University Graduate School of Education.

Tonn, J. L. 2005. Keeping in touch. *Education Week* 24 (39): 30–33.

Uguroglu, M. E., and H. J. Walberh. 1979. Motivation and achievement: A quantitative synthesis. *American Education Research Journal* 16 (4): 375–89.

University of Pennsylvania. 2011. Penn research demonstrates motivation plays a critical role in determining IQ test scores. *Penn News,* April 26. http://www .upenn.edu/pennnews/news/penn-research-demonstrates-motivation-plays -critical-role-determining-iq-test-scores (accessed January 19, 2011).

Usher, A. 2011. Update with 2009–10 data and five-year trends: How many schools have not made adequate yearly progress? Center on Education Policy, April 28. http://www.cep-dc.org/displayDocument.cfm?DocumentID=357 (accessed January 10, 2012).

CHAPTER 6

American Psychiatric Association. 2013. *Diagnostic and statistical manual of mental disorders.* 5th ed. Arlington, Va.: American Psychiatric Publishing.

Bergen, S. E., C. O. Gardner, and K. S. Kendler. 2007. Age-related changes in heritability of behavioral phenotypes over adolescence and young adulthood: A meta-analysis. *Twin Research and Human Genetics* 10 (3): 423–33.

Bouchard, M. F., D. C. Bellinger, R. O. Wright, and M. G. Weisskopf. 2010. Attention-deficit/hyperactivity disorder and urinary metabolites of organophosphate pesticides. *Pediatrics*, 125 (6): e1270–77. http://pediatrics.aappublications.org/content/125/6/e1270.full.

Breggin, P. R. 2002. *The Ritalin fact book: What your doctor won't tell you about ADHD and stimulant drugs.* Cambridge, Mass.: Perseus Publishing.

Burt, S. A. 2009. Rethinking environmental contributions to child and adolescent psychopathology: A meta-analysis of shared environmental influences. *Psychology Bulletin* 135 (4): 608–37. Doi:10.1037/a0015702.

Corrigan, M. W., D. Grove, and P. F. Vincent. 2011. *Multi-dimensional education: A common sense approach to data-driven thinking.* Thousand Oaks, Calif.: Corwin Press.

Herper, M. 2011. A former pharma ghostwriter speaks out. *Forbes*, August 10. http://www.forbes.com/sites/matthewherper/2011/08/10/a-former-pharma-ghostwriter-speaks-out/.

Logdberg, L. 2011. Being the ghost in the machine: A medical ghostwriter's personal view. *PLoS Med* 8 (8): e1001071. Doi:10.1371/journal.pmed.1001071.

Safer, D., R. Allen, and E. Barr. 1972. Depression of growth in hyperactive children on stimulant drugs. *New England Journal of Medicine* 287 (5): 217–20.

Schwarz, A., and S. Cohen. 2013. ADHD seen in 11% of U.S. children as diagnoses rise. *New York Times*, March 31, 2013. http://www.nytimes.com/2013/04/01/health/more-diagnoses-of-hyperactivity-causing-concern.html?pagewanted=all&_r=0.

Singer, N. 2009. Medical papers by ghostwriters pushed therapy. *New York Times*, August 5, A1. http://www.nytimes.com/2009/08/05/health/research/05ghost.html?pagewanted=all.

Thomas, R., G. F. Mitchell, and L. Batstra. 2013. Attention-deficit/hyperactivity disorder: Are we helping or harming? *British Medical Journal* 347 (November 5): f6172, Doi:http://dx.doi.org/10.1136/bmj.f6172.

U.S. Food and Drug Administration. 2007. FDA asks attention-deficit hyperactivity disorder (ADHD) drug manufacturers to develop patient medication guides. February 21. http://www.fda.gov/drugs/drugsafety/postmarketdrugsafetyinformationforpatientsandproviders/ucm107918.htm.

CHAPTER 7

Bandura, A. 1977. *Social learning theory.* Englewood Cliffs, N.J.: Prentice-Hall.

Brown, P. M., M. W. Corrigan, and A. Higgins-D'Alessandro, eds. 2012. *Handbook of prosocial education.* Lanham, Md.: Rowman & Littlefield.

Capara, G. V., C. Barbaranelli, C. Pastorelli, A. Bandura, and P. G. Zimbardo. 2000. Prosocial foundations of academic achievement. *Psychological Science* 11 (4): 302–6.

Cohen, J. 2006. Social, emotional, ethical and academic education: Creating a climate for learning, participation in democracy and well-being. *Harvard Educational Review* 76 (2): 201–37.

Corrigan, M. W. 2012. A body of evidence. In *Handbook of prosocial education*, ed. P. M. Brown, M. W. Corrigan, and A. Higgins-D'Alessandro, 731–66. Lanham, Md.: Rowman & Littlefield.

Corrigan, M. W., D. Grove, and P. F. Vincent. 2011. *Multi-dimensional education: A common sense approach to data-driven thinking.* Thousand Oaks, Calif.: Corwin Press.

Crone, T. M. 2004. What test scores can and cannot tell us about the quality of our schools. *Business Review* Q3: 5–22. Available online at http://www.phil.frb .org/research-and-data/publications/business-review/2004/q3/brq304tc.pdf.

Cruz, F. 1987. *John Dewey's theory of community.* New York: Peter Lang.

Deci, E. L. 2009. Large-scale school reform as viewed from the self-determination theory perspective. *Theory and Research in Education* 7 (2): 244–52.

Deci, E. L., and R. M. Ryan. 1985. *Intrinsic motivation and self-determination in human behavior.* New York: Plenum.

Eisenberg, N., and P. Mussen. 1989. *The roots of prosocial behavior in children.* Cambridge, UK: Cambridge University Press.

Elder, T. E. 2010. The importance of relative standards in ADHD diagnoses: Evidence based on exact birth dates. *Journal of Health Economics* 29 (5): 641–56.

Ellis, K., and P. Shockley-Zalabak. 2003. *Trust in the teacher: Development and validation of an instrument and the relationship to receiver apprehension, motivation, and learning.* Paper presented at the 2003 annual convention of the National Communication Association, Miami, Fla.

Erickson, E. H. 1950. *Childhood and society.* New York: Norton.

Evans, W. N., M. S. Morrill, and S. T. Parente. 2010. Measuring inappropriate medical diagnosis and treatment in survey data: The case of ADHD among school-age children. *Journal of Health Economics* 29 (5): 657–73.

Hart, B., and R. T. Risley. 1995. *Meaningful differences in the everyday experience of young American children.* Baltimore: Paul H. Brookes.

Kohlberg, L., C. Levine, and A. Hewer. 1983. *Moral stages: A current formulation and a response to critics.* Basel, Switzerland: Karger.

Ormrod, J. E. 2006. *Educational psychology: Developing learners.* 5th ed. Upper Saddle River, N.J.: Merrill.

———. 2011. *Essentials for educational psychology.* 3rd ed. Columbus, Ohio: Pearson.

Piaget, J. 1969. *Science of education and the psychology of the child.* New York: Viking.

Skinner, B. F. 1969. *Contingencies of reinforcement.* New York: Appleton-Century-Crofts.

Uguroglu, M. E., and H. J. Walberh. 1979. Motivation and achievement: A quantitative synthesis. *American Education Research Journal* 16(4): 375–89.

Vincent, P. F., and D. Grove. 2012. *Relationships + rules + routines = results: A common sense approach.* Boone, N.C.: Character Development Group.

Wertsch, J. V. 1985. *Vygotsky and the social formation of the mind.* Cambridge, Mass.: Harvard University Press.

CHAPTER 8

Epstein, J. L. 1995. School/family/community partnerships: Caring for children we share. *Phi Delta Kappan* 76 (9): 701–12.

Hart, B., and R. T. Risley. 1995. *Meaningful differences in the everyday experience of young American children.* Baltimore: Paul H. Brookes.

Henderson, A. T., and K. L. Mapp. 2002. *A new wave of evidence: The impact of school, family, and community connections on student achievement.* Austin: Southwest Educational Development Laboratory.

Kruse, K. 1996. *The effects of a low socioeconomic environment on a student's academic achievement* (A research study submitted for the requirements of CNE 579, Research in Education). Huntsville, Tex.: Sam Houston State University. (ERIC Document Reproduction Service No. ED 402380). http://www.eric.ed.gov/PDFS/ED402380.pdf (accessed January 18, 2012).

Langberg, J. M., J. N. Epstein, C. M. Urbanowicz, J. O. Simon, and A. J. Graham. 2008. Efficacy of an organizational skills intervention to improve the academic functioning of students with attention-deficit/hyperactivity disorder. *School Psychology Quarterly* 23 (3): 407–17.

Lee, S., M. Daniels, A. Puig, R. A. Newgent, and S. Nam. 2008. A data-based model to predict postsecondary educational attainment of low-socioeconomic-status students. *Professional School Counseling* 11 (5): 306–16.

McNeal, R. B., Jr. 1999. Parental involvement as social capital: Differential effectiveness on science achievement, truancy, and dropping out. *Social Forces* 78 (1): 117–44.

Miranda, A., S. Jarque, and R. Tarraga. 2006. Interventions in school settings for students with ADHD. *Exceptionality* 14 (1): 35–52.

Rosenthal, R. 1997. Interpersonal expectancy effects: A forty year perspective. Presented as an invited address to teachers of psychology in the secondary schools as part of the American Psychological Association Convention, August, Chicago, Ill.

Rosenthal, R., and L. Jacobson. 1968. *Pygmalion in the classroom: Teacher expectation and pupils' intellectual development.* New York: Holt, Rinehart and Winston.

Vincent, P., Grove, D., and Lamb, J. 2013. *Relationships + Rules + Routines = Results: A Common Sense Approach.* Boone, NC: Character Development Group.

CHAPTER 9

Barkley, R. A. 1987. *Defiant children: A clinician's manual for parent training.* New York: Guilford.

Centers for Disease Control and Prevention. 2013. Childhood obesity facts, July 10. http://www.cdc.gov/healthyyouth/obesity/facts.htm.

Cook, R. E., D. Klein, and A. Tessier. 2008. *Adapting early childhood curricula for children with special needs.* 7th ed. Upper Saddle River, N.J.: Pearson Merrill Prentice-Hall.

Epstein, J. L. 1995. School/family/community partnerships: Caring for children we share. *Phi Delta Kappan* 76 (9): 701–12.

Fan, X., and M. Chen. 2001. Parental involvement and students' academic achievement: A meta-analysis. *Educational Psychology Review* 13 (1): 1–22.

Jones, M., and C. O'Beney. 2004. Promoting mental health through physical activity: Examples from practice. *Journal of Public Mental Health* 3 (1): 39–47.

Lee, S., M. Daniels, A. Puig, R. A. Newgent, and S. Nam. 2008. A data-based model to predict postsecondary educational attainment of low-socioeconomic-status students. *Professional School Counseling* 11 (5): 306–16.

McNeal, R. B., Jr. 1999. Parental involvement as social capital: Differential effectiveness on science achievement, truancy, and dropping out. *Social Forces* 78 (1): 117–44.

Mulrine, C. F., M. A. Prater, and A. Jenkins. 2008. The active classroom: Supporting students with attention deficit hyperactivity disorder through exercise. *Teaching Exceptional Children* 40 (5): 16–22.

Organisation for Economic Co-operation and Development. 2011. What can parents do to help their children succeed in school? http://www.pisa.oecd.org/dataoecd/4/1/49012097.pdf.

Ormrod, J. E. 2006. *Educational psychology: Developing learners*. 5th ed. Upper Saddle River, N.J.: Merrill.

———. 2011. *Essentials for educational psychology*. 3rd ed. Columbus, Ohio: Pearson.

Suglia, S., and S. Solnick. 2013. Soft drinks consumption is associated with behavior problems in 5-year-olds. *Journal of Pediatrics* (August): 1323–28. Doi:10.1016/j.jpeds.2013.06.023. http://www.jpeds.com/article/S0022-3476%2813%2900736-1/fulltext.

Uguroglu, M. E., and H. J. Walberh. 1979. Motivation and achievement: A quantitative synthesis. *American Education Research Journal* 16 (4): 375–89.

CHAPTER 10

Breggin, P. R. 2001. *Talking back to Ritalin: What doctors are telling you about stimulants and ADHD*. Cambridge, Mass.: Da Capo.

Ormrod, J. E. 2006. *Educational psychology: Developing learners*. 5th ed. Upper Saddle River, N.J.: Merrill.

———. 2011. *Essentials for educational psychology*. 3rd ed. Columbus, Ohio: Pearson.

Rosenhan, D. L. 1973. On being sane in insane places. *Science* 179 (4070): 250–58. DOI:10.1126/science.179.4070.250

Lightning Source UK Ltd.
Milton Keynes UK
UKOW01f0653060318

318962UK00001BA/48/P